# The Museum in America

## AMERICAN ASSOCIATION FOR STATE AND LOCAL HISTORY BOOK SERIES



**ABOUT THE SERIES:**

The American Association for State and Local History publishes technical and professional information for those who practice and support history and address issues critical to the field of state and local history. To submit a proposal or manuscript to the series, please request proposal guidelines from AASLH headquarters: AASLH Book Series, 530 Church Street, Suite 600, Nashville, TN 37219. Telephone: (615) 255-2971. Fax (615) 255-2979.

**ABOUT THE ORGANIZATION:**

The American Association for State and Local History (AASLH) is a nonprofit educational organization dedicated to advancing knowledge, understanding, and appreciation of local history in the United States and Canada. In addition to sponsorship of this book series, the association publishes the periodical *History News*, a newsletter, technical leaflets and reports, and other materials; confers prizes and awards in recognition of outstanding achievement in the field; and supports a broad educational program and other activities designed to help members work more effectively. Current members are entitled to discounts on AASLH Series books. To join the organization, contact: Membership Director, AASLH, 530 Church Street, Suite 600, Nashville, TN 37219.

# The Museum in America

## INNOVATORS AND PIONEERS

**by Edward P. Alexander**

ALTAMIRA
PRESS

*A Division of Sage Publications, Inc.*
Walnut Creek • London • New Delhi
PUBLISHED IN COOPERATION WITH
THE AMERICAN ASSOCIATION FOR STATE AND LOCAL HISTORY

For information address:

**AltaMira Press**
A Division of Sage Publications, Inc.
1630 North Main Street, Suite 367
Walnut Creek, CA 94596
explore@altamira.sagepub.com

**Sage Publications Ltd.**
6 Bonhill Street
London EC2A 4PU
United Kingdom

**Sage Publications India Pvt. Ltd.**
M-32 Market
Greater Kailash 1
New Delhi 110 048 India

PRINTED IN THE UNITED STATES OF AMERICA

**Library of Congress Cataloging-in-Publication Data**

Alexander, Edward P. (Edward Porter), 1907–
The museum in America : innovators and pioneers / by Edward Alexander.
p. cm.—(American Association for State and Local History Book series)
"Published in cooperation with the American Association for State and Local History."
Includes bibliographical references and index.
ISBN 0-7619-8946-3 (cloth). — ISBN 0-7619-8947-1 (pbk.)
1. Museums—United States—History. 2. Museum curators—United States—Biography. 3. Museum directors—United States—Biography. 4. Popular culture—Museums—United States—History. 5. United States—Intellectual life—History. I. American Association for State and Local History. II. Title. III. Series.
AM11.A55 1997
069'.0973—dc21 97-21127
CIP

**Cover Design:** Kim Ericsson/Shooting Star Graphics

**Editorial Management:** Virginia Alderson Hoffman

**Typesetting Services:** Kim Ericsson/Shooting Star Graphics

97 98 99 00 7 6 5 4 3 2 1

# Contents

# Dedication

To my daughter, Mary Sheron Alexander, who helped me with part of the research, and without whose persistence and dedication this book would not have come to be published.

# About the Author

Edward Porter Alexander, after receiving his PhD in American History at Columbia University in 1938, directed museums for the New York State Historical Association at Ticonderoga and Cooperstown (editing the quarterly, *New York History*) and the State Historical Society of Wisconsin (editing *The Wisconsin Magazine of History*). He then went to Colonial Williamsburg in Virginia to serve as Director of Interpretation (later Vice President). After 26 years there, he retired on a Friday and the next Monday taught his first class in Museum Studies at the University of Delaware in Newark. In six years he taught more than 300 students, most of whom work in museums in the United States and Canada. He has traveled extensively, visiting museums in such places as China, Japan, and India.

He was a founder and president of the American Association for State and Local History and president of the American Association of Museums.

# Foreword

Most Americans don't go to museums, nor do most, apparently, read books. On the other hand, television and the computer supposedly claim audiences of millions. Starting some years ago, the hard—but not really verified—facts of TV viewership began to influence attendance goals for museums, which as a result made dramatic efforts to reap "popular" audiences in various ways. Vast amounts of money were expended. At the bottom end was overblown design and uselessly complicated mechanical exhibitry, while at the top was a fresh view of interpretation. By far the most enduring of these is the latter, while the former has fallen because of its prohibitive cost, invariably short life, and general impracticality. Where next? The fountains of public money have dried up. Still the museum forms a strong current in American life.

At crossroads like this, institutions look back through the clutter and review basics common to their work that will help them reconsider. This book appears at a perfect time. Edward P. Alexander finds these basics through portraits of people who shaped and, as he puts it, defined the American museum. Alexander's thirteen individuals were passionately committed to ideas, and the pursuit was pervasive in their lives. It is an amazing collection of people.

Some, like Carl Ethan Akeley (1864–1926), followed wild stars. A taxidermist, he traveled the rain forests of Africa with Theodore Roosevelt. We grimace as the baby elephant is shot by TR's son Kermit, and by the time the poor creature, stuffed and waxed with cosmetics, joins its parents and kin in the tableau "Alarm" at the American Museum of Natural History, our modern sensitivities are shaken irreparably. Yet we cannot help but admire what Alexander describes as Akeley's "youthful zest and tremendous nervous energy" and his love of what he called "Brightest Africa" that led to the creation of the distinguished African zoological halls in Chicago and New York.

Alfred Barr's (1902–1981) devotion to modern art prevails in his long shadow, New York's Museum of Modern Art. Alexander found that his work led to "a better treatment of modern art in other museums," which had long shunned it. Reuben Gold Thwaites (1853–1913) brought into flower the State Historical Society of Wisconsin, already an old institution founded in 1846. Thwaites was a newspaper editor, whom Alexander writes became "the most successful historical society director the nation had known."

William Sumner Appleton (1874–1947), a founder of the Society for the Preservation of New England Antiquities in 1910, directed it in the collection of many historic buildings and the rescue of many more from demolition. His antiquarian thirst made him collect fragments of all sorts, from wallpaper to locks, and from his efforts he spawned some of the earliest and most enduring precepts of historic preservation in this country. Frank Oppenheimer (1912–1985), founder of the Exploratorium in San Francisco, was a powerful force in popular education for the science museum.

John Kinard (1936–1989), director of the Smithsonian's Anacostia Neighborhood Museum in Washington, was a bombastic individual who opened America's eyes to the social responsibility of the museum. Katherine Coffey (1900–1972), both serving as director and taking staff functions at the Newark Museum, used all the skills of the profession to make her inner-city museum survive and flourish to the good of all in a context of racial unrest. She and Kinard believed in the power of special exhibitions to attract and educate the public, but more than that, the significance of the museum in the betterment of American life.

Edward P. Alexander's characters were all people who knew what they wanted. Most of them, as originators, mesmerized their patrons effectively, gaining solid support for their programs. But the way was sometimes blocked sufficiently to bring their creative juices to a boil. Alexander's portraits record temper explosions, resignations, rivalries; he describes men and women so determined on the paths to their objectives that most others simply stepped aside and let them go on. Few of his characters were team players, and most had little concern for what they considered extraneous details. Organizations have grown in their wakes, a dozen and more people to realize the objectives first pursued by one.

Their creative spark was not that of the artist but of the educator who would teach and, if necessary, preach. Alexander's museum masters were conveyors and interpreters of knowledge, who believed in the museum as a premier medium of communication. They saw it as more universal, more enduring in application than an ordinary schoolroom, where tensions weakened natural curiosity. "No one ever flunked a museum," writes Alexander. Among his most memorable characters, Anna Billings Gallup (1872–1956), thought museums for children should be "pure fun," and that this was the "Magic key that opens one door of knowledge after another, it is the magic wand that gives each branch of learning a potential of joy, it is the magnet that draws the crowd, the engineer that keeps them busy with efficiency of action."

Reliving these lives with Edward P. Alexander, one can but smile occasionally, thinking how the characters might have fit in to a present-day museum. Accreditation might have raised their hackles as being meddlesome. Political correctness would have offended their sense of independence. These are only surface matters. Alexander's concern is with the universals. He shows us that for all the uniqueness of their stories, we are, in our basics, the professional children of these people. They were the pioneers. All "modern" for their own time—indeed some of them radical—they were as much of their times as we may dearly hope we are of ours.

The book's one glaring omission is understandable: Alexander does not include Alexander. This great innovator in the American museum would have made the masters an even fourteen. He publishes this book at ninety years of age, yet another achievement in a long career that assumes a monumental presence in the history of historical interpretation. After five wartime years as director of the State Historical Society of Wisconsin—the most prestigous position of its kind in the nation— he resigned in 1946 to embark upon a new career as director of the division of education in restored Williamsburg in Virginia.

Colonial Williamsburg was then a restoration not twenty years old, an architecture-driven project not without its sentimental message of a Better Anglo-Saxon Past. Although academic historians remain suspicious and even dubious about historic houses and outdoor museums, their feelings on this subject a half-century ago was utter contempt. History belonged only in lectures and the written word. The source of history lay only in the written document—objects were mute and people who tried to listen to them were playing dolls.

Yet a historian of distinction had now taken up the task of interpreting Williamsburg. Deftly, with time, blazing paths where there had been no trail before, Alexander added another dimension to the physical re-creation of 18th-century life. This was history. With the charms of reenacted cooking, wood chopping, carriage-riding, and the rest, were now the challenges of ideas. What were the beliefs and philosophies generated in this colonial town? Who were the characters and how in the course of everyday life did they help forge a nation, where a ragged row of coastal colonies had been?

Alexander's move from Madison to Williamsburg can be considered one of the major events in the history of American museums. All our historic houses, capitols, courthouses, and other living museum exhibitions follow his lead and, indeed, flatter themselves sometimes that they have built even higher toward the standards he originally set.

*The Museum in America: Innovators and Pioneers* is yet another contribution to the field from Edward P. Alexander. Let him introduce you to people who, like himself, helped make the American museum what it is today.

WILLIAM SEALE

INTRODUCTION

# *Toward a Definition of the American Museum*

THE NUMBER OF MUSEUMS in the United States has grown amazingly, from a half dozen in the colonial period until now with a total exceeding eight thousand, much more numerous than any other nation. The earliest ones were chiefly collections of curiosities and oddments, often the property of one person who depended heavily on admission fees for his support. An exception to this generalization was Charles Willson Peale's Philadelphia Museum of 1786 which stressed natural history, showed more than 250 portraits and paintings, chiefly the creations of Peale and his family, and contained many historical objects. His comprehensive collection of natural science, labeled according to the Linnean nomenclature, attracted many scholars, especially from the American Philosophical Society, but Peale also provided what he called "rational amusement" with demonstrations of electrical machines and chemical experiments, organ recitals, a physiognotrace producing the visitors' silhouettes, and other participatory activities so as to instruct and often entertain as large an audience as possible from the general public.[1]

During the first half of the nineteenth century, a majority of the museums probably belonged to and were operated by very unlearned persons who installed stuffed beasts and serpents, waxwork figures, and electrical machines that gave those touching them a modest shock. These museums also presented farces, songs, dances, and similar vaudeville entertainment as a kind of cheap popular theatre. Examples of such museums were the various versions of the American Museum in New York, the Columbian Museum in Boston, and the Western Museum in Cincinnati with its hellish "Infernal Regions." On the other hand, more serious museums arose with collections that furthered the study of natural history, science and technology, history, or art such as the Academy of Natural Sciences of Philadelphia, the New-York Historical Society, or the Trumbull Gallery at Yale. They usually were governed by boards of directors or trustees and customarily had a supervisor or director who understood the subject matter that they treated. For a time museums that offered chiefly entertainment won out in the competition; their success was exemplified by Phineas T. Barnum, that master of public relations and promotion who dominated the field after acquiring New York City's American Museum in 1841. Though he did gather and display some valuable natural history collections, his emphasis was on pure entertainment. By 1870, however, his successive museums had suffered a series of disastrous fires, and he decided to leave the museum field and devote his energies to the circus.

About that time, a new day dawned with the appearance of important, first-rate institutions such as the American Museum of Natural History and the Metropolitan Museum of Art in New York, the Museum of Fine Arts in Boston, and the Art Institute of Chicago. Soon, serious museums in every field began to spring up all over the country. American museums today, however, differ greatly in size, financial resources, and functions. Some of the larger ones count their collections, yearly attendance, and budgets in the millions, have staffs reaching several thousands, and stay open long hours. Still, about three thousand of the smaller museums are directed by one person (often a volunteer), financed by tiny budgets, and are available only two or three afternoons a week.

I have already had my say in my previous book, *Museum Masters*, about a few American leaders, namely Charles Willson Peale (1741–1827) and his family in his pioneering Philadelphia Museum; George Browne Goode (1851–1896) of the Smithsonian Institution's United States National Museum; Ann Pamela Cunningham (1816–1875) of the Mount Vernon Ladies' Association; and the progressive and innovative John Cotton Dana (1856–1929) of the Newark (New Jersey) Museum. Goode, a skilled scientist himself, still asserted that public institutions like the Smithsonian "are not intended for the few but for the enlightenment and education of the masses." He emphasized the importance of meaningful exhibitions and understandable labels. Cunningham, an early force in the historic house museum field, secured and preserved George Washington's Mount Vernon plantation, to be kept always as he had known it. Dana used special exhibitions and numerous educational activities to lure all elements of the community as well as outside visitors to his museum. He sent its collections and staff members to schools, libraries, clubs, and other organizations in the area, and he devised an apprentice system to train young college graduates in museum work.

My chief purpose in the present volume is to examine carefully how several museum leaders made the education and, to a limited extent, the amusement of the general public their chief aim rather than the accumulation of objects important for the research of scholars and experts. I apply this examination to several well-known types of museums and also consider the subject of museum studies.

I begin with two natural history museum leaders. The first was Henry Fairfield Osborn (1857–1935) who in forty-two years of service made the American Museum of Natural History in New York a model of this type of museum, renowned nationally and internationally. Another master in this field was Carl Ethan Akeley (1864–1926), taxidermist in turn with the Milwaukee Public Museum, Field Museum of Natural History in Chicago, and the American Museum of Natural History. He perfected the habitat group type of exhibition used so extensively in this country and abroad to show naturally posed animals with their accessories such as rocks, soils, plants, and habitations in front of curved background paintings of actual places.

I go on to two art museum leaders. Henry Watson Kent (1866–1948) was a skilled administrator who brought the Metropolitan Museum of Art into the twentieth century with scientific methods of registration, accessioning, cataloguing, communication, and publication, and he succeeded in persuading other museums in America and Europe to use such professional methods. Alfred Hamilton Barr Jr. (1902–1981), the first director of the Museum of Modern Art, through scholarly but popular exhibitions and lucid explanations in his catalogues and books began to arouse enthusiasm for modern art among the public and to influence other museums in its favor.

In the history museum area was Reuben Gold Thwaites (1853–1913), director of the State Historical Society of Wisconsin, who made the society serve the people of that entire state and became the most successful and influential historical society director yet to appear in America. Another historical museum leader was William Sumner Appleton (1874–1947), founder and director of the Society for the Preservation of New England Antiquities, who saved more than fifty important historical and architectural buildings and sites scattered about New England.

Among four masters in specialized fields was Dr. Frank Friedman Oppenheimer (1912–1985) who founded a science and technology museum, which he christened the "Exploratorium." He devised several hundred interactive, "hands-on" exhibits that required participation from the visitors and helped them understand various scientific principles. Anna Billings Gallup (1872–1956) was curator of the Brooklyn Children's Museum, the first of that kind in the world. Her enthusiastic interpretation was known throughout this country and abroad; it helped spread children's museums worldwide. John Robert Kinard (1936–1989) operated the Anacostia Neighborhood Museum in Washington, D.C., as a combination museum, cultural arts center, meeting place for neighborhood groups, and skill training laboratory for youngsters. He expanded its functions so that it became recognized nationally and internationally for its strong civil rights advocacy and its African American history, art, and culture programs. And Katherine Coffey (1900–1972) at the Newark (New Jersey) Museum made a general museum (natural science, art, history, and technology) appeal to a whole community with many ingenious educational programs.

Botanical gardens and zoos are museums that contain living objects. Charles Sprague Sargent (1841–1927) built the Arnold Arboretum near Boston into one of the most outstanding botanical gardens in the nation and the world—a museum of living plants, a scientific station, and a popular educator. William Temple Hornaday (1854–1937) was the first director of the New York Zoological Society which operated the Bronx Park Zoo. He gathered many exotic animals and allowed them to range freely in large enclosures instead of keeping them confined in cages and small paddocks.

Finally, a museum specialist of note was Paul Joseph Sachs (1878–1961) of Harvard University and its Fogg Art Museum, who taught a museum studies course that covered all aspects of art museum work—philosophy, history, buildings, administration, collections, personalities in the art world, politics, and ethics. His students headed American art museums for a generation.

The thirteen leaders featured in this volume did much to transform the American conception of museum purpose. They believed in the collection of objects or specimens, of course, but did not consider their preservation and arrangement as important as the education of the public and service to the community. Studying and researching the objects might at times make contributions to the subject matter of natural science, art, history, or technology, but curators ought not take a supercilious view and devote themselves exclusively to the collection and its research, with their chief clientele scholars and experts. Instead, curators should work actively in the museums' educational programs;

in fact, curators, educators, designers, and administrators ought to form a team to further the educational impact of the whole museum. They should devise exhibitions and other learning activities, create lectures and demonstrations for junior, family, and senior citizen visitors; work closely with the schools to make class journeys to the museum fit in with classroom study; visit schools, libraries, clubs, and other community agencies to give advice or arrange loan exhibits or motion picture showings; and make radio and television appearances. In this way the museum would take its proper place in dispensing education of a special type for its visitors and the surrounding community.

## NOTES

NOTE: Source notes and a selected bibliography are provided at the end of each chapter in this book, listing works referred to in the chapter and especially pertinent to it. Works not listed in the chapter bibliography appear with full publication data at first mention in the chapter notes and as shortened references thereafter.

1. My other writings on this section are on Peale in *Museum Masters: Their Museums and Their Influence* (Nashville: American Association for State and Local History, 1983), 41–77; "Early American Museums: From Collection of Curiosities to Popular Education," *International Journal of Museum Management and Curatorship* 6 (1987): 337–51; "The American Museum Movement Chooses Education," *Curator* 31 (March 1988): 61–80.

## SELECT BIBLIOGRAPHY

Alexander, Edward P. *Museum Masters: Their Museums and Their Influence*. Nashville: American Association for State and Local History, 1983, 41–77.

_____. "Early American Museums: From Collection of Curiosities to Popular Education." *International Journal of Museum Management and Curatorship* 6 (1987): 337–51.

_____. "The American Museum Movement Chooses Education." *Curator* 31 (March 1988): 61–80.

CHAPTER 1

# Henry Fairfield Osborn *Develops a Model Natural History Museum*

## I

HENRY FAIRFIELD OSBORN, at age thirty-four a promising young scientist, left his teaching post at Princeton University in 1891 to accept a joint appointment as professor of biology at Columbia University and curator of a new department of mammalian paleontology at the American Museum of Natural History. His post enabled the museum and university to begin to cooperate in the natural history field. Through the years, the two institutions worked together ever more closely, university professors often using the museum's collections in their research and museum curators frequently teaching at the university.[1]

The American Museum, to which Professor Osborn came, was founded in 1869 as a result of the prescience and infectious enthusiasm of Albert Smith Bickmore, who had studied at Harvard with Louis Agasiz and worked in his Museum of Comparative Zoology. Bickmore thought Cambridge too small a place for the great museum of natural history that he envisioned; he chose New York City as the ideal spot. He enlisted the aid of wealthy leaders of the metropolis, such as Theodore Roosevelt, father of the late president; Joseph H. Choate, the lawyer; Morris K. Jesup and J. Pierpont Morgan, bankers; Robert Colgate, the soap magnate; and Alexander T. Stewart, the department store entrepreneur. Afraid that Boston, Philadelphia, Washington, and Chicago were outstripping their beloved city in cultural attainments, they secured a charter from the state legislature, made Bickmore the museum's superintendent (the title used by the prestigious British Museum), and persuaded the Commissioners of Central Park, headed by the imaginative and cooperative Andrew H. Green, to allow them to house exhibits in the second and third stories of the old Arsenal Building in the park, and later to give them some eighteen acres at Central Park West and 79th Street for a permanent home.

The trustees of the American Museum and the even younger Metropolitan Museum of Art in 1871 joined to petition the state legislature to allow the city to tax itself $500,000 to pay for a building for the two museums. In support, they presented a petition signed by several thousand property owners. The movement resulted in an important compromise, in which the city agreed to own and pay for the two separate buildings that resulted, along with their maintenance and security, while the boards of trustees financed the collections, their preservation and interpretation. About one hundred municipalities throughout the country since then have adopted similar joint public and private support arrangements for their museums.

The American Museum at first put its emphasis upon public instruction rather than scientific research. It stated that the museum was "to be second to none" and "while affording amusement and instruction to the public," would "be the means of teaching our youth to appreciate the wonderful works of our Creator."[2] Bickmore was not a skillful administrator, and in 1881 he stepped down as superintendent to give courses of lectures to public school principals and teachers, and soon after to head a Department of Public Instruction. A facile and fascinating speaker, he used hand-painted stereoptican lantern slides to illustrate his lectures.

Morris K. Jesup, multimillionaire supplier of railroad equipment and a prominent banker, became president of the Board of Trustees in 1881 and took over the museum's administration. He came to the office almost daily and handled the smallest details. He insisted upon sound financial procedures, immaculate cleanliness and order in the building, and exhibits directed toward the general public. He asserted: "I am a plain, unscientific business man; I want the exhibits to be labelled so that I understand them, and then I feel sure that others can understand."[3] He also slowly came to appreciate the museum curators' devotion to scientific research and the need for funds to support it. He persuaded the board to back research projects and expeditions, even though many trustees continued to regard the museum as their own private property and often wished to finance exhibits that were showy and spectacular, not necessarily scientific and educational. Jesup brought Frederic Ward Putnam, director of Harvard's Peabody Museum of Archaeology and Ethnology, to the American Museum in 1894 on a part-time basis to organize a strong department of anthropology, and Putnam appointed the brilliant young Franz Boas as his assistant. Jesup also personally financed several projects that included the six-year-long Jesup North Pacific Expedition of 1897, directed by Boas. Jesup and his wife, during their lifetimes and in their wills, contributed nearly seven million dollars to the museum, mainly to the endowment fund, by far the largest gift that it had received.

Professor Osborn brought a strong scientific background and imaginative ideas about popular exhibition to the museum. President Jesup appreciated his educational and research contributions and was impressed by his willingness to handle personnel and business matters. Thus, in 1899, Jesup asked Osborn to become his administrative assistant. From that time forward, Osborn had a two-sided career at the museum as curator/scientist and administrator.

## II

Henry Fairfield Osborn was born at Fairfield, Connecticut, into a wealthy, socially prominent family. His father, William Henry Osborn, was a founder and long-time president of the Illinois Central Railroad. His mother, born Virginia Reed Sturges, was firm and charitable, and young Osborn's close companion. He spent most of his boyhood in New York City, where he attended Columbia Grammar School (he later said that the discipline there was rigid) and Lyon's Collegiate Institute. His father built a summer home called Castle Rock (later Professor Osborn's favorite residence), on a hilltop overlooking the Hudson River at Garrison, New York, and added "Woodsome Lodge" as an outbuilding where his son could pursue his varied interests. At age fourteen, he published sixteen issues of *The Boys' Journal*, for which he provided most of the copy, composition, and printing. Young Theodore Roosevelt and Osborn were close friends, and their intimacy lasted into later life.

In 1873 Osborn entered Princeton University, where he studied geology with Dr. Arnold Guyot, and philosophy with the dynamic President James McCosh, a Presbyterian divine, one of the first scholars to accept the theory of evolution. He also did hard manual work in the Geology Museum, helped form a student Natural Science Association, and organized a geological camping expedition in the Catskills with two other students during the summer following their junior year. Upon graduation, the three of them made two summer treks to Colorado and Wyoming to collect fossils. In 1878–1879 Osborn studied anatomy and histology with Dr. William H. Welch at Bellevue Medical College and the College of Physicians and Surgeons. Dr. Welch thought him the best student he had ever had. The next year, he decided to go to England instead of Germany to complete his graduate laboratory work in embryology and comparative anatomy with Francis Maitland Balfour at Cambridge and Thomas Huxley in London. The Huxleys invited Osborn to their Sunday evening high teas, where Huxley complained that he was children-pecked as well as hen-pecked. Huxley introduced the awestruck young man to Charles Darwin himself, and he met many other leading scientists. He returned to Princeton to receive his Sc.D. in 1881 and begin a decade of teaching there. He tried to carry on Balfour's and Huxley's methods of informal, lively class discussion followed by closely supervised laboratory work; he urged his students not merely to memorize facts but rather to cultivate observation and creative thinking. He rose to be professor of comparative anatomy and then moved to Columbia in 1891 to teach anatomy and zoology and serve as dean of the Faculty of Pure Science. At the two universities, he taught twenty-eight classes of undergraduates and graduates; he liked to refer to them as his "biological sons," who in this country and abroad were instructing "a young army of biological grandsons."[4]

In 1880 Osborn went on a field expedition to Texas and Louisiana in search of a fossil alligator and other long-tailed amphibians. He was disappointed with his work there and decided that he lacked facility for good field exploration. He commented philosophically: "It is well to realize one's inaptitudes, so that one may better advance in the direction of which his talent does lie. *If you cannot find your research way in one direction, turn to another in which you may be successful.*"[5]

Osborn in 1881 was married to Lucretia Thatcher Perry, the daughter of General A. J. Perry. The Osborns were a charming couple, always ready to entertain their numerous friends and acquaintances; they remained unperturbed on special occasions, as when he chartered a steamboat and brought the entire meeting of the International Congress of Eugenics to "Castle Rock" for a reception. Lucretia bore five children and later wrote three books, one of them a biography of George Washington in his own words.

At Princeton, Osborn began to become a skilled paleontologist. He decided that "*the discovery of new principles is the chief end of research*," not the routine assemblage of facts; throughout his long career, he rejoiced in making generalizations, based on exacting scientific observation and reasoning but always in language that the general public could understand. He thought that his paleontological observations were usually accepted but was not disturbed when they were considered controversial. He said that "*if new principles are sound they will finally gain universal acceptance; if unsound the less widely accepted they are the better*."[6] He studied the work of Joseph Leidy, the first great American paleontologist, and knew intimately Edward Drinker Cope and Daniel Charles Marsh of Yale. The last two were the leading collectors of American fossils but deadly enemies. Osborn and Cope worked closely together at the Academy of Natural Sciences of Philadelphia and maintained friendly relations, though Cope could often be combative. On one occasion, he and a close friend engaged in fisticuffs, and Cope told Osborn the next day, "If you think my eye is black, you ought to see Frazer this morning."[7] In addition to studying fossils found in America, Osborn made a trip to Europe in 1886 to examine those of some tiny Mesozoic animals. He sent his graduate student, Barnum Brown, who was employed at the American Museum, to seek fossils in Como Bluff, Wyoming, thus precipitating a bitter quarrel with Professor Marsh, who accused Osborn of encroaching upon his territory. But he continued dispatching his assistants on persistent expeditions in both America and Europe and, as a result, the American Museum's holdings of vertebrate prehistoric fossils were second to none in the world.

Professor Osborn had a fresh, even radical approach for a paleontologist toward exhibition; he wished to mount the huge fossilized skeletons of the prehistoric monsters and display them to the public. He met considerable opposition from scientists, both within and outside his staff, who argued that the bones ought to be arranged in drawers and used only for study by experts. Osborn was right, of course, so far as the general public was concerned; he made "dinosaur" a household word, and the massive fossils have remained to this day the most impressive and popular of all the museum's exhibits.

After Osborn became President Jesup's assistant, it soon was clear that the aging president was slowing down. In 1901, at Osborn's suggestion, he brought Dr. Herman Carey Bumpus from Brown University and Wood's Hole Biological Laboratory to become his full-time assistant and soon made him the museum's first director; at about the same time, Osborn was elevated to the Board of Trustees and elected its second vice-president. Bumpus made great contributions to the educational program, such as sending out small collections of "nature cabinets" to the schools; they soon reached more than one million students yearly. As Jesup's health failed, he came to the museum only occasionally in his wheelchair, but it was the clever, calculating Osborn rather than Bumpus who wielded the real administrative power. Osborn turned down his election as secretary of the prestigious Smithsonian Institution in 1905, and upon Jesup's death the next year became president of the trustees, whereupon he soon retired from active teaching at Columbia.

Bumpus was jealous of Osborn's control of the museum and dared publicly to accuse him of "financial mismanagement and subtle dishonesty."[8] In 1910, the trustees investigated, found Osborn innocent of the charges, and dismissed Bumpus. Osborn then appointed Frederic A. Lucas, at that time director of the Brooklyn Museum, as director. The two men worked together somewhat more harmoniously, though Osborn continued to insist upon making the important decisions. Dr. Lucas, writing later of his fifty years as a museum man, remarked ruefully that "the director of a large museum is frequently, or largely, director in name only."[9]

## III

During President Osborn's long administration of some twenty-seven years, the American Museum became recognized as a national and international institution. In the 1920s it was at its height with a growing collection nourished by about one hundred expeditions per year, excellent exhibitions that attracted heavy popular attendance, strong research and publications, and a varied educational program that reached not only the schools but family and community groups. The museum was indeed a model in the natural history field; it was ahead of its two chief American competitors—the Smithsonian Institution's National Museum of Natural History and the Field Museum of Natural History in Chicago—and competed well with the British Museum of Natural History in London.

The museum's financing was unusual and somewhat disorderly, based mainly upon gifts from the trustees and Osborn's friends. He took no salary and even contributed $40,000 to building the fossil collection. J. Pierpont Morgan's first wife was Osborn's aunt, and Morgan for a time gave $15,000 yearly to the paleontology program, a fact which Osborn kept secret. Morgan also financed the work of Charles R. Knight, the freelance painter and sculptor whom Osborn persuaded to provide striking, exciting murals and other pictures and models of prehistoric animals. Osborn obtained private funds for important expeditions, such as Carl Akeley's to obtain specimens for his planned African Hall or several trips of Martin and Osa Johnson to secure motion and still pictures of African animal life. The museum managed to support three expeditions by Roy Chapman Andrews to China, Tibet, Burma, and Outer Mongolia. The last of those tours with a fleet of automobiles and 125 camels found seventy-million-year-old dinosaur eggs, some of them with unhatched babies, in the Gobi Desert in 1943, along with other rare fossils. Osborn was overjoyed to have a prediction that he had made in 1900 fulfilled— that many prehistoric mammals would be found in Asia—and Mrs. Osborn and he hastened to visit the expedition. Osborn's keen eye even found a rare mammal tooth during the trip.

But Osborn thought that the museum's chief purpose was education, not collection. A good museum was no longer "a sanctuary or refuge, a safety deposit vault for curios"; instead it was a "progressive educational force" that "succeeds if it teaches." Before the American Association of Museums in 1917, he declared that "museum folk are educators of a special type," and he developed that idea as follows:

> We enlist in a form of education which is, in fact, most difficult, since its ideals are to present visually the laws of nature and of art in such a way as both to educate and to create a strong impression on the mind of the visitor. In other words, museum folk . . . seldom have an opportunity of speaking to their students; the expression of their thoughts and their ideals is through the exhibits which they arrange. The successful museum teacher is the one who is able to teach without speaking, as nature teaches or art teaches. He may speak only through labels on his specimens.[10]

The exhibitions at the museum were outstanding. Akeley joined its staff as taxidermist and designer in 1909 to install habitat groups, and stunning new halls of mammals opened for North America, South America, and Southern Asia. Between 1880 and 1915 the education program expanded greatly with lectures to school teachers at the museum; nature study collections and lantern slides sent to the schools; visiting school classes; special presentations for the blind; and talks by staff members at the schools. George H. Sherwood became curator of public instruction after 1906 and later was the museum's executive director. He estimated in 1926 that the education program was reaching six million persons each year. The museum also operated a trailside museum at Bear Mountain with nature trails. Osborn himself took delight in viewing the classes of school children streaming into the museum and in stopping boys and girls to ask them their impressions. He often told with much laughter of inquiring of a little red-headed fellow in the elevator, "What do you like best in the Museum?" and of his reply, in a sepulchral voice: "Fossil fishes."[11]

Osborn always encouraged his staff to do scientific investigation, and he helped establish publications to serve as outlets for research of both the staff and outside scholars. The various series included the *Bulletin* (1881–), *Memoirs* (1893–), *Anthropological Papers* (1907–), and *Novitiates* [New Acquaintances] (1921–). He began issuing the magazine *Natural History* in 1900 (at first as the *American Museum Journal*) with popular articles for the members and general public. He also contributed 7,000 volumes of his private library. Still, some biologists, especially those in genetics and physiology, considered the museum old-fashioned in its research and thought that the staff contained too many administrators and field workers without enough graduate training, and produced too few worthwhile publications.

Osborn himself set a fast pace in research and publication. During his career, he produced 940 titles with about 12,000 pages. They covered a broad field indeed—geology, paleontology, comparative anatomy, embryology, neurology, anthropology, evolution of man, biology and principles of evolution, education, conservation of forests and mammals, and biographies of men of science and letters. His two most original paleontological contributions were *The Titanotheres* [mainly fossil horses and rhinoceroses] *of Ancient Wyoming, Dakota, and Kansas*, published in two volumes by the U.S. Geological Survey in 1929, and *The Proboscides* [fossil elephants and mammoths]: *Evolution, Phylogeny, and Classification*, in two volumes which appeared after Osborn's death. His numerous more popular books included *From the Greeks to Darwin* (1894); *The Age of Mammals in Europe, Asia, and North America* (1910); *Men of the Old Stone Age: Their Environment, Life, and Art* (1915); *The Origin and Evolution of Life* (1917); *Evolution and Religion* (1923); *Impressions of Great Naturalists* (1924); *Evolution and Religion in Education* (1926); and *Creative Education in School, College, University, and Museum* (1927). A host of honors came to him from this scholarship—twelve medals, nine honorary degrees, and membership in sixty-one learned societies in fifteen countries.

All together, during Osborn's presidency, the American Museum's building area doubled, the city appropriation tripled, the endowment increased sevenfold, the scientific staff some three times, and membership more than four times. He managed to expand the physical plant so that it contained nearly twenty interconnected structures, perhaps the most important the monumental entrance building honoring Theodore Roosevelt, which the State of New York financed, with a thirty-foot-high statue in front showing Roosevelt mounted on a horse and protecting an American Indian and an African-American. One of Osborn's favorite later plans was an intermuseum promenade 160 feet wide through

Central Park to connect the American Museum and the Metropolitan Museum of Art. He considered the defeat of that project one of the greatest failures of his life.

With his broad interests, Osborn kept the museum in touch with the main movements of American life. During the First World War, he ordered all male employees to perform military and bayonet drill in the parking lot, so that they could defend the museum "against the barbarous Teutonic Horde."[12] In the 1920s, he opposed William Jennings Bryan and the crusade against teaching the theory of evolution in the Tennessee schools that resulted in the Scopes Trial. A lifelong communicant and church-goer, Osborn was startled to find himself classed publicly with Voltaire, Thomas Paine, and Robert Ingersoll as a subversive-atheist. The minister of one large New York church painted the lurid picture of obscenities in some of the plays produced in the city and of the immorality rampant there. He asked, "Who is responsible for this lewdness and this animalism?" and answered, "Henry Fairfield Osborn."[13]

Osborn was involved in a more serious dispute arising from the eugenics movement. His fellow trustee and friend, Madison Grant, in 1916 wrote *The Passing of the Great Age*, which upheld the Nordic race as superior to other Europeans, Negroes, and Orientals. He argued that the United States ought to repudiate its sentimental boast that recognized no distinction in "race, creed, or color" or else write "Finis Americae." Maudlin romanticism had made the country "an asylum of the oppressed" and was sweeping the nation toward a racial abyss.[14] Grant went on to show himself strongly anti-Semitic, anti-Negro, and a believer in sterilization of the unfit. Osborn's preface to the book praised his friend's correct scientific method and declared that the true spirit of eugenics would conserve and multiply the best spiritual, moral, intellectual, and physical forces of heredity to maintain the integrity of American institutions in the future.

When the Second International Conference of Eugenics, with Osborn as president, met at the museum in 1921, he declared that the war had "left the finest racial stocks in many countries so depleted that there is danger of their extinction" and that "our own race is threatened with submergence by the influx of other races." His address at the National Immigration Conference of 1923 continued in the same vein. He thought that the Army intelligence tests had shown that blacks had inferior minds, while "the oriental civilization, the oriental soul, is fundamentally different from the American"; and the Nordic nations were superior to Italy or the Balkans. The government ought to send skilled agents to examine those wishing to come to the United States and thus avoid the calamity of having immigrants constitute one-third the population of our insane asylums.[15]

Osborn and many of the other trustees shared the view that the American Museum ought to promote the proper education of immigrants. He wished to make it a teaching "nature institution" so as to preserve rural and old-time American virtues against immigration and urbanization. Somewhat less prejudiced than Grant, as a practical matter he added a Jewish man, Felix Warburg, to the museum board in 1910 and found him an able and devoted trustee. Osborn took a vocal part in the movement to restrict immigration, and two newspaper articles were headed: "Osborn Calls U. S. Europe's Dump" and "Lo, the Poor Nordic: Professor Osborn's Petition on the Immigration Question." He also was somewhat of an anti-feminist and insisted that women made inferior schoolteachers. After his retirement from the museum, he visited Germany in 1934 and enthusiastically praised the Nazi racial ideas. But he died the next year at his home in Garrison.

## IV

Dr. Margaret Mead, for long the museum's outstanding anthropologist, made a just evaluation of Professor Osborn as president and personality. She said:

> Osborn *ran* the museum. Since then, the president has been . . . well, *normal*. The last days of Osborn were very capricious. He was powerful and capricious. Salaries were thousands of dollars apart because of his capriciousness. Osborn was a magnificent old devil. This was his dream, and he built it. He was arbitrary and opinionated. . . . he was a wealthy man, who was also a scientific explorer. . . . We would never have had the Museum without him.[16]

Dr. Sherwood, who worked under Osborn as curator and director and who sometimes was criticized as being sycophantic to him, thought that Professor Osborn's chief characteristics were breadth of vision, tenacity of purpose, fertility of mind, sympathy with youth, and eternal optimism. Perhaps he should have added something about "limitless energy."

Osborn himself insisted that a scientist could combine research investigation, teaching, and creative institutional work without doing injustice to any of them. In a scientific career, he deemed research by far the highest goal but that institutional work was justified, especially "when it is chiefly directed toward collecting materials for original research in every branch of natural history and in inspiring and training younger men in those branches."[17] In Osborn's case, creative institutional work included not only the American Museum (and for a time Columbia University), but also the New York Zoological Society which was developing the Bronx Zoo. He was a charter member there in 1895, served with Madison Grant on the executive committee, and was its hardworking president from 1909 to 1924.[18]

The American Museum of Natural History was controlled and administered by two presidents of its Board of Trustees, Jesup and Osborn, for half a century, from 1881 to 1933. They did a good job on the whole, but with power concentrated as it was, they could be arbitrary and unreasonable; that was especially true in Osborn's case. Financing was also often indefinite and uncertain when it was so dependent upon the whims of wealthy board members and their friends. Though Osborn retired during the great depression, which gravely cut back the museum's programs for a period, from that time forward, the president and the Board of Trustees usually confined themselves to raising funds and approving general policies, while the director did the everyday administration, carried out policies, handled personnel problems including appointments and dismissals, with the curators had charge of the museological functions of collection, preservation, research, exhibition, and education, and suggested policies for board consideration. The American Museum, however, recently has joined several of the larger American museums in employing as president a paid administrator, whose chief function is fundraising and other financial concerns, and placing under him the subject-matter specialist, the director. No doubt, Henry Fairfield Osborn would have approved heartily of that arrangement.

## NOTES

1. This chapter is based on the following sources: American Museum of Natural History *Annual Report* 1 (1870); Roy Chapman Andrews, *On the Trail of Ancient Man: A Narrative of the Field Work of the Central Asiatic Expeditions* (New York: G. P. Putnam's Sons, 1926); William Adams Brown, *Morris Ketchum Jesup: A Character Sketch* (New York: Charles Scribner's Sons, 1910); Ralph W. Dexter, "The Role of F. W. Putnam in Developing Anthropology at the American Museum of Natural History," *Curator* 9 (1976): 303–10; Madison Grant, *The Passing of a Great Race, or the Racial Basis of European History*, 4th rev. ed. (New York: Charles Scribner's Sons, 1929); William King Gregory, "Henry Fairfield Osborn," American Philosophical Society *Proceedings* 76 (1936): 395–408; Gregory, "Henry Fairfield Osborn, 1857–1935," National Academy of Sciences *Biographical Memoirs* 19 (1938): 50–119; Gregory, "Henry Fairfield Osborn: An Appreciation," *Scientific Monthly* 41 (Dec. 1935): 567–69; Geoffrey T. Hellman, *Bankers, Bones & Beetles: The First Century of the American Museum of Natural History* (Garden City, N.Y.: Natural History Press, 1969); John Michael Kennedy, "Philanthropy and

Science in New York City: The American Museum of Natural History, 1868–1968" (New Haven: Yale University Ph.D. Dissertation, 1968); Frederic Augustus Lucas, *Fifty Years of Museum Work: Autobiography, Unpublished Papers, and Bibliography* (New York: American Museum of Natural History, 1933); *Natural History: The Journal of the American Museum of Natural History, New York* 1 (1900); Henry Fairfield Osborn, *The American Museum of Natural History: Its Origin, Its History, the Growth of Its Departments to December 31, 1909*, 2d edition (New York: Irving Press, 1911); Osborn, "Biographical Memoir of Edward Drinker Cope, 1840–1897," National Academy of Sciences *Biographical Memoirs* 13 (1930): 124–317; Osborn, *Creative Education in School, College, University, and Museum: Personal Observation and Experience of the Half-Century, 1877–1927* (New York: Charles Scribner's Sons, 1927); Osborn, *Evolution and Religion in Education: Polemics of the Fundamentalist Controversy of 1922–1928* (New York: Charles Scribner's Sons, 1928); Osborn, *Fifty-two Years of Research, Observation and Publication, 1877–1929: A Life Adventure in Breadth and Depth*, ed. by Florence Milligan (New York: Charles Scribner's Sons, 1930); Osborn, *Impressions of Great Naturalists: Darwin, Wallace, Huxley, Leidy, Cope, Balfour, Roosevelt, and Others*, 2d edition revised (New York: Charles Scribner's Sons, 1928); Osborn, "Morris K. Jesup," *Science* 27 (Feb 7, 1908): 235–36; "Henry Fairfield Osborn . . . Tributes Paid at Memorial Meetings," *Natural History Supplement* 37 (Feb. 1936): 1–14; Douglas J. Preston, *Dinosaurs in the Attic: An Excursion into the American Museum of Natural History* (New York: St. Martin's Press, 1987); Nina J. Root, "The Library of the American Museum of Natural History," *Journal of the Society for the Bibliography of Natural History* 9 (Apr. 1980): 587–91; George Gaylord Simpson, "Henry Fairfield Osborn," *Dictionary of American Biography* (New York: Charles Scribner's Sons, 1940), Supplement 1: 584–87.

2. Osborn, *American Museum of Natural History*, 11.
3. Brown, *Jesup*, 153.
4. Osborn, *Creative Education*, 4–5.
5. Gregory, "Henry Fairfield Osborn, 1857–1935," 61.
6. Osborn, *Fifty-two Years*, 63.
7. Osborn, *Impressions of Great Naturalists*, 179.
8. Hellman, *Bankers, Bones & Beetles*, 112.
9. Ibid., 152.
10. Osborn, *Creative Education*, 235, 242–46.
11. "Henry Fairfield Osborn Tributes," 5; Osborn, *Creative Education*, 22.
12. Root, "Library of the American Museum," 589.
13. "Henry Fairfield Osborn Tributes," 12–14; Osborn, *Impressions of Great Naturalists*, 163.
14. Grant, *Passing of the Great Age*, xxxiii, 263.
15. American Museum, *Annual Report*, 1921: 31–33; Henry Fairfield Osborn, "The Approach to the Immigration Problem through Science," National Immigration Conference *Proceedings* (Dec. 13–14, 1923): 3–11.
16. Hellman, *Bankers, Bones & Beetles*, 204.
17. Osborn, *Fifty-two Years*, 62.
18. William Bridges, *Gathering of Animals: An Unconventional History of the New York Zoological Society* (New York: Harper and Row, 1974).

## SELECT BIBLIOGRAPHY

American Museum of Natural History. *Annual Report* 1 (1870).

Andrews, Roy Chapman. *On the Trail of Ancient Man: A Narrative of the Field Work of the*

*Central Asiatic Expeditions*. New York: G. P. Putnam's Sons, 1926.
Bridges, William. *Gathering of Animals: An Unconventional History of the New York Zoological Society*. New York: Harper and Row, 1974.
Brown, William Adams. *Morris Ketchum Jesup: A Character Sketch*. New York: Charles Scribner's Sons, 1910.
Dexter, Ralph W. "The Role of F. W. Putnam in Developing Anthropology at the American Museum of Natural History." *Curator* 9 (1976): 303–10.
Grant, Madison. *The Passing of a Great Race, or the Racial Basis of European History*. 4th rev. ed. New York: Charles Scribner's Sons, 1929).
Gregory, William King. "Henry Fairfield Osborn." American Philosophical Society *Proceedings* 76 (1936): 395–408.
_____. "Henry Fairfield Osborn, 1857–1935." National Academy of Sciences *Biographical Memoirs* 19 (1938): 50–119.
_____. "Henry Fairfield Osborn: An Appreciation." *Scientific Monthly* 41 (Dec. 1935): 567–69.
Hellman, Geoffrey T. *Bankers, Bones & Beetles: The First Century of the American Museum of Natural History*. Garden City, N.Y.: Natural History Press, 1969.
Kennedy, John Michael. "Philanthropy and Science in New York City: The American Museum of Natural History, 1868–1968." New Haven: Yale University Ph.D. Dissertation, 1968.
Lucas, Frederic Augustus. *Fifty Years of Museum Work: Autobiography, Unpublished Papers, and Bibliography*. New York: American Museum of Natural History, 1933.
*Natural History: The Journal of the American Museum of Natural History, New York* 1 (1900).
Osborn, Henry Fairfield. *The American Museum of Natural History: Its Origin, Its History, the Growth of Its Departments to December 31, 1909*. 2d edition. New York: Irving Press, 1911.
_____. "Biographical Memoir of Edward Drinker Cope, 1840–1897." National Academy of Sciences *Biographical Memoirs* 13 (1930): 124–317.
_____. *Creative Education in School, College, University, and Museum: Personal Observation and Experience of the Half-Century, 1877–1927*. New York: Charles Scribner's Sons, 1927.
_____. *Evolution and Religion in Education: Polemics of the Fundamentalist Controversy of 1922–1928*. New York: Charles Scribner's Sons, 1928.
_____. *Fifty-two Years of Research, Observation and Publication, 1877–1929: A Life Adventure in Breadth and Depth*. Edited by Florence Milligan. New York: Charles Scribner's Sons, 1930.
_____. *Impressions of Great Naturalists: Darwin, Wallace, Huxley, Leidy, Cope, Balfour, Roosevelt, and Others*. 2d edition revised. New York: Charles Scribner's Sons, 1928.
_____. "Morris K. Jesup." *Science* 27 (Feb 7, 1908): 235–36.
_____. "The Approach to the Immigration Problem through Science." National Immigration Conference *Proceedings* (Dec. 13–14, 1923): 3–11.
"Henry Fairfield Osborn ... Tributes Paid at Memorial Meetings." *Natural History Supplement* 37 (Feb. 1936): 1–14.
Preston, Douglas J. *Dinosaurs in the Attic: An Excursion into the American Museum of Natural History*. New York: St. Martin's Press, 1987.
Root, Nina J. "The Library of the American Museum of Natural History." *Journal of the Society for the Bibliography of Natural History* 9 (Apr. 1980): 587–91.
Simpson, George Gaylord. "Henry Fairfield Osborn." *Dictionary of American Biography*. New York: Charles Scribner's Sons, 1940, Supplement 1: 584–87.

# CHAPTER 2

# Carl Ethan Akeley *Perfects the Habitat Group Exhibition*

## I

When Carl Akeley as a young man in the 1870s became enamored of taxidermy, the ordinary practice of that craft was, by modern standards, extremely primitive. The hide of the animal would be steeped in a bath of salt, alum, and arsenical soap, and the dried, tanned skin then hung upside down. The carcass was stuffed with straw or rags, and the wired and wrapped leg bones inserted. The process killed pests, but shrinkage of the tanned hide could give the animal's face a comical leer, and the carcass usually was overstuffed. In any case, the animal did not look natural. Akeley asserted that taxidermy had been started by upholsterers, and he and his friend William Wheeler once burst into gales of laughter when they saw a lumpy stuffed lynx upholstered to four times its normal size and with a glass eye that peered off at an absurd angle.

Akeley soon began to try to make the animals that he worked on appear more natural. At Ward's Establishment in Rochester, New York, he used a plaster cast for a zebra's body and managed to avoid splitting the skin of its legs, but his conservative fellow taxidermists threw the experiment out on the dump. At the Milwaukee Public Museum, Akeley succeeded in mounting a muskrat colony in its proper watery element, a true habitat group that is still on display there. Later, at the Field Museum in Chicago, he achieved a modern and greatly improved taxidermy. For a time, how to substitute a light papier-maché and wirecloth manikin for a heavy cast puzzled him, but one day, on a streetcar bound for the museum, he suddenly cried out, "I've got it!" much to the amusement of the other passengers.

His final procedure called for the taxidermist to study the animal's anatomy as well as its habits in the field, and to make full photographic records of the carcass, often with a death mask of the head and casts of other portions of the body. The animal was skinned carefully; a small slit in the belly allowed the leg bones to be removed without splitting the skin of the legs; and the whole hide was scraped, fleshed, and dried. Everything was then packed in zinc-lined cases and poisoned with disulfide of carbon. In the field also, flora such as leaves, branches, mosses, and flowers were preserved in formalin or reproduced in plaster casts with color notes. Sketches were made of the area to be used as painted background.

Back in the museum workroom, Akeley fashioned a clay model that showed each muscle and tendon of the animal as well as sectional plaster molds, each lined with a thin coating of glue and muslin. When the glue had dried, papier-maché was molded in the plaster form, reinforced with wirecloth, and placed in water to melt the glue. The result was a lightweight but strong manikin. The pelt, having been treated and softened with a vegetable tanning agent, then was fitted over the manikin and shellacked to make it impervious to moisture. The bones or metal supports on the interior held the manikin in place, and the preserved animal would last indefinitely. Akeley also invented metal molds to reproduce the environmental foliage in wax.

Akeley's "enduring passion for artistic taxidermy" thus produced an authentic faunal habitat group. An artificially lighted exhibit case or diorama with a glass front showed the animal or animals with realistic anatomy and in lifelike poses. The plastic foreground of rocks, soil, plants, and accessories reconstructed the natural habitat and merged, in the rear, into a curved canvas painting of an actual scene.[1] His friend Wheeler explained Akeley's reasoning thus:

> He was thoroughly convinced that an animal is meaningless, except to a hard-shelled zoologist, unless it is presented in such a manner as to convey something of its real character, or *ethos*, which is manifested by its specific motor behavior in a specific natural environment.[2]

The director of the Milwaukee Public Museum, Henry L. Ward, asserted that Akeley was "the man of whom I can say without fear of accusation of flattery that he has done more for taxidermy in America than any other person." According to Dr. Wilfred H. Osgood, chief curator of zoology at the Field Museum, "By utilizing the methods of the sculptor, in connection with ingenious devices of his own invention, he revolutionized taxidermy and raised it to the level of a high art." And Dr. Henry Fairfield Osborn of the American Museum of Natural History said that he wished

> to express the everlasting debt which all museums in America owe to the life work of this remarkable man. We may only estimate the full measure of our debt by considering what the standards, not only of this Museum but of all museums in America, would have been without the sweep of his great achievements, which gave us a wholly new conception of the mammalian kingdom and of the close portrayal of nature in animal habitat groups.

Professor Osborn also told his staff: "This Museum has benefited throughout more than half a century by high talent among men and women in its service, but Akeley was the only genius who has been among us."[3]

Akeley's wife, Mary, was exaggerating, however, when she called his muskrats at the Milwaukee Public Museum the "first true habitat group." Several exhibitors had already produced or were producing museum groups. Charles Willson Peale, in his Philadelphia Museum in the eighteenth century, exhibited naturally posed birds and small animals with environmental features such as reproduced plants and with accurately painted backgrounds. Others exhibited less true-to-nature storytelling groups, for instance, Jules Verreaux's "Arab Courier Attacked by Lions" shown at the Paris Exposition of 1867. William Temple Hornaday in 1879, while still working at Ward's and after an expedition to India and Borneo, prepared a group of five orangutans, entitled "Battle in the Treetops," that created a sensation when shown at a meeting of the American Association for the Advancement of Science. Later, as chief taxidermist at the Smithsonian's United States National Museum, he added several outstanding groups there, employing many of the same principles that Akeley was to follow.[4]

## II

Carl Ethan Akeley was born on a farm in Orleans County west of Rochester, New York, on May 20, 1864. His father, Daniel Webster Akeley, had come from Vermont, and his mother, born Julia Glidden, was a member of a somewhat aristocratic family of the Rochester area. He attended country school, did farm chores, and was an enthusiastic hunter and student of birds. At age twelve, Carl read an advertisement in the *Youth's Companion* for a book on taxidermy; it cost one dollar, but he managed to borrow a copy from an older boy. He stuffed a canary for a woman and, at age sixteen, had some business cards printed that read: "Carl E. Akeley—Artistic Taxidermy in All Its Branches." He took some lessons in painting in a nearby town and then, for some six weeks, attended Brockport Normal School during the day and, in the evening, observed an Englishman, David Bruce, painter, decorator, and amateur taxidermist, as he worked.

Bruce suggested that he go to see Professor Henry A. Ward, who ran Ward's Natural History Establishment at Rochester, collecting and selling specimens and other objects to colleges and museums and employing several taxidermists, among whom was Frederic A. Lucas, to be in turn director of the Brooklyn Museum and the American Museum of Natural History. Hornaday later described Ward as having "the nervous energy of an electric motor, the imagination and vision of Napoleon, the collecting tentacles of an octopus, and the poise of a Chesterfield."[5] Akeley walked three miles to take the train to Rochester, and then went beneath the arch made by the jaws of a sperm whale and past a big stuffed gorilla in front of the fifteen buildings of Ward's Establishment. He paced back and forth shyly and finally entered Ward's office, to be greeted with a gruff "What do you want?" Ward hired him as a student taxidermist at only $3.50 per week, though his room and board cost $4.

Akeley got to know the other taxidermists and became a close friend of William North Wheeler from Milwaukee, also aged nineteen, whom Ward had hired at $9 weekly. The two young men read the classics aloud together, took long walks, attended the Universalist Church, and went to lectures, one of them on "Which Way?" by the agnostic Robert Ingersoll, whom they found inspiring and witty. Wheeler was to meet many scientists during his long and successful career, but he later asserted that, "Of all the men I have known," Carl seemed "to have the greatest range of innate ability."[6] Akeley spent four years at Ward's, but his experimental approach to taxidermy was not always appreciated. Ward fired him after his first year, and for six months he worked in the New York taxidermy shop of John Wallace. Ward then rehired him, saying that his dismissal had been based on false reports.

Akeley decided that he would like to enter the Sheffield Scientific School at Yale, but failed the entrance examination. Wheeler, who had returned to Milwaukee to teach in the German Academy, urged him to come there and offered to tutor him. Akeley delayed leaving Ward's because "Jumbo," P. T. Barnum's famed elephant, had been killed in Canada in an encounter with a railroad locomotive, and Ward's was to treat the remains. Akeley took the leading role in preparing the huge carcass for exhibition with Barnum's circus (it later went to the Museum at Tufts University) and also in articulating the skeleton for the American Museum of Natural History.[7]

In the fall of 1886, Akeley moved to Milwaukee and set up a taxidermy shop in a barn that belonged to Wheeler's mother. He did much work for the Milwaukee Public Museum and was added to its staff, while Wheeler became the museum custodian (director) there. Akeley studied animal anatomy and experimented with producing manikins for the mounted bodies. One of the museum board members obtained a sledge from lapland, and Akeley modeled a reindeer to pull it and an authentically dressed Laplander as driver with waxen face and hands. He also did the group of orangutans from Borneo and planned a series on Wisconsin fur-bearing animals. He completed "Muskrats at Home" in 1893 and later, in his shop, prepared a horse for the Smithsonian Institution to show at the Columbian Exposition in Chicago, and a buck's head, entitled "The Challenge," that won first prize in a Sportsman's Show at New York (where, incidentally, Theodore Roosevelt was one of the judges). Akeley stayed in Milwaukee for eight years, and his friend Wheeler was the cause of his leaving. While traveling in Europe, Wheeler called on Sir William Fowler, director of the British Museum of Natural History, and told him of his friend's superior talent in taxidermy, whereupon Sir William offered Akeley a position.[8]

When Akeley left Milwaukee in 1895 on his way to London, he stopped at the Field Columbian Museum in Chicago. Dr. Daniel Giraud Elliot, the curator of zoology, offered him several taxonomic commissions, which he decided to accept, and in the next year he went to Africa with Dr. Elliot on a collecting expedition. At Chicago, Akeley perfected his procedure for producing habitat groups. He did a series on Virginia deer—life-sized dioramas showing them in spring, summer, fall, and winter. He planned several extensive habitat halls for the Field's new building, but when they failed to receive financing, he moved on in 1909 to work for the American Museum of Natural History in New York, where he remained until his death. He kept in touch with the Field Museum, however, and the two institutions often cooperated on projects.[9]

While in Chicago, Akeley was married, in 1902, to Delia J. Denning of Beaver Dam, Wisconsin. She accompanied him on two African expeditions and nursed him after an almost fatal encounter with an elephant. After World War I, the marriage deteriorated and the couple separated, Carl living in New York bachelor quarters with two companions, Vilhjamar Stefansson, the explorer, and Herbert

J. Spinden. This was probably the period that Robert Cushman Murphy recalled when coteries of writers, painters, savants, and creative men of affairs would sit late at dinner in the Century Club and get "Ake" to talk about his varied experiences.[10] In March 1923, Delia accused him of mental cruelty, and an acrimonious divorce ended the marriage. Carl was wed to Mary L. Jobe in October 1924. He was sixty years old and she, thirty-eight. Mary was an experienced mountain climber and explorer, who had made seven expeditions in the Canadian Rockies, and the Canadian Government had named a high peak there "Mount Jobe" in her honor. She also conducted Camp Mystic in Mystic, Connecticut, in summers to teach young girls physical fitness and outdoor survival skills.[11] Stefansson took her to the American Museum to meet Akeley in 1922, and she described him at work on a gorilla group as follows:

> Carl came in. He was wiping his hands on a wad of tow. His shirt sleeves were rolled above his elbows and his clothes were bespotted with plaster. Behind his flecked spectacles his eyes smiled—almost twinkled. Little did either of us dream that one day, we would be together climbing the high forested mountains of his beloved Africa.[12]

Akeley got along well with young people, and he trained several staff members to be taxidermists. Louis P. Jonas, who worked with him for three years at the American Museum, admired his "constant supply of surprising ideas" and well described him:

> The old khaki trousers he wore when he worked, the corn cob pipe he smoked but more frequently allowed to grow cold in his absorption in his task, I remember as part of his beloved personality. To me then as now it seems that the encouragement and inspiration which Akeley gave to the rising naturalists of his day were among his most valuable gifts to his fellow men—contributions which will leave a profound influence for many years to come upon those who worked with him.[13]

Akeley himself told Mary during his last African expedition: "I want twenty more good years for work. Then African Hall [his great conception for the American Museum] will be so nearly finished that the men who know my methods and have worked with me can carry it on to final completion."[14] His life was to end on that journey, but James L. Clark, Robert H. Rockwell, Richard G. Raddatz, and others completed his dream.

Akeley was also an ingenious inventor. At Chicago about 1909, the old building for the Columbian Exposition that then housed the Field Museum was losing patches of stucco. Akeley modified an air spray gun that he used in building manikins so that it could spread liquid cement and gave the building a fresh coating. His patented Cement Gun was employed on the Panama Canal and many other projects. After experiencing, on his African expedition of 1909–1910, the limitations of the motion picture camera then in use, he devised and patented the Akeley Camera, which would pan up and down, from side to side, and diagonally. It also easily made use of telescopic lens and had a faster shutter that permitted photography in poorer light. With his new camera, Akeley photographed elephants, lions, gorillas, and other African wildlife, and the team of Martin and Osa Johnson used it on their photographic explorations in Africa for the American Museum. The camera also recorded the last race of Man O'War and the Dempsey-Carpentier heavyweight fight. Robert L. Flaherty employed it for *Nanook of the North* and *Moana*, and it became the favorite of many other documentary filmmakers. The Franklin Institute of Philadelphia awarded Akeley its Scott Medal for inventing the Cement Gun and its John Price Wetherill Medal for the camera.[15]

During World War I, Akeley was a dollar-a-year man in the Engineer Corps, solving many problems. His camera photographed battlefield scenes, and the Cement Gun lined trenches and helped produce concrete boats, which, however, proved unsuccessful. He worked on large searchlights, furnishing them with a mirror system, and on an improved tank. He was constantly on call to the Shipping Board, Bureau of Standards, Ordnance Department, and National Research Council. The engineers would often remark about a problem: "Let's see what Akeley says."[16]

## III

Carl Akeley was one of those fortunate broadly-based human beings whose touch of genius expressed itself in varied fields. He was equally at home in the arts of taxidermy and sculpture or the practicalities of mechanical invention. The real governing force of his life, however, became a deep, even passionate love for Africa and its wildlife. It irritated him to have it called the "Dark Continent," and he entitled his book *In Brightest Africa*. He insisted that gorillas were not the fierce, aggressive creatures they were sometimes pictured, but generally gentle and would attack humans only if defending their young. Elephants usually avoided conflicts with hunters, and the courageous lion "is a gentleman," not at all vindictive and rarely "man-eating." Akeley soon forgot the voracious mosquitoes, rampant malaria, stifling heat of the tropics, and cold, heavy rain of the mountains. He rejoiced in the Kivu area of the high Belgian Congo with its three smoking volcanic cones—Bisoke, Karisimbi, and Mikeno.

He told his wife there: "This is the Kivu at last. Here the fairies play: Isn't this forest the most beautiful, the most ancient in all the world?" He often said that he wanted "to die in the harness" and "to be buried in Africa."[17]

On Akeley's first African trip, to British Somaliland in 1896 for the Field Museum as Dr. Elliot's assistant, he was enchanted by the great herds of game that he saw. He did not kill lightly but only to secure museum specimens, to provide food for the expedition, or for bait. On that trip he obtained examples for fifteen large groups that he mounted for the museum on his return. They included the African buffalo, mountain nyala, Swayne's hartebeast, rare dibatag (Clark's gazelle), beim (small antelope), wild ass, zebra, wart hog, spotted and striped hyenas, jackal, cheetah, leopard, white-tailed gnu, quereza monkey, aardvark, black forest hog, bongo, and giant sable antelope. A dangerous high point of the tour was his hand-to-hand battle with a leopard, which, as he was hunting ostriches, sprang on him suddenly and knocked his gun to the ground after he had fired a shot that hit one paw. The beast bit him along his arm, but Akeley got his hand down its throat to keep it from biting elsewhere, partially strangled it, fell on top of it breaking several of its ribs, and finally killed it with a knife brought by one of the native bearers. Akeley's hand was mangled, his body covered with bloody scratches and bruises, upon which he poured disinfectants liberally.[18]

In 1905–1906 Akeley made his second journey, this time to British East Africa. He took a young Kikuyu lad of twelve or thirteen, Uimba Gikungu, whom he called "Bill," on the safari, and Bill served him well, usually as gun boy, on subsequent trips. Akeley was his *Bwana*, and, on the last expedition, Mary Akeley his *Memsahib*. Akeley took the white hunter, Richard J. Cunningham, with him on the first part of the tour to teach him how to hunt elephants. He then went to Uganda on his own and collected thirteen species of animals for the Field Museum's African Hall. Upon his return, he mounted the two huge elephants, "The Fighting Bulls," that still dominate the Field's entrance hall.[19]

Akeley's third African venture was for the American Museum of Natural History, in 1909–1910. He studied then mainly elephants, lions, and the lion-spearing hunts of the natives and wished to obtain elephants for an outstanding group for the museum. Theodore Roosevelt was also on safari with his son Kermit, and the two expeditions joined for a time. T. R. shot a cow elephant for Akeley's proposed group, and Kermit, a baby elephant, while Carl secured a magnificent old bull and a younger male. Upon his return to New York, he mounted an impressive group of the four, entitled "The Alarm."

James L. Clark, whom the American Museum had earlier sent to Chicago to study with him, was astonished when he joined Akeley in Africa to find him well along in treating three elephant hides. Clark commented thus: "How Akeley had done it, I cannot guess, but by dint of working all night himself and by working the natives as well, he had managed to get the skins of three of those huge beasts before we arrived."[20] Such bursts of energy were typical of Akeley, and he frequently labored all night in the field or later at the museum when mounting specimens.

On that expedition, Akeley was attacked and almost killed by a raging bull elephant when his gun jammed. He had the presence of mind to grasp the two tusks and swing between them, but the beast mashed his chest with its trunk and pushed the tusks into the ground, intent upon crushing him to death. Fortunately, the tusks struck a stone or other impediment, and the elephant left him for dead in order to attack some of the bearers. Akeley was unconscious for about six hours; the natives thought he had expired and superstitiously refused to touch him. They did send word to the camp, and Delia Akeley pressed through the night to reach him. He had suffered a broken nose, his cheek cut open to the teeth, one eye closed, his forehead bleeding, and several ribs cracked and protruding into the lungs. He spent several months recovering, and some of his friends thought that he was slowed down permanently by the attack. One positive result of the incident was that, upon his return home while still recuperating, he began to plan a great African Hall for the American Museum.[21]

Akeley's fourth tour to Africa, in 1921–1922, went to the high gorilla country of the Belgian Congo. Mr. and Mrs. Herbert E. Bradley of Chicago accompanied him along with their five-year-old daughter, Alice, a governess, and a woman secretary. Akeley took the women and the child along to show that Africa, with its gorillas, was a relatively safe place. He was intent upon obtaining a mountain gorilla group for his African Hall. Bradley shot a huge male, known as the "Giant of Karisimbi," and Akeley secured a younger male, a female, and her four-year-old son. The male he shot came crashing down a steep incline but was stopped by a tree, and Akeley skinned it in that precarious position. The female took a similar fall into a deep abyss, where he had difficulty in securing the hide.

Mrs. Bradley was worried about his health and wrote:

> We reached the camp and found Mr. Akeley looking as if years instead of days had intervened. He was very worn; he had done the work of ten men under particularly trying conditions; he had started with a fever, had been infected with jiggers . . .; he had killed his gorillas in most inaccessible places where his natives

> had balked at following; he had skinned and skeletonized and dissected without rest, and now energy and appetite had deserted him. We felt troubled when we saw him, but a good dinner . . . began to make him feel better.[22]

Akeley was transported by the beauty of the volcanic Kivu region and vowed to return to gather proper surface and plant accessories and to bring along an artist to paint the awe-inspiring scene for background. Upon his return to the museum, he mounted the four gorillas in a naturally posed group with the old bull thumping its chest.[23]

During the next few years, Akeley completed drawings and blueprints for his African Hall and made a scale model. The main room was to be 152 feet long, 60 feet wide, and 30 feet high. On a platform in the center would stand the great elephant group, "The Alarm," flanked by black rhinoceroses at one end, and white rhinos at the other. By this time Akeley had become a skillful sculptor. He planned to install life-sized bronzes that showed three Nandi natives hunting lions while armed only with spears. In one sculpture, two of the natives had thrown their spears, wounding one of the lions, while the third hunter stood ready to meet their onset. Another bronze had the lion and lioness charging, and the third portrayed the hunters chanting a requiem over the dead beasts. Stanley Field, president of the Field Museum, was so impressed by the sculptures that he agreed to pay for two bronze copies of each plaster original, one set to be exhibited in each of the two African Halls. At the other end of the American Museum's installation, one would see other Akeley bronzes—of a combat between a lion and buffalo; "At Bay," showing an elephant caught in a trap; and "Jungle Football," with four baby elephants playing with a dirt ball, a fragment of a sun-baked ant hill.

The hall was to be dimly illuminated but with two levels of forty well-lighted habitat groups in hermetically sealed alleyways behind glass so as to provide uniform temperature and humidity. Four larger corner groups on the first floor showed a dozen species on the equatorial river Tana; a plains group with baboons, zebras, and elands; a Congo forest with gorillas, okapi, and chimpanzees; and a desert water hole with a sixteen-foot-high reticulated giraffe drinking while surrounded by other animals. Below the second level, a bronze bas-relief in twenty-four panels portrayed African natives in their villages with their domestic animals or on the hunt.

President Osborn of the American Museum was enthusiastic about Akeley's plan for the new hall, and agreed to ask the City of New York to finance a new wing to contain the African Hall; he urged Akeley to secure funding for another tour to obtain animals. In 1925, Daniel E. Pomeroy, a wealthy friend of Carl's from New York, took him to meet George Eastman, the Kodak photographic entrepreneur, who also was a big game hunter. Akeley described his project to Eastman with unrestrained enthusiasm and at once, undiplomatically, asked him for a million dollars. The outcome was that Eastman put up $100,000 for four habitat groups, Pomeroy $25,000 for one, and his friend, Colonel Daniel B. Wentz of Philadelphia, $25,000 for another. The three men were to go on safari in Africa with Akeley to secure animals for their groups; unfortunately, Colonel Wentz died before he could leave, but his contribution remained. The American Museum also sent two preparators—Robert H. Rockwell and Richard C. Raddatz—and two artists to paint background scenes—Arthur A. Janson and William R. Leigh.[24]

Carl and Mary (it was her first journey to Africa) left in January 1926 for London, where they completed gathering supplies. They then stopped in Brussels to meet King Albert. Carl had suggested in 1922 that the king set aside an area ten miles square in the Kivu region as a sanctuary for mountain gorillas and other wildlife, and the king had established Parc National Albert in 1925. He now asked Carl to survey the plot during the expedition, and he agreed to have Dr. Jean M. Derscheid, the Belgian zoologist, go along.

The Akeleys went on by way of Genoa, the Suez Canal, and Mombasa to Nairobi in Kenya. There they soon met Eastman and Pomeroy as well as Martin and Osa Johnson, who were photographing African animals. When the Akeleys in three lorries and a Chevrolet car began to gather specimens, Carl was depressed to see that wildlife was disappearing under the onslaughts of farmers, ivory poachers, and greedy big game hunters. The Akeleys met an old Boer farmer, who emphatically wished to see the "vermin zebra" exterminated. After hunting buffalo fruitlessly in the Tana River region, Carl said: "I have not appreciated the absolute necessity of carrying on the African Hall . . . as I do now after this painful revelation. *The old conditions, the story of which we want to tell, are now gone and in another decade the men who knew them will be gone.*"[25]

The expedition had some lighter moments, as in May on Carl's birthday, when Mary arranged a surprise party with a wonderful cake, a bouquet of wildflowers gathered by Leigh, clever place cards drawn by Jansson, and special drinks concocted by Raddatz.[26] There were also some solid successes. Mary Akeley was a good executive (she called herself a "proper safari manager and general factotum") and soon took over the difficult task of dealing with the native bearers. Carl shot a magnificent reticulated giraffe bull and a female, and in Tanganika they saw a total of 146 lions, of which Carl obtained excellent motion pictures. Bill, the gun boy, sighted a fine black-maned lion that *Memsahib* shot. But by August, Carl was running a high fever, apparently typhoid, and was alarmingly weak. Mary had him loaded into a lorry and sat beside him as they set out over 300 miles of rough country for Nairobi. After treatment at the hospital there, Carl reluctantly spent three weeks in the Kenya Nursing Home.

On October 14, despite Mary's protests, he insisted that he had recovered, and they started for the Kivu. Carl still was far from well but always outdistanced Mary on the trail; he told her what his secret was: "There is only one way to get through. I just put my head down and go." On October 18, they celebrated their second wedding anniversary. The native porters sang to them and received the customary *baksheesh*, or gratuity. The expedition reached the Kivu in November, but Carl frequently had to be carried in a hammock, with Mary walking beside him. By November 13, he was spending the day in bed, and on November 17, he died, perhaps from pneumonia, dysentery, typhoid, or exhaustion. He was buried on Mount Mikeno in a grave cut eight feet into the soft lava rock; a concrete slab covered the coffin of native mahogany, bearing the simple inscription: "Carl Akeley/November 17, 1926."

Rockwell, the preparator, and Leigh, the artist, later wrote books that described the expedition. Both men were enchanted by the African countryside and awed by Akeley's personality and his driving determination. Rockwell said that "Carl saw as his great mission in life the preservation for posterity of a monumental and lifelike record of the fauna of this great bright continent. To the best of my ability I dedicated myself to the same ideals that had fired this creative genius."[27] Leigh thought that he "was in the company of a great—a tremendous temperament . . . a great soul—a blazer of new trails." He added: "Such a spirit as Akeley's does not often appear in this world. He had the rare quality—seldom understood or appreciated because it is so unusual—of complete devotion to art. It was his God."[28] Both men observed that he did not get along with Eastman, who refused to give him an additional $500,000 for his project. Rockwell described personalities well. He found Pomeroy a jovial, happy companion in contrast to the somber, cold, and dour Eastman, and he thought "feminine little Osa [Johnson], a courageous daredevil if I ever saw one."[29] Akeley gave Rockwell much responsibility and had him shoot specimens in addition to gathering plants and other environmental material for the habitat groups.

Mary Akeley was determined that the expedition should be completed, and she assumed its leadership. She later wrote: "We had to keep faith with him who had such faith in us. There was nothing else to do." She located the spot that Carl had chosen as background for his gorilla group (he had thought it the "most glorious scene in Africa") and set Leigh to making sketches, while Raddatz and she photographed the rocks, trees, and foliage of the site and took samples in formalin or plaster casts that would enable the preparators to create an accurate foreground. In April 1927, the Akeley-Eastman-Pomeroy Expedition reached the United States, sixteen months after it had departed.[30]

The Akeley African Halls at the American Museum and the Field Museum, both of them conceived and partially mounted by Carl Akeley, were dedicated in 1927, but the New York one was not opened in largely completed form until 1938. Mary Akeley did much to keep her husband's memory alive. She was an accomplished writer, capturing the African scene much more vividly than Carl. She produced seven good books on Africa, between 1929 and 1951, mainly on Akeley's work, using Carl's journals and her own daily diary as a basis. Delia Akeley threatened to sue Mary for libel because, in telling of Carl's deadly encounter with the bull elephant, she had credited the courageous dash through the night to reach him to Bill, the gun boy, instead of Delia. The first Mrs. Akeley made an African expedition of her own in 1925 and wrote a book about it, and an earlier work of hers was devoted to J.T., Jr., a pet monkey that Carl and Delia had acquired on one trip. Both wives thus took advantage of their African experiences to claim a share in Akeley's fame.

Mary Akeley continued to take a deep interest in the Parc National Albert in the Belgian Congo. King Albert formally inaugurated it in 1929 with an enlarged area of 500,000 acres. An American Committee for the park was formed with President Osborn a member and Mary Akeley as secretary. The king bestowed upon her the Cross of the Knights of the Order of the Crown of Belgium. She took two more African trips, one to South Africa to inspect wild animal sanctuaries and another to the Congo, during which she revisited Carl's grave.[31]

Carl Akeley's contributions to museums were outstanding. He perfected the habitat group that showed animals and their environment accurately, effectively, and hopefully permanently. Careful study of animal anatomy and *ethos*, of the rocks, soil, and plants of the habitat, and of scenic backgrounds would guarantee the naturalness and liveliness of the exhibit. Attention to the use of lasting materials in the whole display, safe lighting, and nonfluctuating temperature and humidity would insure a high degree of permanence. Good natural history museums in America and throughout the world adopted Carl Akeley's version of the habitat group.

But Akeley had come to have a higher personal aim. His youthful zest and tremendous nervous energy, tempered with kindliness and blessed with a whimsical sense of humor, found a passionate outlet. As his friend Pomeroy put it: "Akeley lived for Africa. He knew the primitive Africa and he saw it being destroyed. Then to preserve and portray Africa for posterity became the single purpose of his life. He dedicated his life to the task of bringing Africa to America."[32] And as one surveys the two African memorial halls, in Chicago and New York, one must conclude that he succeeded brilliantly.

## NOTES

1. Carl E. Akeley, *In Brightest Africa*, memorial edition (Garden City, N.Y.: Garden City Publishing Co., 1932), 4–5; Mary Jobe Akeley, *Carl Akeley's Africa: The Account of the Akeley-Eastman-Pomeroy African Hall Expedition of the American Museum of Natural History* (New York: Dodd, Mead & Co., 1929), 300–08; Mary Akeley, *The Wilderness Lives Again: Carl Akeley and the Great Adventure* (New York: Dodd, Mead & Co., 1940), 14–19, 196–99, 223–24; "Akeley's African Hall," *Mentor* 13 (Jan. 1926): 1–52; "Akeley Memorial Number," *Natural History* 27 (1927): 133–60; Nancy Oestrich Lurie, *A Special Style: The Milwaukee Public Museum* (Milwaukee: Milwaukee Public Museum, 1983), 14–20; Robert Cushman Murphy, "Carl Ethan Akeley, 1864–1926," *Curator* 7 (Dec. 1964): 307–20; Douglas J. Preston, *Dinosaurs in the Attic: An Excursion into the American Museum of Natural History* (New York: St. Martin's Press, 1986), 78–93; Mary L. Jobe Akeley Papers, American Museum of Natural History, 6 boxes.
2. Mary Akeley, *Wilderness Lives Again*, 35.
3. Ibid., 76, 361–62; Murphy, "Carl Ethan Akeley," 307.
4. Mary Akeley, *Wilderness Lives Again*, 30–32; Edward P. Alexander, *Museum Masters: Their Museums and Their Influence* (Nashville: American Association for State and Local History, 1983), 43–77; William Temple Hornaday, *Taxidermy and Ecological Collecting: A Complete Handbook* (New York: Charles Scribner's Sons, 1891), 99–178, 218–304. The "Arab Courier Attacked by Lions" is illustrated in *Curator* 6 (1963): 178.
5. Sally Gregory Kohlstadt, "Henry A. Ward: The Merchant Naturalist and American Museum Development," *Journal of the Society for the Bibliography of Natural History* 9 (Apr. 1980): 651.
6. Mary Akeley, *Wilderness Lives Again*, 20–21; William Morton Wheeler, "Carl Akeley's Early Boyhood and Environment," *Natural History* 27 (1927): 135.
7. Carl Akeley, *Brightest Africa*, 1–8; Mary Akeley, *Wilderness Lives Again*, 4–12, 39–101; "Carl Ethan Akeley," *Dictionary of American Biography*, 1: 132–33.
8. Carl Akeley, *Brightest Africa*, 8–10; Mary Akeley, *Wilderness Lives Again*, 22–39; Lurie, *Milwaukee Public Museum*, 14–20.
9. Carl Akeley, *Brightest Africa*, 10–19; Mary Akeley, *Wilderness Lives Again*, 12–26, 202–07; Chesly Manly, *One Billion Years on Our Doorstep;...Six Articles on the Chicago Museum of Natural History* (Chicago: Chicago Museum of Natural History, 1959), 55–64.
10. Murphy, "Akeley," p. 308.

11. New York *Times*, Oct. 21, 1923; New York *World*, Oct. 19, 1924; New York *Herald*, Oct. 19, 1924; New York *Herald Tribune*, Apr. 15, 1927; Lewis E. Akeley to Roy Chapman Andrews, Dec. 12, 1936, all in Mary L. Jobe Akeley Papers.

12. Mary Akeley, *Wilderness Lives Again*, 189–201; Preston, *Dinosaurs in the Attic*, 86–88; "Mary Jobe Akeley," *Geographical Journal* 12 (Dec. 1966): 597–598; *Notable American Women: The Modern Period* (Cambridge, Mass.: Harvard University Press, 1980), 8—10.

13. Mary Akeley, *Wilderness Lives Again*, 215, 362–63.

14. Ibid., 220. See also 378–85.

15. Carl Akeley, *Brightest Africa*, 164–68; Mary Akeley, *Wilderness Lives Again*, 114–16, 141–43; F. Trubee Davidson, "Akeley, the Inventor," *Natural History* 27 (1927): 124–29; Clyde Fisher, "Carl Akeley and His Work," *Scientific Monthly* 24 (Feb. 1927): 109–11.

16. Carl Akeley, *Brightest Africa*, 168–72; Mary Akeley, *Wilderness Lives Again*, 210–12.

17. Mary Akeley, *Carl Akeley's Africa*, 189–90.

18. Carl Akeley, *Brightest Africa*, 63–67, 97–103, 114–38; Mary Akeley, *Wilderness Lives Again*, 39–59; Mary Akeley, *Carl Akeley's Africa*, 1–4; Carl Akeley and Mary L. Jobe Akeley, *Adventures in the African Jungle* (New York: Dodd, Mead & Company, 1930), 68—95; Carl and Mary Akeley, *Lions, Gorillas, and Their Neighbors* (New York: Dodd, Mead & Company, 1933), 217–36.

19. Carl Akeley, *Brightest Africa*, 131–33; Mary Akeley, *Wilderness Lives Again*, 78–101; Carl and Mary Akeley, *Adventures in the African Jungle*, 25–46; Manly, *One Billion Years*, 55–64.

20. Mary Akeley, *Wilderness Lives Again*, 105.

21. Carl Akeley, "Elephants," *World's Work* 41 (Nov. 1920): 77–92; Mary Akeley, *Wilderness Lives Again*, 103–07, 119–26, 135–37; Carl and Mary Akeley, *Adventures in the African Jungle*, 1–24, 180–94.

22. Mary Akeley, *Wilderness Lives Again*, 181.

23. Carl Akeley, *Brightest Africa*, 188–210, 221–24, 229–32; Carl and Mary Akeley, *Lions, Gorillas and Their Neighbors*, 124–48; Mary Hastings Bradley, "In Africa with Akeley," *Natural History* 27 (1927): 161–73.

24. Carl Akeley, *Brightest Africa*, 251–67; Akeley, "African Hall: A Monument to Primitive Africa," *Mentor* 13 (Jan. 1926): 10–22; Mary Akeley, *Wilderness Lives Again*, 208–12, 223–43, 378–85.

25. Mary Akeley, *Wilderness Lives Again*, 290.

26. Robert E. Rockwell, *My Way of Becoming a Hunter* (New York: W. W. Norton & Co., 1955), 216–18.

27. Ibid., 216.

28. William R. Leigh, *Frontiers of Enchantment: An Artist's Adventures in Africa* (New York: Simon and Schuster, 1938), 6, 252.

29. Rockwell, *Becoming a Hunter*, 208–09, 232.

30. Mary Akeley, *Wilderness Lives Again*, 244–314, 322–23, 340–41.

31. Ibid., 342–58, 378–85; Mary Akeley, *Carl Akeley's Africa*, 247–58; Manly, *One Billion Years*, 55–64; "Akeley Memorial African Hall," 1–89; Carl Akeley, "African Hall" and "Have a Heart: A Statement and Plea for Fair Game Sport in Africa," *Mentor* 13 (Jan. 1926): 10–22, 47–50; Baron de Cartier de Marchienne, "Akeley, the Conservationist," *Natural History* 27 (1927): 115–17; Fisher, "Akeley and His Work," 117; "Mary Jobe Akeley," *Geographical Journal* 112 (Dec. 1966): 597–98; Delia J. Akeley's books are *"J.T., Jr.," the Biography of an African Monkey* (New York: Macmillan Company, 1928) and *Jungle Portraits with Original Photographs* (New York: Macmillan Company, 1930). See also her "She Feels Safer in the Jungle!" Kansas City *Journal-Post*, July 15, 1928, in Mary Jobe Akeley Papers. Mary Akeley's

books, in addition to those cited above, are *Restless Jungle: With Many Illustrations* (New York: R. N. McBride and Company, 1936); *Rumble of a Distant Drum: A True Story of the African Hinterland* (London: George C. Harrap & Co., 1948); and *Congo Men: Historical Background and Scientific Aspects of the Great Game Sanctuaries of the Belgian Congo* (London: Victor Gallancz, 1951).

32. Mary Akeley, *Wilderness Lives Again*, 223–24.

## SELECT BIBLIOGRAPHY


Akeley, Carl E. "African Hall: A Monument to Primitive Africa." *Mentor* 13 (Jan. 1926): 10–22.

_____. "Elephants." *World's Work* 41 (Nov. 1920): 77–92.

_____. "Have a Heart: A Statement and Plea for Fair Game Sport in Africa." *Mentor* 13 (Jan. 1926): 47–50.

_____. *In Brightest Africa*. Memorial edition. Garden City, N.Y.: Garden City Publishing Co., 1932.

Akeley, Carl and Mary L. Jobe. *Adventures in the African Jungle*. New York: Dodd, Mead & Company, 1930.

_____. *Lions, Gorillas, and Their Neighbors*. New York: Dodd, Mead & Company, 1933.

Akeley, Delia J. *"J.T., Jr.," the Biography of an African Monkey*. New York: Macmillan Company, 1928.

_____. *Jungle Portraits with Original Photographs*. New York: Macmillan Company, 1930.

Akeley, Mary Jobe. *Carl Akeley's Africa: The Account of the Akeley-Eastman-Pomeroy African Hall Expedition of the American Museum of Natural History*. New York: Dodd, Mead & Co., 1929.

_____. *Congo Men: Historical Background and Scientific Aspects of the Great Game Sanctuaries of the Belgian Congo*. London: Victor Gallancz, 1951.

_____. *Restless Jungle: With Many Illustrations*. New York: R. N. McBride and Company, 1936.

_____. *Rumble of a Distant Drum: A True Story of the African Hinterland*. London: George C. Harrap & Co., 1948.

_____. *The Wilderness Lives Again: Carl Akeley and the Great Adventure*. New York: Dodd, Mead & Co., 1940.

"Akeley Memorial Number." *Natural History* 27 (1927): 133–60.

"Akeley's African Hall." *Mentor* 13 (Jan. 1926): 1–52.

Alexander, Edward P. *Museum Masters: Their Museums and Their Influence*. Nashville: American Association for State and Local History, 1983.

Bradley, Mary Hastings. "In Africa with Akeley." *Natural History* 27 (1927): 161–73.

"Carl Ethan Akeley." *Dictionary of American Biography*, 1: 132–33.

Davidson, F. Trubee. "Akeley, the Inventor." *Natural History* 27 (1927): 124–29.

de Marchienne, Baron de Cartier. "Akeley, the Conservationist." *Natural History* 27 (1927): 115–17.

Fisher, Clyde. "Carl Akeley and His Work." *Scientific Monthly* 24 (Feb. 1927): 109–11.

Hornaday, William Temple. *Taxidermy and Ecological Collecting: A Complete Handbook*. New York: Charles Scribner's Sons, 1891.

Kohlstadt, Sally Gregory. "Henry A. Ward: The Merchant Naturalist and American Museum Development." *Journal of the Society for the Bibliography of Natural History* 9 (Apr. 1980): 651.

Leigh, William R. *Frontiers of Enchantment: An Artist's Adventures in Africa*. New York: Simon and Schuster, 1938.

Lurie, Nancy Oestrich. *A Special Style: The Milwaukee Public Museum*. Milwaukee: Milwaukee Public Museum, 1983.

Manly, Chesly. *One Billion Years on Our Doorstep;...Six Articles on the Chicago Museum of Natural History*. Chicago: Chicago Museum of Natural History, 1959.

"Mary Jobe Akeley." *Geographical Journal* 12 (Dec. 1966): 597–598.

Mary L. Jobe Akeley Papers. American Museum of Natural History. 6 boxes.

Murphy, Robert Cushman. "Carl Ethan Akeley, 1864–1926." *Curator* 7 (Dec. 1964): 307–20.

*Notable American Women: The Modern Period*. Cambridge, Mass.: Harvard University Press, 1980.

Preston, Douglas J. *Dinosaurs in the Attic: An Excursion into the American Museum of Natural History*. New York: St. Martin's Press, 1986.

Rockwell, Robert E. *My Way of Becoming a Hunter*. New York: W. W. Norton & Co., 1955.

Wheeler, William Morton. "Carl Akeley's Early Boyhood and Environment." *Natural History* 27 (1927): 135.

CHAPTER 3

# Henry Watson Kent *Standardizes Functions of the Art Museum*

## I

HENRY WATSON KENT became the paid assistant secretary of the Metropolitan Museum of Art in 1905. He was recruited by Robert W. de Forest, sometimes referred to as New York's first citizen, who was serving as trustee and secretary of the museum during a period of reorganization. "General" Luigi di Cesnola (1832–1904) was a previous trustee and secretary, and then its first salaried director from 1879 until his death. He was a master of self-promotion (for example, he used the title of general when he had been only a colonel in the Civil War), and he unsuccessfully schemed to sell the museum two collections of Phoenician, Greek, Assyrian, and Egyptian artifacts that he had excavated while serving as United States Consul in Cyprus. Cesnola was hard working and spent long hours in the museum, but he ruled his small staff in autocratic and volatile fashion. He was accused of indiscriminately placing heads, arms, legs, and other features on the statues in the Cypriote Collection, and he resisted opening the museum on Sunday afternoons, though the trustees finally reluctantly did so in 1891. The younger trustees disliked the way Cesnola tactlessly antagonized trustees, staff, and the public and made a determined effort to dismiss him in 1895, but he managed to weather the storm.[1]

The founders of the Metropolitan in its charter of 1870 agreed to conduct a museum and library of art, to encourage and develop the study of fine arts and the application of arts to manufactures and practical life, and to furnish popular instruction and recreation. Though the trustees gave some lip service to having the museum serve the community, no great effort was made in the educational area, aside from offering some elementary art courses to students for a time and providing occasional special exhibitions and lectures.

The reorganization of the museum after Cesnola's death greatly expanded its scope and operations. J. Pierpont Morgan soon became president of the trustees; not only was he a world-class financier but the greatest art collector of his day. He persuaded wealthy friends to join him as trustees and, when an annual deficit occurred, would go around the board room table, his intense black eyes commanding gifts. He secured as the new director Sir Caspar Purdon Clarke, head of the South Kensington (Victoria and Albert) Museum in London. Edward Robinson, director of the Museum of Fine Arts in Boston, became assistant director. Sir Caspar was largely a figurehead and Robinson, the museum's chief executive, became director in 1910. But the everyday administration was in the hands of Kent, strongly backed by de Forest, who succeeded Morgan as president. Kent lived near the de Forests, and he would stop often for a working breakfast on his way to the museum.

Kent was appalled by the lack of system that he found. Cesnola had tried to make all the decisions himself. There was only one typewriter and one telephone (in the library), no information desk, little communication with the staff, and animosity among the three curators that occasionally led to fisticuffs. Kent set up normal business procedures and regarded himself as "the *entrepreneur* between the initiators of all action, the trustees, and their employees."[2] He instituted scientific methods of registration, accessioning, cataloguing, communication, and publication. De Forest and he were determined to make the museum an educational institution. Kent, long a close friend of John Cotton Dana, director of the Newark (New Jersey) Museum, said that their friendship "was also an education for me in public relationships, of which he was a master."[3] The two men vied to see which one could do the most to make his museum serve its community. Dana in 1920 needled Kent, saying that the Metropolitan's attendance was just under one million yearly, the same as the Newark library and museum in "a God-forsaken town in the estimation of many, in a still more God-forsaken state, in the estimation of others; and a very unimportant museum therein."[4]

In the curatorial field, Kent made many contributions, especially in the collection of American antiques that resulted in the American Wing. Meanwhile, Morgan and de Forest backed Egyptian expeditions and obtained other outstanding collections that began to make the Metropolitan a museum of national and even international importance. It started gradually to abandon many of the materials in the Cypriote Collection and in its comprehensive holdings of plaster casts.

All in all, Kent was the "dean" of American museum education for many years. He lived up to his motto of "art for the people's sake . . . for the enjoyment, for the study, and for the profit of the people." And Calvin Tomkins probably is right in considering him "without doubt, the greatest museum man of his generation."[5]

## II

Henry Watson Kent was born on September 28, 1866, at Boston, the son of Robert Restieaux and Eliza (Watson) Kent and a descendant of sturdy New England Puritan families. He attended Boston Latin School for a time and then, from 1881, the Free Academy of Norwich, Connecticut. He and his sister roomed there with the Rev. Charles T. Weitzel, and Kent studied German with him. He worked at the Boston Public Library during the summer of 1884 and, that fall, embraced the "profession of Librarianship" by entering the experimental library science course at Columbia College, taught by Melvil Dewey, whose students served as interns in the Columbia Library and became thoroughly familiar with innovative library procedures that included decimal classification. Kent pointed out later that Dewey's library students were trained first of all as public servants, while museum curators and directors of that day had no such background and thus "few of them seem to have imbibed the notion of the importance of that relationship."[6] Ill health caused Kent to drop out of the program and go to Florida in 1886, but he returned two years later, to work in the card catalogue section of the library. Professor William R. Ware, who headed the department of architecture at Columbia, then made a crucial suggestion, that Kent ought to try museum work. His opportunity came in 1888 when he was offered the position of librarian at the Peck Library of the Norwich (Connecticut) Free Academy and curator of the newly established Slater Memorial Museum there. Both institutions occupied the impressive Slater Memorial Building, which contained academy classrooms and an auditorium that provided the community with an atheneum and lyceum for lectures, music, and small study groups.

Edward Robinson, at that time the learned curator of classical collections at the Museum of Fine Arts, was brought in to select, purchase, and arrange in chronological order 124 plaster casts of Greek sculpture and architecture and 103 of Italian, some of them on revolving pedestals. They comprised the main collection of the museum, though in addition there were electrotypes of Greek coins, small Renaissance plaster reproductions, and numerous photographs of paintings and European architecture. According to a speaker at the opening ceremonies, the museum had "a collection unsurpassed, perhaps unequaled, by any that is owned by any college in the land."[7] One of Kent's first tasks was securing a plasterer to install fig leaves in the right places on the casts before the opening of the museum.

During his twelve years at the Norwich library and museum, Kent carried on a vigorous and varied program. He arranged twenty-seven special exhibitions in order to secure repeat visitation from the community and to attract viewers from many states and several foreign countries. Among the subjects treated were Barbizon paintings; rugs, tapestries, embroideries, and brocades; portraits of men and women of early Norwich; local silversmiths; Norwich publications; children's books; and fine bindings. Yearly attendance at the museum during the period reached as high as 12,000.

The academy established an Art School, Normal School, and manual training department, all of which worked closely with the museum. The art classes stressed design and its application to industries; some academy graduates became designers in the textile and jewelry factories that were so numerous in the region. Kent taught various academy and Art School classes, often in the museum galleries, on history of art, history of sculpture, and Greek sculptures. He had for long been enthusiastic about fine printing and bookbinding, and he persuaded the academy to secure a small press and establish a course in printing that sometimes provided labels and did other small jobs for the museum. On one occasion, he helped the students stage seven tableaux from the *Iliad*, making their own costumes and constructing a Greek chair.

Kent arranged several public school class visits, not a usual museum activity in that day. First graders made sketches of the casts and toured the museum; one time, "an almost terrified hush" took place when a small black boy, wide-eyed, pointed at a huge centaur and whispered: "There is God!"[8] Pupils from more advanced grades made visits, and a Saturday morning art class included sketching and stories about the casts. Nor did Kent neglect the Peck Library. He built it up to contain 12,000 volumes and 65 periodicals and newspapers, with author and title catalogue. The students used it constantly, and the public was invited to do so every afternoon. It was one of the largest school collections in the country and, in the field of art, ranked with college libraries.

Meanwhile, Kent was studying early American history, architecture, and arts and crafts, so respected in the community, and meeting prominent early collectors of decorative arts. Among them were H. Eugene Bolles and Dwight Blaney of Boston, George S. Palmer of New London, and Harry Harkness Flagler of New York. They were collecting paintings, furniture, silver, textiles, and other examples of Americana at a time when the art museums of the country were devoted almost exclusively to European and Near Eastern art from ancient times to the nineteenth century. In 1883, Kent made an extensive, eight-month European tour, visiting museums from Turkey, Greece, and Italy to Germany and Britain, taking notes accompanied by sketches of administration, services to the public, catalogues, exhibit displays, publications, and such practical matters as chairs, benches, pedestals, and bulletin boards. He was impressed by the historical period rooms he saw in Zurich, Nuremberg, and Munich, which sought to give visitors a journey through history, and by Director Wilhelm Bode's period rooms and other innovations in Berlin.

At home, Kent was in demand to advise museums on collecting and installing casts—at the Rhode Island School of Design; the Metropolitan Museum, which sent its special committee on casts to Norwich and had Kent arrange its exhibition; the Buffalo Fine Arts Academy; the City Library Association in Springfield, Massachusetts, where he began his friendship with John Cotton Dana; and, somewhat later, the Carnegie Institute in Pittsburgh.

At that time, art historians were convinced that original ancient sculptures were no longer obtainable and that American museums ought to form comprehensive cast collections for the sake of art students, aspiring artists, and the many high school and college pupils studying Greek and Latin. Thus, Pierre Le Brun, the architect assembling casts for the Metropolitan, expressed the common wisdom when he wrote in 1885:

> Collections of casts are springing up in all the older communities, and they have a completeness and a unity not found possible in museums of originals. Such collections must undoubtedly be the main dependence of our American fine-art institutions. . . . We cannot hope to stock them adequately with antiquities. Chances of acquiring valuable collections of originals are rare and will become rarer.[9]

Such predictions underestimated the efforts of archaeological expeditions, the expansion of museum collections to include Oriental, European, and even American decorative arts, and the tremendous increase of American wealth that allowed collectors and museums to take advantage of revolutionary changes in Europe which released treasures thought to be permanently fixed there.

Kent was a well-organized administrator who gave meticulous attention to detail and the completion of projects. Those qualities impressed de Forest, and led to Kent eventually being hired by the Metropolitan. His personality is fascinating to examine: a bachelor, he was later renowned for his icy reserve and rigid self-control, but he had a multitude of good friends in the Norwich community as well as among collectors of Americana throughout the region and the bibliophiles who cherished fine printing and the arts of book production. He got along well with the students in his classes, especially the young women, and he later hired several of them at the Metropolitan.

In 1900, Kent left Norwich to become assistant librarian of the Grolier Club in New York. That organization had been formed in 1884 to promote the arts involved in the production of books and to advance the use of good paper, typography, presswork, illustrations, and binding. Its founders were either students of fine printing or practitioners of the printing trades. They admired French progress in that field and named their club after Grolier, the French sixteenth-century bibliophile. They were also wealthy and maintained a comfortable clubhouse, where they accumulated a superb library, held well-attended stereoptican lectures and special exhibitions, and issued handsomely crafted publications.

Kent admitted that he had moved to the Grolier "with the hope that I might go on to the Metropolitan Museum,"[10] but he delighted in bibliographical work and in 1903 became librarian of the club. He formed close friendships with the great bookmen of the day, such as Robert Hoe, manufacturer of rotary printing presses; William Loring Andrews, collector of New York historical prints; and Samuel P. Avery, successful art dealer and philanthropist. Kent also became acquainted with the leading typographers and printers, including the veteran Theodore L. Devine, Daniel Berkeley Updike, Bruce Rogers, and Carl P. Rollins, as well as the engravers Rudolph Ruzica and August Jaccaci; afterwards, he used such talent in issuing Metropolitan publications.

Kent enjoyed living in New York, and he joined the Century Club and, for a time, the Players Club. He was never happier than he was at the Grolier, and he maintained his enthusiasm for the printing arts for the remainder of his life. He served as president of the Grolier Club for six years and of the American Institute of Graphic Arts for three years. The institute gave him its gold medal in 1930 "in appreciation of a career of notable influence in the field of graphic arts" and "the deepest influence on typography."[11] The Pierpont Morgan Library in 1938 arranged a special exhibition of printing done at the Metropolitan under Kent's supervision and praised him for "raising the standard of institutional printing to that of one of the Fine Arts."[12] The extent of his interest and influence is glimpsed in the bibliography of his publications prepared by Lois Leighton Comings for his autobiography, *What I Am Pleased to Call My Education*; of a total of 185 entries, some 75 are devoted to the art of bookmaking.

## III

As assistant secretary of the Metropolitan, Kent took the minutes of the trustee meetings, and his attendance there kept him fully informed of policies and let the trustees know him well and appreciate his services. As soon as he arrived at the museum, he began to devise businesslike systems for handling its usual activities. Not only was his own position added to the staff, but also those of a registrar and a photographer. If an object was offered by gift or bequest and was accepted by the trustees after favorable recommendations by the director, the curator concerned, and the trustee committee, Kent notified the director with copies to the curator and registrar, who already had received the object. The number placed in the accession book and on the object itself included the year and the numeral indicating its order in the annual accessions. A catalogue card was then prepared with the photograph of the object reproduced on the back. Secretary, registrar, photographer, curator, and sales department all saw the card, added information and made what entries they needed from it. Purchases were treated somewhat similarly, though the price was included in the record. Kent in 1911 gave a full account of the system to the annual meeting of the American Association of Museums in Boston and urged his listeners to use such an arrangement in their museums and let him have any suggestions for improvement.[13]

Kent established an information desk at the entrance to the museum. It answered members' and visitors' questions and sold post cards, photographs, slides, and museum publications. He edited the museum *Bulletin*, which began publication late in 1905; it carried articles on acquisitions and art history matters by the curators and full accounts of educational activities so as to keep members, staff, and other museums informed. It began as a quarterly but was so popular that, within a year, it changed to a bimonthly and then a monthly, ultimately attaining a circulation of 16,000. Kent also secured a small press to print labels, announcements, menus, and the like. He arranged for the *Bulletin* and other larger printing jobs, including books, to be done by good designers and printers so that, beginning in 1921, the museum usually had one or more titles listed in the *Fifty Best Books of the Year* chosen by the American Institute of Graphic Arts. The Morgan Library's special show of Metropolitan publications said that Kent had "added to his other duties the fostering of the Museum Press . . . with such enthusiasm and genuine love for beautiful printing that it has become an artistic asset to the Museum."[14]

A reading of the *Bulletin* during Kent's administration shows that he gave attention to the smallest details. Among many possible examples of his care, a "rolling-chair" was offered for those who could not walk, and later on, someone could be hired to push it for fifty cents an hour. Alterations were made to improve the electric wiring, and rest rooms were rejuvenated. Changes were frequently noted for the museum's restaurant, and it finally was turned into a cafeteria. Chairs were provided in the galleries to decrease visitors' "museum fatigue." Of great importance, a Metropolitan Museum Employees Association was begun, and years later it staged a minstrel show for de Forest's eightieth birthday, while several special exhibitions were held of the art work of the employees. Kent looked after such details as part of the duties of his entrepreneurship.[15]

Even more significant, however, were Kent's efforts, always backed by de Forest, to provide a strong educational program. First of all, he analyzed the museum's audience and classified it as follows:

1. The idle and curious, who came on holidays with their friends to see what it was all about.
2. The people who came with a desire to learn.
3. The real students of art and archaeology, who knew what they wanted and how to study.
4. The teachers and pupils of the public schools, who came because the School Board told them to do so.
5. The practical people, manufacturers and designers, who employed the arts of design as part of their business.
6. The artist who wanted to widen his knowledge, and the copyist.
7. Museum members who paid for their privileges or inherited them.[16]

Kent at once began to improve facilities for handling visitors in accord with his analysis. In the school field, for example, the friendly Sir Caspar spoke to high school teachers of English one Saturday on how the museum could help their students, and a similar session was held for teachers of economics and history. A classroom accommodating 250–300 with stereoptican equipment, blackboard, and easels was set aside for teacher and student groups, who were admitted free of charge while ordinary visitors usually paid. A new lecture hall with improved acoustics would hold 400 listeners. In 1908, Kent added an expert guide to the staff, who took school classes studying chiefly art, history, dress-making, or applied design about the collection. School classes were free, but individuals were charged 25 cents. Kent thus was following the example of the Museum of Fine Arts in Boston, which a year earlier had established its office of "docent." As attendance increased, a second guide was added who also visited the schools. The class tours elicited favorable comments from the students, such as: "How soon may we come again?" and "I was here yesterday, and I saw the armor myself, and now I am bringing my mother to see it."[17] Kent also began to send slides, mounted photographs, textiles, casts, and other objects to the schools for classroom use and to lend such materials at the Information Desk to libraries, hospitals, and other community centers at a modest charge. The city superintendent of schools cooperated by assigning Dr. James P. Haney, supervisor of art in the high schools, to work with the museum.

Kent inaugurated a broad-based lecture program designed to appeal to all the different audiences. It reached members; members' children; the general public with art history sessions every Saturday and more popular talks on Sunday; public school teachers and pupils; students in the New York art schools; and aspiring designers along with department store buyers and sales-people. Story hours were held for children every Saturday morning, as well as special classes for the disabled. The speakers came from the staff—for example, Director Robinson with six lectures on Greek art and Albert Lythgoe and Herbert Winlock on Egyptian excavations—or were visiting authorities from home or abroad. The teachers heard educational leaders, such as Dr. G. Stanley Hall, president of Clark University, or Professor Frank Jewett Mather of Princeton, and they also learned what other museums were doing in the field from Louise Connolly of Dana's Newark Museum or the charismatic Anna Billings Gallup, curator of the Brooklyn Children's Museum. New York University, Columbia Teachers College, and City College offered lecture courses at the museum, for which tuition was charged. In 1918, musical concerts, with David Mannes as conductor, were held on certain Saturday evenings and became most popular; they were financed by private contributions, often by John D. Rockefeller, Jr.[18]

Kent was especially interested in using the museum, in accord with its charter, to assist industrial design. Not only were lectures provided for designers, furniture makers, interior decorators, weavers, other craftspeople, and department store supervisors and sales clerks, but a series of industrial exhibitions was begun. Its thirteenth edition, held in 1934, drew 139,296 visitors in 63 days, record attendance for a show of that length. Kent also experimented with lending museum materials widely, at first with traveling exhibitions in the country east of the Mississippi through the American Federation of Arts. Then, in 1935, after a branch museum he planned failed to receive financing, he sent circulating exhibits on Chinese and Japanese art, European armor, and ancient Egypt to community groups in the city. He was hoping to develop a chain of branch exhibit centers, and by 1938 there were seven collections on tour, serviced by Works Progress Administration workers, in one college, four high schools, one branch library, one museum, and one "Y" branch, that reached a total of 474,912 viewers. These community exhibits, a conscious effort to meet demands for the decentralization of the museum's collection, now included motion pictures, many of them made by the museum, and it also added radio broadcasts to its extension activities.[19]

The expansion of the education program enhanced Kent's position at the Metropolitan. In 1907 he was appointed supervisor of museum instruction and six years later, upon de Forest's accession to presidency of the trustees, Kent became secretary. He also headed the department of industrial relations. He received assistance with his heavy load when Richard F. Bach, formerly of the Columbia School of Architecture, came in 1918 to work with trade journals, manufacturers, and designers, and when Huger Elliott, former principal of the Pennsylvania Museum's School of Industrial Art, arrived in 1925 to handle museum instruction. Kent also appointed George Lauder Greenway to be assistant secretary.[20]

Kent's skillful and energetic administration changed the whole concept of the purposes of the Metropolitan Museum. When he began work, it was a traditional art museum of that day devoted to the collection, conservation, and research of art objects, but de Forest and he made its first aim to provide visual instruction. As Bach expressed it, the Metropolitan became a museum of service, a museum of daily use, a museum to aid industry, and a museum that was an instrument of education. The New York *Times* declared that the museum's annual report of 1923

> makes it clear that this Museum is not a mere repository for things gathered out of the past from many civilizations, but that it is a live educational force. It is not a place alone of conserving and recording; it is an institution for teaching

> through its collections the love of [art] . . . The diffusion of art in its highest forms will not only be helpful to the students and artisans of every branch of industry, but will "tend directly to humanize, to educate and refine a practical and laborious people."[21]

Kent was determined that the new concept of the museum should be understood nationally and internationally. As early as 1908, he organized a session at the London meeting of the Third International Art Congress on museums and the schools. Roger Fry of London, Alfred Litchtark of Hamburg, and others spoke. Viscount Sudeley, a member of the British House of Lords, was so impressed that he secured an act of Parliament appointing guide lecturers for London museums with special emphasis on teachers and school pupils. Kent attended sessions of the Museums Association of Great Britain and sent Elliott and Bach to other meetings, such as that of the Sixth International Congress on Art Education held in Prague. Kent also took a leading part in the formation of the American Association of Museums in 1906 and regularly attended its annual meetings. In the *Bulletin*, he followed the activities of American and European museums and the annual meetings and special seminars of their professional organizations. He was determined to see that a skilled museum profession should develop both in America and abroad.[22]

Kent often left the collections and research upon them to the director and curators, but he was the chief force in persuading the Metropolitan to gather and exhibit American paintings and decorative arts in period room settings. While at Norwich, he had come to appreciate Americana and to know its chief collectors. In 1909 when the Hudson-Fulton Celebration was held in New York, the Metropolitan decided to offer a special exhibition of Dutch old master paintings by Rembrandt, Hals, Vermeer, and others as well as some decorative arts. Kent pointed out that the show ought to include Americana for the Fulton part of the celebration. Edward Robinson, soon to become the director, opposed the idea because he shared the common opinion of art historians of the day that European or ancient art was far superior to that of America. Robinson consulted his former co-workers and friends at the Museum of Fine Arts, who supported his opinion. Kent, however, convinced de Forest, chairman of the commemoration committee, of the soundness of his concept and assured him that such an exhibition would attract popular enthusiasm and attendance. The result was that the museum borrowed American paintings, furniture, silver, and other art objects of the period 1625–1825 from the leading collectors of the day. The materials, arranged along the walls in the museum galleries, constituted the first exhibition of American antiques to be held in the city. It aroused great public excitement in the forty-one days it was shown and attracted greater attendance than did the Dutch masterpieces.

During the exhibition, H. Eugene Bolles told Kent that he would like to sell his collection then on display. Kent at once went into action. He invited Mr. and Mrs. de Forest and R. T. Haines Halsey to be his guests on a trip to New England. They talked with George Francis Dow, curator of the Society for the Preservation of New England Antiquities in Boston, and visited the three pioneer American period rooms that he had done in 1907 while curator at the Essex Institute in Salem. They saw other such installations at Danvers, Topsfield, Beverly, and Boston. When they returned home, Mrs. Russell Sage (de Forest was her lawyer) agreed to purchase the Bolles Collection for the museum, which also began to acquire such rooms with their interior architecture intact. Mr. Halsey, an experienced collector who had become a museum trustee and chairman of the committee on American decorative arts, took the lead in assembling those materials.

In 1922, Mr. and Mrs. de Forest (her father had been the first president of the museum) announced that they were financing entirely, at no cost to the city, a new wing to house the American rooms. They purchased the 1822–1824 facade of the old United States Assay Office (originally the United States Branch Bank) on Wall Street and gave it to the museum to serve as an entryway for the new wing. Kent pored over the plans, using Swiss and German museums as precedents. In 1924 the American Wing was opened with about a dozen eighteenth- and early nineteenth-century original rooms and two reproduced seventeenth-century ones from Massachusetts. Halsey, who worked harmoniously with Kent and de Forest, was the chief designer and curator of the project. The American Wing was an immediate hit with the public and had great influence on the dozens of historic houses being opened as museums, on many art museums, and later upon Colonial Williamsburg and the Henry Francis du Pont Winterthur Museum.[23]

Kent backed George Gray Barnard and his medieval cloister collection and rejoiced when John D. Rockefeller, Jr., financed its purchase for the Metropolitan. It opened in 1938 as The Cloisters in the elevated Fort Tryon Park site overlooking the Hudson. Kent also played an important role as consultant for the Cleveland Museum of Art, opened in 1916, helping design its building and plan its collection. He took a more cautious stance when it came to contemporary art at the Metropolitan; his warning was that "to buy the modern in haste is to repent at leisure."[24] Kent's later years at the Metropolitan were a period for receiving honors. The Architectural League of New York awarded him its Michael Friedman medal for "his service in the cause of industrial art." He was a leader in the Walpole Society of connoisseurs that he helped start in 1909, and he was elected a vice-president of the American Association of Museums. Hamilton College and Brown University gave him honorary degrees. He was sounded out for the directorships of art museums in Boston, Philadelphia, Buffalo, Indianapolis, and Cleveland, and for the librarianship of Williams College.[25]

But along with the honors went some disappointments. Kent's always carefully maintained reserve and his cultivated British accent brought some accusations that he was a frightful snob, and his young women assistants who called themselves his "willing slaves" could also be a source of ridicule. Kent in the beginning welcomed William M. Ivins, the museum's first curator of prints, for the two men shared a common interest in fine printing, but they came to quarrel loudly and bitterly. Kent's letter of introduction for one of his young women going abroad to study museum methods in London, Vienna, Berlin, and Paris stated that she "will occupy herself with the process of reproduction in those cities." The letter filled Ivins with malicious glee. More seriously, he once accused Kent of pushing him out of a taxi and causing him to fall on the curb. Kent also had to put up with Alan Priest, curator of Eastern art and a confirmed practical joker. Learning of the ship on which Kent was returning from Europe, he wrote the immigration officials that a notorious narcotics smuggler was aboard and gave them an exact description of Kent with his white hair and thin mustache. Kent had to undergo a searching examination from head to toe.[26]

Affairs took an unpleasant turn for Kent when Francis Henry Taylor became director of the Metropolitan in 1940. He had had a brilliant administration at the Worcester Art Museum with fascinating special exhibitions that attracted much interest from professionals as well as the public. Taylor, however, was a very different person from the seventy-four-year-old Kent—outgoing, impetuous, and given to telling humorous stories, many of them indelicate. He also had positive ideas about museum administration and considered Kent's methods old-fashioned and somewhat precious. He appointed Laurence S. Harrison his business administrator and had him report on each of the museum's departments. Kent demanded to see the reports on his sections, but Harrison said that only Taylor could approve that action. Kent went to see Taylor but submitted his resignation a few days later, to take effect at year's end. The Board of Trustees accepted the resignation with reluctance, made Kent secretary emeritus, praised his "unselfish, devoted, and untiring energy and intelligent and constructive foresight," and continued to call on him occasionally for advice. Though he undoubtedly felt that he had been treated shabbily after his thirty-five years of service, Kent maintained his reserve and did not complain in his autobiography. He died from a heart attack on August 28, 1948, in the summer hotel he regularly frequented.[27]

Kent was a most distinguished museum man for his day. He did much to make the premier aim of the American museum educational, but he did not neglect its collection, preservation, and research functions. In fact, he could be proud of his business-like organizational improvements that were so badly needed when he began work. And he did much to add professional standards to museum undertakings, not only in his own institution but also nationally and internationally. The museum world that he left in 1940 was a very different and much improved place from that of fifty years earlier, and he had played a responsible and valiant part in the change. To the end, his great ideal had been that "most austere of all mental qualities, a sense of style" based upon "attainment and restraint."[28]

## NOTES

1. The chief sources on Kent and the Metropolitan Museum are Nathaniel Burt, *Palaces for the People: A Social History of American Art Museums* (Boston: Little, Brown, 1977); Stephen Mark Dobbs, "Dana and Kent and Early Museum Education," *Museum News* 50 (October 1971): 38–41; Howard Hibbard, *The Metropolitan Museum of Art* (New York: Harper & Row, 1980); Winifred E. Howe, *A History of the Metropolitan Museum of Art*, 2 vols. (New York: Metropolitan Museum of Art, 1913, 1946); Henry Watson Kent, *What I Am Pleased to Call My Education*, edited by Lois Leighton Comings (New York: Grolier Club, 1949); Henry Watson Kent and Florence N. Levy, *Catalogue of an Exhibition of American Paintings, Furniture, Silver, and Other Objects of Art, 1625–1825* (New York: Metropolitan Museum of Art, 1909); Leo Lerman, *The Museum: One Hundred Years of the Metropolitan Museum of Art* (New York: Viking Press, 1969); Calvin Tomkins, *Merchants and Masterpieces: The Story of the Metropolitan Museum of Art* (New York: E. P. Dutton, 1970). For Cesnola, see also Elizabeth McFadden, *The Glitter and the Gold: A Spirited Account of the Metropolitan Museum of Art's First Director, the Audacious and High-Handed Luigi Palma di Cesnola* (New York: Dial Press, 1971).
2. Tomkins, *Merchants and Masterpieces*, 116.
3. Kent, *My Education*, 102. See also Edward P. Alexander, "John Cotton Dana and the Newark Museum: The Museum of Community Service," in *Museum Masters: Their Museums and Their Influence* (Nashville, Tennessee: American Association for State and Local History, 1983), 377–411.
4. Dobbs, "Dana and Kent," 40.
5. Ibid., 39–40; Tomkins, *Merchants and Masterpieces*, 115.
6. Kent, *My Education*, 17.
7. Ibid., 49.
8. Ibid., 63.

9. Ibid., 108–09.

10. Ibid., 114. See also Brander Matthews, "The Grolier Club," *Century* 39 (Nov. 1889): 86–97.

11. Kent, *My Education*, 132–33.

12. Ibid., 152.

13. Metropolitan Museum *Bulletin* 2 (1907): 54–57; 6 (1911): 169–70; Kent, *My Education*, 141–43.

14. Metropolitan Museum *Bulletin* 33 (1938): 265–67.

15. Metropolitan Museum *Bulletin* 2 (1907): 85; 3 (1908): 233; 4 (1909): 85–86, 140; 5 (1910): 100; 7 (1912): 198–99; 10 (1915): 34; 13 (1918): 227–28; 17 (1922): 221; 20 (1925): 111; 23 (1928): 166; 30 (1935): 254; 38 (1939): 25–26.

16. Kent, *My Education*, 144–45.

17. Metropolitan Museum *Bulletin* 6 (1911): 63–64. See also 2 (1907): 85; 3 (1908): 46–47, 180; 5 (1910): 63–64, 201–07; 6 (1911): 148, 176; 7 (1912): 158–61; 8 (1913 supplement, Sept.): 6; 9 (1914): 223; 12 (1917): 205–06; 21 (1926): 202–17; Kent, *My Education*, 146–47.

18. Metropolitan Museum *Bulletin* 3 (1908): 46–47; 4 (1909): 230–31; 5 (1910): 63–64; 6 (1911): 63–64, 240; 7 (1912): 20–21, 158–61; 8 (1913): 110–11, 252, supplement (Sept.), 6–11; 9 (1914): 132, 190–94; 10 (1915): 112, 128–29, 241–42; 11 (1916): 182–204; 13 (1918): 52, 290; 15 (1920): 169; 16 (1921): 39; 17 (1922): 86; Kent, *My Education*, 147–49.

19. Metropolitan Museum *Bulletin* 4 (1909): 231; 6 (1911): 158; 9 (1914): 132; 10 (1915): 33; 11 (1916): 111, 189; 12 (1917): 93–94, 121; 13 (1918): 205–06, 290; 18 (1923): 311–12; 21 (1926): 20, 202–17; 22 (1927): 61; 23 (1928): 59; 24 (1929): 96–97, 158–67; 28 (1933): 183–84; 29 (1934): 186, 162, 182–84; 30 (1935): 18, 92–93; 31 (1936): 148–49; 33 (1938): 249–52; 35 (1940): 74–76; Howe, *Metropolitan Museum History*, 2: 203–05; Kent, *My Education*, 153–58.

20. Metropolitan Museum *Bulletin* 3 (1908): 46–47; 13 (1918): 288; 20 (1925): 137; 27 (1932): 147; Kent, *My Education*, 135, 156–57; Howe, *Metropolitan Museum History*, 2: 22, 69, 177.

21. Metropolitan Museum *Bulletin* 19 (1924): 91–92. See also 22 (1927): 238.

22. Kent, *My Education*, 145–46; Metropolitan Museum *Bulletin* 22 (1927): 224–25; 31 (1936): 149.

23. Metropolitan Museum *Bulletin* 4 (1909): 75–76, 181–83, 189, 196–97, 219–20, 230–31; 5 (1910): 5–16, 60; 17 (1922, part II): 1–23; 19 (1924): 251–65; Kent, *My Education*, 83–84, 160–64; Kent and Levy, *Catalogue of an Exhibition*; Howe, *Metropolitan Museum History*, 2: 22, 35–38; Wendy Kaplan, "R. T. H. Halsey: An Ideology of Collecting American Decorative Arts," *Winterthur Portfolio* 17 (Spring 1987): 43–53; Tomkins, *Merchants and Masterpieces*, 195–204.

24. Metropolitan Museum *Bulletin* 20 (1925): 166–77; 21 (1926): 114–20; 30 (1935): 98–100; Kent, *My Education*, 164–65; Tomkins, *Merchants and Masterpieces*, 249–50.

25. Metropolitan Museum *Bulletin* 20 (1925): 189; 27 (1932): 262; 29 (1934): 183–84; 31 (1936): 149; Kent, *My Education*, 161–62, 165–66.

26. Tomkins, *Merchants and Masterpieces*, 212–13, 241–42, 279.

27. Ibid., 266–76.

28. Kent, *My Education*, 167–68.

## SELECT BIBLIOGRAPHY

Alexander, Edward P. "John Cotton Dana and the Newark Museum: The Museum of Community Service." In *Museum Masters: Their Museums and Their Influence*. Nashville, Tennessee: American Association for State and Local History, 1983.

Burt, Nathaniel. *Palaces for the People: A Social History of American Art Museums*. Boston: Little, Brown, 1977.

Dobbs, Stephen Mark. "Dana and Kent and Early Museum Education." *Museum News* 50 (October 1971): 38–41.

Hibbard, Howard. *The Metropolitan Museum of Art*. New York: Harper & Row, 1980.

Howe, Winifred E. *A History of the Metropolitan Museum of Art*. 2 vols. New York: Metropolitan Museum of Art, 1913, 1946.

Kaplan, Wendy. "R. T. H. Halsey: An Ideology of Collecting American Decorative Arts." *Winterthur Portfolio* 17 (Spring 1987): 43–53.

Kent, Henry Watson. *What I Am Pleased to Call My Education*. Edited by Lois Leighton Comings. New York: Grolier Club, 1949.

Kent, Henry Watson, and Florence N. Levy. *Catalogue of an Exhibition of American Paintings, Furniture, Silver, and Other Objects of Art, 1625–1825*. New York: Metropolitan Museum of Art, 1909.

Lerman, Leo. *The Museum: One Hundred Years of the Metropolitan Museum of Art*. New York: Viking Press, 1969.

Matthews, Brander. "The Grolier Club." *Century* 39 (Nov. 1889): 86–97.

McFadden, Elizabeth. *The Glitter and the Gold: A Spirited Account of the Metropolitan Museum of Art's First Director, the Audacious and High-Handed Luigi Palma di Cesnola*. New York: Dial Press, 1971.

Metropolitan Museum *Bulletin*. Vols. 2–38 (1907–1939).

Tomkins, Calvin. *Merchants and Masterpieces: The Story of the Metropolitan Museum of Art*. New York: E. P. Dutton, 1970).

CHAPTER 4

# Alfred Hamilton Barr Jr.
# *Brings Modern Art to the Museum*

## I

A NEW MUSEUM OPENED in New York on the afternoon of November 7, 1929. Six small galleries on the twelfth floor of the Hecksher Building on Fifth Avenue and 57th Street contained a special loan exhibition entitled *Cezanne, Gauguin, Seurat, and van Gogh* to introduce the Museum of Modern Art. The first afternoon was reserved for invited guests, but, next day, the general public came flooding in. Such openings of the museum's special exhibitions from the beginning were considered chic social events, and many of those attending were dressed to the nines. The times were not auspicious for the new venture, for the precipitous and alarming collapse of the stock market in the previous month had signaled the start of the worst economic depression of the twentieth century. But the museum founders and the participating public were unaware that industrial and social blight would encompass the whole globe and, ten years later, merge into catastrophic world war.

The founders of the new museum were three women, familiarly known as "The Ladies." All three were wealthy collectors of art produced from the latter part of the nineteenth century to their own day. Miss Lillie (often called "Lizzie") P. Bliss, whose father was a rich textile merchant and manufacturer, attended the famed Armory Show of 1913 devoted to advanced European art of the time. Its most shocking single piece was Marcel Duchamps's *Nude Descending a Staircase*. Miss Lillie admired Arthur B. Davies, the romantic artist who was the chief organizer of the show and, under his guidance, purchased five of the paintings—two Redons, two Degases, and a Renoir. She went on to obtain other works by these artists and by Cezanne, Seurat, Matisse, Picasso, and Toulouse-Latrec, more than one hundred examples in all. Miss Lillie was shy and retiring but may be considered the intellectual leader of the founding trio.

The second lady was Abby Aldrich (Mrs. John D., Jr.) Rockefeller, daughter of a powerful United States senator, sister of a leading banker, and wife of the wealthiest philanthropist in the country. She had collected the productions of modern American and European artists for many years and, since her husband had more conventional tastes, she made her purchases with her "Aldrich" money and had a private gallery upstairs in their home for her own and her children's enlightenment and pleasure. Mrs. Rockefeller was the trio's most capable organizer, a skillful problem solver full of energy, and a calm, warm person who communicated well with others. The third lady was Mary Quinn (Mrs. Cornelius J.) Sullivan. She had taught art for many years and, at age forty, had married a successful lawyer. Lillie Bliss and she were close friends, who helped Davies finance the Armory Show and listened to his pleas for the establishment of a museum to promote the new art. As a person, Mary Quinn was the most enthusiastic of the founders, described by another of her friends as a "whizbang" and "sparkplug."[1]

Lillie Bliss and Abby Rockefeller were vacationing in Egypt during the winter of 1928 and talked about founding the new museum; when Mrs. Rockefeller returned from Europe later that spring on the same ship with Mrs. Sullivan, they exchanged views on the subject. Back home, the three continued their discussions, and, late in May, Mrs. Rockefeller invited A. Conger Goodyear to luncheon with them. A colonel in the first World War, he had business interests in Buffalo. The Ladies were attracted by his enthusiasm for modern art, of which he had an extensive collection. He had served as trustee of the Albright Gallery in Buffalo and briefly as president until the trustees voted him off the board when he purchased a Picasso for the gallery. In the middle of the lunch, Mrs. Rockefeller, speaking for the Ladies, asked Goodyear to become chairman of a committee to organize "a new gallery or museum in New York that would exhibit works of art of the modern school."[2] Goodyear asked for a week to think over the proposal but called the next day to accept.

The new chairman added three members to the committee—Frank Crowninshield, the editor of *Vanity Fair*, a collector of modern paintings and sculpture, and an experienced publicist; Professor Paul J. Sachs, teacher of the well-known "museum course" at Harvard, curator of the Fogg Museum there, and a leading collector of drawings; and Josephine Boardman (Mrs. Winthrop

Murray) Crane, widow of an executive of the Crane Paper Company; he had been governor of Massachusetts and a United States senator. The committee decided upon "The Museum of Modern Art" as a name and petitioned the Regents of the University of the State of New York for a charter. They stated that the purposes of the new institution were "establishing and maintaining in the City of New York, a museum of modern art, encouraging and developing the study of modern arts and the application of said arts to manufacture and practical life, and furnishing popular instruction." The Regents granted a provisional charter on September 19. With the Board of Trustees official, it added several new members, all leading collectors of modern art—Stephen C. Clark, Samuel A. Lewisohn, Chester Dale, Duncan Phillips of Washington, and three others. Of these, only Clark and Lewisohn took prominent parts in the new museum. The trustees raised $115,000 for each of the first two years and rented space in the Heckhser Building at $12,000 per annum.[3]

The next important step was the appointment of a director. Professor Sachs, who was well acquainted with the art museum field and had trained many of its personnel, recommended Alfred Hamilton Barr Jr., twenty-seven years old and teaching art history at Wellesley College. After he had visited Mrs. Rockefeller twice at her summer home in Seal Harbor, he was appointed director in 1929, with a salary of $10,000 plus $2,500 for travel, and made a member of the board. His friend Jere Abbott became associate director, and there were three other paid staff members and one volunteer.

Goodyear went abroad to try to borrow works for a French exhibition, but he, Crowninshield, Sachs, and Barr had wished to open the museum with the work of modern American artists. The Ladies, however, insisted adamantly upon a French show. Its thirty-five Cezannes, twenty-six Gauguins, seventeen Seurats, and twenty-seven van Goghs attracted long waiting lines and overburdened the Heckhser elevators. When the exhibition closed a month later, some 47,000 persons had seen it. The newspapers and art critics found it superb. And Barr was responsible, not only for its attractive arrangement, but for the handsome catalogue that contained pictures and descriptions of each work as well as his perceptive and thoughtful Foreword.

## II

Alfred Hamilton Barr Jr. was born in Detroit on January 28, 1902, the son of Barr, Sr., and Annie Elizabeth (Wilson) Barr. The father, a Presbyterian minister, was a graduate of Princeton and its Theological Seminary, and the mother had attended Vassar for two years. The home's emphasis on serious intellectual achievement had much to do with the son's scholarly thoughtfulness and zeal. The family moved in 1911 to Baltimore, where Alfred attended the Boys' Latin School. He collected tin soldiers (with his friends refighting the battles of Gettysburg and Waterloo), played chess, and engaged enthusiastically in birdwatching. He edited the *Inkwell*, the school paper, and was graduated *cum laude* in 1918 as the Head Boy who delivered the class valedictory. That fall he entered Princeton with a four-year scholarship and, the next year, decided to major in art, largely because of a class he took in medieval art with Professor Charles Rufus Morey that included architecture, sculpture, painting, the minor arts, and crafts. He then had "Modern Painting" with Professor Frank Jewett Mather and upheld Matisse's worth in arguments with his teacher. Barr graduated a Phi Beta Kappa with high honors in 1922 and attended graduate school there the next year, receiving his M.A.

In 1923 Barr began teaching art history at Vassar and, in the next spring, staged an *Exhibition of Modern European Art* there with sixty-one items borrowed from New York dealers. He spent the summer in Europe and, in the fall, entered Harvard Graduate School as fellow and teaching assistant. He took courses with Professor Sachs on drawings of the old masters and on engraving and etching. In the spring of 1925 he passed his oral examination for the doctorate, and Professor Sachs wrote Professor Morey at Princeton to congratulate him "on the perfectly splendid student you have developed" in Barr. In the examination, Sachs thought "that he acquitted himself better than any candidate during the time I have been here" and "that he had thought deeply and ranged widely over the whole field" of art history.[4]

That fall, Barr returned to Princeton for a year as preceptor in art and archaeology, and in 1926 he became associate professor of art history at Wellesley, living in Cambridge and attending Professor Sachs's "museum course." He also organized an exhibition on modern art for the Fogg Museum. In the spring of 1927, Barr taught with missionary zeal the first undergraduate course in modern art offered in this country; it included architecture, graphic design, photography, music, the theatre, motion pictures, decorative arts, and crafts. He devised an unusual entrance examination for the course and referred to its seven young women students as his "children." He put on an *Exhibition of Progressive Modern Painting from Corot to Daumier to Post-Cubism* at Wellesley's Farnsworth Museum with thirty-five pictures.

In the fall of 1927, Barr set out for a year in Europe, for which Professor Sachs arranged a grant, with his friend Jere Abbott. They visited London, Holland, and Germany, where they spent four days at the Bauhaus in Dessau and were impressed by the way it interrelated painting, graphic arts, architecture, crafts, typography, theatre, cinema, photography, and industrial design. They went on to Russia (Moscow, Leningrad, and Novgorod), Warsaw, Vienna, and Paris, visiting museums and closely inspecting architecture everywhere. Upon his return, he taught another year at Wellesley and, in the spring, received a prestigious Carnegie fellowship to the Institute of Fine Arts at New York University but, before he could begin work there, accepted the directorship of the Modern Museum.[5]

Barr obviously had learned much about modern art during his university and teaching experience. (He went on to receive his doctorate from Harvard years later with his book on Picasso serving as his dissertation.) He had visited museums here and abroad and knew how to borrow art works for exhibition, install them tellingly, and write convincing catalogues about them. As a person, he was low-keyed and somewhat shy, but his knowledge was great, his enthusiasm unlimited, and his approach to modern art almost religious in its crusading intensity.

Professor Agnes Ringe, who taught art at Vassar, brought her associate and friend, Margaret Scolari, to see the museum's opening exhibition and introduced her to Barr. She was a native of Italy; her father Virgilio was an antiques dealer in Rome, and her mother, born Mary Fitzmaurice, was Irish. "Marga," as Barr soon called here, was fluent in most European languages and was teaching Italian at Vassar. She also was a knowledgeable art historian. Marga and Alfred were married in May 1930, at first by a New York justice of the peace and then in Paris at the American Church so as to satisfy his mother. Marga was of the greatest help to Barr, who was not adept at foreign languages. She acted as interpreter with European artists, collectors, museum directors and curators, and dealers; her study of art and her sociability also helped make her an invaluable member of the Barr team. In addition she handled the practical concerns of the household and shared the economic burden, teaching art at the Spence School for thirty-seven years beginning in 1943. The Barrs had one child, Victoria, but neither of them attained much intimacy with her. Barr dedicated his book on Picasso to Marga, and, in acknowledging her enormous help with research and translation for his volume on Matisse, he wryly concluded: "In fact, without her, the author might not have survived his book."[6]

## III

Special exhibitions were from the first the main concern of the Modern Museum, and the trustees and small staff worked furiously to stage two of them in the last two months of 1929 and six more the following year. Alfred and Marga began to go to Europe in the summer to secure art for future shows. The second exhibition on *Paintings by Nineteen Living Americans* attracted only about half the attendance of the opening one and received much adverse criticism from the art establishment, including, of course, the artists not invited to exhibit. The next show on *Painting in Paris from American Collections* with Picasso and Matisse as the stars more than regained public popularity, but *Forty-six Painters and Sculptors Under Thirty-five Years of Age* and *Painting and Sculpture by Living Americans* again secured fewer viewers and aroused considerable hostile comment. Still, everyone could agree that the museum was presenting exciting, even when controversial, exhibitions. Barr's mixture of scholarship and showmanship was making a large audience aware of the new art.

But the museum wished to be more than a gallery for special exhibitions. The Founders' Manifesto had promised a series of shows of the modern work of American and European artists for the first two years but also stated their intention "to establish a permanent public Museum which will acquire, from time to time, collections of the best modern works of art."[7] Much discussion took place among trustees and staff as to whether they should pass on to other more historically oriented museums, such as the Metropolitan, works that time showed to have permanent worth, just as the Luxembourg Gallery did in Paris for the Louvre. The idea of such an established relationship was dropped for the moment, but Goodyear talked of the collection as a kind of river with new works coming in now and then, and others going on elsewhere, while Barr defined the ideal permanent collection as a torpedo with its nose "the ever advancing present, its tail the ever receding past." He said later:

> The Museum is aware that it may often guess wrong in its acquisitions. When it acquires a dozen recent paintings it will be lucky in ten years if three will still seem worth looking at, and if in twenty years one should survive. For the future the important problem is to acquire this one; the other nine will be forgiven . . . and forgotten. But meanwhile we live in the present, and for the present these other nine will seem just as necessary and useful, serving their purpose by inclusion in exhibitions so long as their artistic lives shall last. Sooner or later, time will eliminate them.[8]

The permanent collection at first was tiny—five paintings and eight sculptures—and Barr's proposal to show it in a separate room was voted down. In 1931, however, Lillie Bliss died and left the museum most of her splendid collection. One condition of the bequest required that, within three years, the museum raise an endowment large enough to assure its continuation. The executors of the will at first placed that goal at $1 million, but later, in view of the raging economic depression, reduced it to $600,000, and the trustees succeeded in raising it.[9]

In 1932 the Rockefellers gave the former home of John D., Sr., on 53rd Street to the museum, and it moved there from its crowded quarters in the Hecksher Building. By then, Barr had worked himself to the edge of a nervous breakdown; assisted by his small staff, he had organized sixteen exhibitions and issued sixteen catalogues, carefully planned, enticingly written, and beautifully illustrated. The trustees wisely granted him a year off with half pay, and the Barrs spent the time in Europe, visiting artists, collectors, and museums, and still making arrangements for future shows. He was shocked to learn how Hitler, who had just come to power in Germany, was destroying modern art, and he wrote a series of articles entitled "Hitler and the Nine Muses" expressing his alarm but could find publication for only one of them, in Lincoln Kirstein's small *Hound & Horn* magazine at Harvard.[10]

A van Gogh exhibition in 1935 attracted nearly 125,000 viewers who, at 25 cents a head (the first time the museum charged admission), brought in more than $20,000. The police had to be called to keep the long waiting lines in order. Department stores sold color transparencies and ladies' dresses in van Gogh colors. The exhibition went on a triumphal tour to the Pacific coast and back; it reached a total of nearly 900,000 persons.[11]

Often, the shows stirred controversy, especially two in 1936 on *Cubism and Abstract Art* and *Fantastic Art, Dada, and Surrealism*. The latter contained Meret Oppenheim's *The Fur-lined Teacup*, complete with fur-lined saucer and teaspoon, and Duchamp's *Why Not Sneeze* with a small cage filled with sugar lumps and a thermometer. Barr's preface in the catalogue for the second exhibition explained that "Surrealism as an art movement is a serious affair and for many it is a philosophy, a way of life, a cause to which some of the most brilliant painters and poets of our age are giving themselves with consuming devotion." But the newspapers and the general public had a humorous field day. The show was to travel, and Goodyear and some other trustees tried to get Barr to eliminate what they considered ridiculous objects, but he refused to do so, and the museum's policy of not interfering with the decisions of a director of any exhibition was upheld, no matter how reluctantly.[12]

In 1938, after six years of negotiation by Goodyear, the museum sent *Three Centuries of American Art* to be exhibited at the Louvre's Jeu de Paume in Paris. In addition to the customary works of art selected mainly by Goodyear, the show contained exhibits of architecture, motion pictures, and photography. The French critics were "absolutely vicious" in judging both the historical and modern paintings and sculpture but found the architecture stimulating and praised Barr's catalogue. The movie showings (five times daily) frequently generated long lines and were recognized as a peculiarly American form of art. Unfortunately, though, attendance at the main exhibition was meager.[13]

As early as 1929, Barr had proposed to the trustees the extension of the museum's activities to cover architecture, industrial design, photography, stage settings, decorative arts, and motion pictures. He had taught his undergraduate class at Wellesley modern art based on that broad definition, and on his European trips had admired the way the Bauhaus was furthering that conception. The trustees postponed the plan, but in 1932 Barr began to implement it. With his friends Philip Johnson and Henry-Russell Hitchcock, he presented the *Modern Architecture: International Exhibition* that featured what Barr called the "International Style." They had been working on the show for two years, and it contained the designs of more than fifty modern architects including Wright, Gropius, Le Corbusier, Oud, and Mies van der Rohe; the new functionalism was emphasized with many models and photographs. It was the museum's first traveling exhibit and circulated among eleven other museums and a department store. As a result, Barr succeeded in establishing a new Department of Architecture with Philip Johnson as its unpaid director.[14]

Other parts of the broader art plan appeared through the years, the organization of new departments usually following important special exhibitions. *Motion Pictures, 1914–1934* resulted in the Film Library, which soon was showing old movies in the auditorium. Several smaller photographic shows and then *Photography, 1839–1937* preceded the organization of the Department of Photography. Philip Johnson's exhibition on *Machine Art* in 1934 and a series on industrial design that began with *Useful Household Objects Under $5* led to the Department of Industrial Art in 1940.[15]

In 1935 the museum established a Department of Circulating Exhibits with Elodie Courter, a Wellesley graduate, at its head. It sent out shows, the contents approved by Barr himself, chiefly to colleges, universities, libraries, museums, and department stores throughout the country. In its first six years, nearly one hundred exhibitions were displayed more than one thousand times in 222 cities of the United States, Canada, and Hawaii. Thus, thousands of persons, many of them enthusiastic college students, learned of the attractions of modern art. The museum also developed many educational activities for the schools, though Barr was not too interested personally in that area. But Victor d'Amico, a wonderfully warm art educator, joined the staff in 1937. He sent exhibits and slides to the New York high schools, conducted tours for their students at the museum, set up a Young People's Gallery with Saturday classes, and helped organize a National Committee on Art Education that improved the teaching of art in many schools of the region.[16]

The museum moved into greatly enlarged quarters in 1939. The old Rockefeller house was torn down, and a sleek, modern, functional building took its place. It had six floors with auditorium and lounge in the basement; three stories with movable partitions and flexible lighting for exhibits; two floors for Library, Film Library, and offices; and a penthouse Members' Lounge with a terrace. A Sculpture Garden visible from the building was situated in the rear. Philip L. Goodwin, a board member, had been the chief architect, but his traditionalism had been modified by his assistant, the young Edward Durrell Stone, a convinced modernist. Barr, then in Paris, had tentatively promised to employ Mies van der Rohe, but Goodyear and Nelson A. Rockefeller had chosen an American architect instead. Barr resigned from the building committee in protest, though his ideas continued to be transmnitted through staff members. He was largely responsible for the use of a new translucent material (Thermolux) on the entrance side of the museum and for the natural lighting employed throughout. The building committee and architects had opposed these features, and it was necessary later to build a false wall because the Thermolux let in too much light.[17]

At a trustee dinner two days before the opening of the new building, a changing of the guard took place. Goodyear (probably reluctantly) and Mrs. Rockefeller resigned as president and vice-president, and Stephen Clark became chairman with Nelson Rockefeller as president. Professor Sachs, who had been Barr's strongest backer on the board, urged the trustees in the next decade to devote more energy and funds to films, architecture, photographs, the Library, and a choice permanent collection. He warned against "*the danger of timidity*" and insisted that the museum "must continue to take risks" and "continue to be a pioneer . . . bold and uncompromising." Goodyear, who had often been Barr's chief opponent on policy matters, said at the dinner:

> The pituitary gland, you know, has a very profound influence in the growth of the body. The skeleton cannot prosper without it, and when its activity is diminished, this leads to obesity and mental defects. Our pituitary gland is Alfred Barr. . . . It is useless for me to attempt to tell you what Alfred has done for us. I need only say, look about you.[18]

The change in the board leadership was the beginning of serious trouble for Barr. The trustees had always taken a greater share in the museum's administration than he would have preferred. When young Edward M. M. Warburg was appointed to the board in 1932, he argued unsuccessfully that the director ought to be given a free hand with exhibitions and other administrative matters; he thought that "Mrs. Rockefeller, Goodyear, Sam Lewisohn, and some of the others were frustrated museum directors."[19] Nelson Rockefeller, as the new president, brought some efficiency experts to analyze the staff and whether expenditures could be reduced. As a result, two upper staff members were dismissed, and another one resigned. All this was done without consulting Barr, who was then in Paris. Rockefeller went to Washington in 1940 as coordinator of the Office of Inter-American Affairs, and John Hay Whitney, who replaced him, joined the Air Force in 1942. Stephen Clark then became both chairman and president.[20]

Mr. Clark was a quiet, somewhat shy man who did not communicate well nor understand Barr. As a collector and connoisseur, he found Barr's taste erratic and sometimes frivolous, as when he exhibited Joe Milone's fantastically tinsel-bedecked shoeshine stand. Clark also was a good businessman, much concerned about the museum's finances and convinced that Barr was a careless administrator. Barr, on his part, could be uncommunicative and difficult. Goodyear referred to his fine Italian hand, and some critics called him a Svengali or Tallyrand in his relations with the trustees, but the fact is that he was often unperceptive and untactful. Despite Clark's worries about finances, Barr asked for raises for his staff and even sought a salary of $15,000 for himself. (He withdrew that request after Clark's shocked terse response.) The confrontation between the two men came to a head on October 16, 1943, when Clark wrote Barr that "in these difficult times the relatively unimportant work you are doing does not justify a salary of $12,000 a year." He ought to give his time to writing books and "assume the position of Advisory Director at a salary of $6,000 a year."[21] The letter was written with the approval of the more active and influential trustees. Mrs. Rockefeller tried to soften the blow somewhat by pointing out how important it was to the cause of modern art for Barr to write definitive books on the subject. But he was denied an office in the museum and apparently was expected to do his writing mainly at home. Barr simply refused to leave and fitted out a small cubicle for himself in the Library. He wrote his mentor Sachs that he was "still pretty damn sore" about the demotion and asked: "Were all the planning and all the exhibitions, and all the paintings I have bought and the standards I have fought for—was it someone else?"[22]

Most of the staff continued to consult Barr as if he were still director. By the time of the annual meeting in 1946, Clark had softened his animosity considerably. He reported that freeing Barr from administrative routine had had good results, as the trustees had hoped. He had organized a fine exhibition of the collection of paintings and sculpture; his book on Picasso was about to appear; he was to deliver the Mary Flexner lectures at Bryn Mawr; and he was providing the editorial supervision of the Penguin series on American artists. All in all, Clark said, Barr was continuing to contribute "more than anyone to the strict maintenance of the Museum's integrity and artistic standards."[23] In June 1946, Clark retired as chairman and president, to be succeeded by John Hay Whitney and Nelson Rockefeller.

Barr was a talented writer with a facility for clothing his innovative ideas in clear, easily understood language. His catalogues of the museum's exhibitions, which brilliantly explained aspects of modern art, were eagerly sought after by art museums, both here and abroad, so that they soon went out of print. But for Barr, always the perfectionist, writing was extremely difficult. He was never satisfied but insisted on many versions; he indulged in much procrastination and often missed deadlines. He failed to produce an authoritative, comprehensive book on modern art, its history and meaning, though he did write an excellent forty-eight page booklet, issued in 1943 and entitled *What Is Modern Painting?* It seductively broke down the barriers between modern art and the ordinary person, was lauded by scholars, and became a best seller with the public. After many struggles, he managed to produce two full-length and definitive masterpieces—*Picasso: Fifty Years of His Art* in 1946 and *Matisse: His Art and His Public* in 1951.[24]

Barr's position began to improve markedly with the coming of René d'Harnoncourt to the staff in 1944, at first with the peculiar title of vice-president in charge of foreign activities and director of the Department of Manual Industry. A former Austrian count, he was an authority on Mexican and American Indian art and unusually skilled in museum installation. More important, he was a "gentle giant" (six feet seven and 230 pounds) who understood people and knew how to obtain harmony in an institution. His social rank impressed the trustees, and he came to be cherished by the staff. He appreciated Barr's great ability and insisted that he be a member of his five-man Coordinating Committee that had the direction of the museum from 1946 until d'Harnoncourt was promoted to the directorship three years later.[25]

A woman trustee in the inner circle described what was happening thus:

> No one else could have become director and at the same time kept Alfred, who is really the backbone of the Museum, happy and functioning. René set out to reinstate Alfred, and built the whole thing around him. René can cope with Alfred, and he can hold a group of prima donnas together. Specialists, such as museum curators, are perfectionists, you know, and they get into a state of nerves. It's hard for them to meet a deadline. They're dedicated people, but they're edgy, and René gives them a sense of excitement and drama that enhances their feeling for their work.

And Barr himself had this to say:

> René is a man I have enormous affection for. And appreciation. This place is a madhouse, because of the pressures, the number of people who want to get into the act, and a temperamental board of trustees and staff. He holds it together. . . . I think he's the most patient man I've ever known—Lincolnian really—and I'm an authority on testing patience, since I'm chronically irritable and tend to need people to complain to.[26]

## IV

At d'Harnoncourt's firm suggestion, Barr was made director of collections in 1947, and he continued at that post until his retirement twenty years later. His major contributions were in the paintings and sculpture department, and he passed judgment on every item added to those collections. But, of course, he had much influence in other areas, especially architecture, industrial design, photography, and films. Though Barr still sometimes felt bitter about his demotion, his new position took advantage of his main talents as idea man, inspirational innovator, and maintainer of quality standards, while relieving him from the administrative minutiae that he handled less well.

The museum collection had first become important with Lillie Bliss's bequest and then expanded with Mrs. Rockefeller's substantial gifts of paintings, drawings, and sculpture and of the museum's first sizeable purchase fund of more than $30,000. Another generous donor was Mrs. Simon Guggenheim, who in 1937 of her own volition came to see Barr and began to finance specific purchases for him, such as Picasso's *Mirror*, *Three Musicians*, and *She-goat* bronze, Rousseau's *Sleeping Gypsy*, and Chagall's *I and the Village*. Altogether, she furnished more than two million dollars for such acquisitions. The trustees and many other collectors contributed more and more modern masterpieces. Barr and others on the staff were always glad to advise and help serious collectors, many of whom gratefully remembered the museum with gifts or bequests.[27]

The question of passing along works of art to other museums concerned the museum for many years. In 1934, President Goodyear and William Sloan Coffin, president of the Metropolitan Museum of Art, entered into a series of negotiations. Coffin suggested that the Metropolitan's Hearn Fund, of about $15,000 yearly for the purchase of paintings by living American artists, be administered by a committee of the two institutions. Any paintings acquired should be shown at the Modern for ten years or more and then, if the Metropolitan wished, pass on to it. The trustees of the Modern approved the suggested arrangement, but Coffin died before his trustees could discuss the matter, and it was dropped.[28]

In 1944 the museum, under Stephen Clark's administration and partly for financial reasons, decided to sell at public auction some of its holdings considered less permanent. The funds received were to be used to purchase twentieth-century art, chiefly by living artists, and no work by a living North or South American artist was included in the sale. In all, 108 items were disposed of, though 63 of them were contributed by the trustees from their own collections. The museum discards included four Cezanne oils and watercolors, two Seurat drawings, and one Matisse. The museum received only a disappointing $55,189 from the sale.[29]

When Henry Francis Taylor became director of the Metropolitan in 1940, he began to hold conversations with both the Modern and the Whitney Museum in an effort to harmonize their collecting and exhibition practices. Taylor was a much different personality from Barr, his humor and expressions of opinion often bawdy, as when he referred to the Modern as "the whorehouse on Fifty-third Street" or to "those pansies" who worked there. He, however, left the negotiations with the other museums to his president, Roland L. Redmond, who was an accomplished lawyer; Stephen Clark and Nelson Rockefeller were also trustees of both the Modern and the Metropolitan. Redmond worked closely with Barr and with Juliana Force of the Whitney to secure the *Three Museum Agreement of 1947*. Under it, the Metropolitan was to concentrate on classic art; the Whitney, on American art; and the Modern, on both American and foreign modern art. The three were to exchange items from their holdings for special exhibitions. The Modern sold the Metropolitan twenty-six works of art for $191,000, and the Metropolitan sent the Modern on extended loan Maillol's *Chained Action* sculpture and Picasso's *Portrait of Gertrude Stein*. But the agreement, which was to last for five years, was an uneasy one. The Whitney had talked of building next to the Metropolitan but, when disputes arose, dropped out of the arrangement after a year. The Modern decided not to renew the pact in 1952, chiefly because it had become convinced that important donors might not wish to leave their cherished masterpieces to a museum that might pass them along. The next year, President John Hay Whitney announced the important change in policy that abandoned the transferral of collections to other institutions. It promised to keep on view in the museum's own galleries masterpieces of the modern movement, though works judged not to have that quality would still be sold or traded. The failure of the *Three Museum Agreement* probably did not harm the cause of modern art, for the Metropolitan began to build on its own collection in that field and the two other museums continued their vigorous efforts.[30]

When Barr retired in 1967 after thirty-eight years of service, the Board of Trustees appointed him its counselor, and he continued to advise occasionally on various matters. Numerous honors came to him, and his recommendations were often sought on important decisions in the art museum field. Unfortunately, however, his memory, which had always been so remarkable and served him so well, began to fail, and he came to suffer the ravages of Alzheimer's disease. Despite Marga's constant devoted care and her frantic attempts to find some medical cure, he was forced to spend his last six years in a convalescent home, where he died on August 15, 1981.

Barr's career had indeed been a remarkable one. In 1929 modern art had been looked down upon in the United States by the art world and most artists as well as by the general public. Many had agreed with Dean Inge, who thought "the revolting productions of the modernist school" resembled "now the work of a very unpleasant child, now the first efforts of an African savage, and now the delirious hallicunations of an incurable lunatic."[31] But Barr's exhibitions of the French Impressionists and post-Impressionists together with the clear, reasonable explanations of his catalogues attracted public interest and aroused enthusiasm. Similarly, American nineteenth-century artists like Homer, Ryder, Eakins, Whistler, and George Caleb Bingham were, in general, well received. The backing of the museum that such shows produced stood it in good stead when more radical works were exhibited, such as cubism, abstract art, fantastic art, and surrealism. Barr had done much to alter the whole art field. When he retired, *Newsweek* commented: "In the old days, a museum was a stately cenotaph for defunct genius, full of the hush and odor of sanctity. Barr changed all that and literally seduced the public off the street with showmanship and genius." Professor Sachs said that the museum had become "a telling instrument in the field of general education" and had "liberalized the policies of every one of our leading museums . . . even the most complacent." And Hilton Kramer wrote in 1987 that Barr gave the art museum a new role. No longer was it to be regarded as a refuge from the conflicts and controversies of contemporary life. Henceforth it would take up its mission at the very crossroads where tradition and innovation meet, and act as a guide to the present as well as the past.[32]

The success of the Modern also led to better treatment of modern art in other museums. In New York, the Whitney Museum of American Art (1930) and the Solomon R. Guggenheim Museum (1937) appeared on the scene with strong commitment to the modern movement, and the Metropolitan in 1949 set up its own Department of Contemporary (now Twentieth Century) Art. Elsewhere in the United States, other museums friendly to the modern approach were strengthened, such as the Art Institute of Chicago, Albright-Knox Gallery of Buffalo, Phillips Gallery in Washington, and Boston's Institute of Contemporary Art. The international influence of the Modern Museum was also great. American travelers sometimes were surprised to find that many Europeans regarded it as the premier museum in the new world. The museum's International Council reinforced that impression by sending exhibitions to Asia, Africa, Australia, Latin America, and Europe, and lending art works to American ambassadors. All these developments made Barr one of the most influential museum masters yet to flourish in this country.

## NOTES

1. The most readily available sources on the museum and Barr are: Alfred H. Barr Jr., *Defining Modern Art: Selected Writings of Alfred H. Barr Jr.*, edited by Irving Sandler and Amy Newman (New York: Abrams, 1986); Barr, *Painting and Sculpture in the Museum of Modern Art, 1929–1967* (New York: MOMA, 1977); Margaret Scolari Barr, "Our Campaigns," *New Criterion* (Summer 1987): 23–74; *Contemporary Authors: A Bibliographical Guide to Current Authors and Their Work*, edited by Clara D. Kinsman (Detroit: Gale Research Company, 1975), vols. 49–52: 47–48; Emily Genauer, "The Fur-lined Museum," *Harper's Magazine* 189 (July 1944): 129–38; A. Conger Goodyear, *The Museum of Modern Art: The First Ten Years* (New York: MOMA, 1943); Geoffrey T. Hellman, "Imperturbable Noble: René d'Harnoncourt," *New*

*Yorker* 36 (May 7, 1960): 49–112; Hellman, "Profile of a Museum," *Art in America* 40 (Feb. 1964): 27–64; Hilton Kramer, "Alfred Barr at MOMA: An Introduction," *New Criterion* (Summer 1987): i–iii; Russell Lynes, *Good Old Modern: The Museum of Modern Art* (New York: Atheneum, 1973); Dwight Macdonald, "Profiles: Action on West Fifty-Third Street," *New Yorker* 29 (Dec. 12, 1953): 49–82; *New Yorker* 29 (Dec. 19, 1953): 35–72; Alice Goldfarb Marquis, *Alfred H. Barr Jr.: Missionary for the Modern* (Chicago: Contemporary Books, 1989); Museum of Modern Art *Bulletin* 1–30 (1933–1962); Museum of Modern Art, *The Lillie B. Bliss Collection, 1934* (New York: MOMA, 1934); Museum of Modern Art, *The Museum of Modern Art, New York: The History and the Collection* (New York: Abrams, 1984); Rona Roob, "1936: The Museum Selects an Architect," *Archives of American Art Journal* 23, No. 1 (1983): 22–30; Roob, "Alfred H. Barr Jr.: A Chronicle of the Years 1902–1929," *New Criterion* (Summer 1987): 1–19; John Russell, "Visionary Curator, Cautionary Tale," New York *Times*, July 26, 1989.

2. Lynes, *Good Old Modern*, 9.

3. Goodyear, *First Ten Years*, 12, 16.

4. Lynes, *Good Old Modern*, 20; Marquis, *Barr*, chap. 2.

5. Marquis, *Barr*, 2–3, chap. 3; Roob, "Barr, 1902–1929," 1–19.

6. Margaret Barr, "Our Campaigns," 24; "Margaret Scolari Barr," New York *Times*, Dec. 31, 1987; Marquis, *Barr*, 71–76, 161–62, 269–70; Roob, "Barr, 1902–1929," 19.

7. Goodyear, *First Ten Years*, 15, 84.

8. Hellman, "Profile of a Museum," 27; Marquis, *Barr*, 116–17.

9. Barr, *Modern Museum Painting and Sculpture*, xi; Goodyear, *First Ten Years*, 82; Marquis, *Barr*, 115–16.

10. *Magazine of Art* (Oct. 1945): 212–22; Marquis, *Barr*, 102–09.

11. Goodyear, *First Ten Years*, 54–57; Lynes, *Good Old Modern*, 132–36; Marquis, *Barr*, 131–35.

12. Goodyear, *First Ten Years*, 57–59, 62–64 (quotation on p. 63); Lynes, *Good Old Modern*, 137–46; Marquis, *Barr*, 149–61.

13. Goodyear, *First Ten Years*, 73–82; Lynes, *Good Old Modern*, 183–85; Marquis, *Barr*, 161–67.

14. Margaret Barr, "Our Campaigns," 28; Goodyear, *First Ten Years*, 137–39; Lynes, *Good Old Modern*, 285; Marquis, *Barr*, 85–87.

15. Lynes, *Good Old Modern*, 180–81, 318.

16. Goodyear, *First Ten Years*, 93; Lynes, *Good Old Modern*, 117–20, 260–61; Marquis, *Barr*, 122–23, 161.

17. Goodyear, *First Ten Years*, 125–32; Lynes, *Good Old Modern*, 171, 193–95, 355; Marquis, *Barr*, 167–70; Museum of Modern Art, *History and Collection*, 19; Roob, "Museum Selects an Architect," 22–30.

18. Goodyear, *First Ten Years*, 96; Lynes, *Good Old Modern* 199–203 (quotations on pp. 200–01); Marquis, *Barr*, 171–73.

19. Lynes, *Good Old Modern*, 153.

20. Margaret Barr, "Our Campaigns," 54–56, 60, 64; Genauer, "Fur-lined Museum," 132; Lynes, *Good Old Modern*, 213–14, 222, 224.

21. Margaret Barr, "Our Campaigns," 68; see also 67–73; Lynes, *Good Old Modern*, 240–43; Marquis, *Barr*, 200–10.

22. Lynes, *Good Old Modern*, 246–47.

23. Marquis, *Barr*, 211–12; Museum of Modern Art *Bulletin* 13 (Feb. 1946): 4, 20.

24. Marquis, *Barr*, 91–92, 215–18, 265–67; *Matisse: His Art and His Public* (New York: MOMA, 1951); *Picasso: Fifty Years of His Art* (New York: MOMA, 1946); *What Is Modern Painting?*

(New York: MOMA, 1943).

25. Lynes, *Good Old Modern*, 265–71; Marquis, *Barr*, 284–86, 345; Museum of Modern Art *Bulletin* 15, No. 4 (1948): 25.

26. The quotations are in Hellman, "René d'Harnoncourt," 27, 50, 52.

27. Lynes, *Good Old Modern*, 295–96; Marquis, *Barr*, 11, 117–18.

28. Goodyear, *First Ten Years*, 39–40.

29. Margaret Barr, "Our Campaigns," 73; Lynes, *Good Old Modern*, 295–97; Marquis, *Barr*, 223–24.

30. Lynes, *Good Old Modern*, 250, 287–91; Marquis, *Barr*, 245–47; Museum of Modern Art *Bulletin* 15 (Fall 1947): 20; Calvin Tomkins, *Merchants and Masterpieces: The Story of the Metropolitan Museum of Art* (New York: E. P. Dutton, 1970), 304–10.

31. Goodyear, *The First Ten Years*, 26; Marquis, *Barr*, 347, 355–56.

32. The quotations are in Lynes, *Good Old Modern*, 352, 405.

## SELECT BIBLIOGRAPHY


Barr, Alfred H., Jr. *Defining Modern Art: Selected Writings of Alfred H. Barr Jr.* Edited by Irving Sandler and Amy Newman. New York: Abrams, 1986.

_____. *Painting and Sculpture in the Museum of Modern Art, 1929–1967*. New York: MOMA, 1977.

Barr, Margaret Scolari. "Our Campaigns." *New Criterion* (Summer 1987): 23–74.

*Contemporary Authors: A Bibliographical Guide to Current Authors and Their Work*. Edited by Clara D. Kinsman. Detroit: Gale Research Company, 1975. Vols. 49–52.

Genauer, Emily. "The Fur-lined Museum." *Harper's Magazine* 189 (July 1944): 129–38.

Goodyear, A. Conger. *The Museum of Modern Art: The First Ten Years*. New York: MOMA, 1943.

Hellman, Geoffrey T. "Imperturbable Noble: René d'Harnoncourt." *New Yorker* 36 (May 7, 1960): 49–112.

_____. "Profile of a Museum." *Art in America* 40 (Feb. 1964): 27–64.

Kramer, Hilton. "Alfred Barr at MOMA: An Introduction." *New Criterion* (Summer 1987): i–iii.

Lynes, Russell. *Good Old Modern: The Museum of Modern Art*. New York: Atheneum, 1973.

Macdonald, Dwight. "Profiles: Action on West Fifty-Third Street." *New Yorker* 29 (Dec. 12, 1953): 49–82; and 29 (Dec. 19, 1953): 35–72.

Marquis, Alice Goldfarb. *Alfred H. Barr Jr.: Missionary for the Modern*. Chicago: Contemporary Books, 1989.

Museum of Modern Art *Bulletin* 1–30 (1933–1962).

_____. *The Lillie B. Bliss Collection, 1934*. New York: MOMA, 1934.

_____. *Matisse: His Art and His Public*. New York: MOMA, 1951.

_____. *The Museum of Modern Art, New York: The History and the Collection*. New York: Abrams, 1984.

_____. *Picasso: Fifty Years of His Art*. New York: MOMA, 1946.

_____. *What Is Modern Painting?* New York: MOMA, 1943.

Roob, Rona. "1936: The Museum Selects an Architect." *Archives of American Art Journal* 23, No. 1 (1983): 22–30.

_____. "Alfred H. Barr Jr.: A Chronicle of the Years 1902–1929." *New Criterion* (Summer 1987): 1–19.

Russell, John. "Visionary Curator, Cautionary Tale." New York *Times*, July 26, 1989.

Tomkins, Calvin. *Merchants and Masterpieces: The Story of the Metropolitan Museum of Art*. New York: E. P. Dutton, 1970.

# CHAPTER 5

# Reuben Gold Thwaites *Makes a Historical Society Reach the People of a State*

## I

AMERICAN HISTORICAL SOCIETIES appeared soon after the end of the Revolution and the adoption of the Constitution. They aimed to collect the books, newspapers, manuscripts, and objects, at first both of natural science and history, that would keep the American experience alive and through meetings and publications disseminate that history throughout the country and even abroad. The earliest organizations were the Massachusetts Historical Society (1791) in Boston, the New-York Historical Society (1804), and the American Antiquarian Society (1812) in Worcester, Massachusetts. By the time of the Centennial Exposition at Philadelphia in 1876, there were more than seventy societies, extending from Texas through every state to the Atlantic.[1]

Nearly all the historical societies were independent, private membership bodies governed by a Board of Trustees and Executive Committee and receiving their financial support from membership dues and donations. The Massachusetts and Antiquarian ones were unusual in that their members were elected because of their scholarly contributions or publications. The three pioneer organizations placed chief emphasis upon building research libraries, but all of them in the beginning gathered museum materials. Massachusetts sought "specimens of natural and artificial curiosities, and a selection of every thing which can improve and promote the historical knowledge of our country, either in a physical or political view."[2] The New York Society's constitution stated that its object "shall be to discover, procure, and preserve whatever may relate to the natural, civil, literary, and ecclesiastical history of the United States in general, and of this State in particular," and it promised to collect not only library materials but "specimens of the various productions of the American Continent and of the adjacent Islands, and such animal, vegetable, and mineral objects . . . deemed worthy of preservation."[3] The American Antiquarian Society wished "to preserve such relics of American Antiquity as are portable, as well as to collect and preserve those of other parts of the Globe" and "specimens, with written accounts respecting them, of fossils, handicrafts of the Aborigines,&c."[4] For a time it collected actively, especially in the fields of American Indian archaeology and antiquities.

Only the New York Society continued for long to amass museum materials. Massachusetts soon gave away everything except portraits and some valuable New England historical artifacts. The Antiquarian Society agreed with its librarian Christopher Columbus Baldwin that "a library should contain nothing but books, coins, statuary, and pictures" and that it was "absurd to pile up old bureaus and chests, and stuff them with old coats and hats and high-heeled shoes."[5] By 1854 it was bestowing its natural history and anthropological collections upon other institutions. New York from the start secured American portraits and paintings, decorative arts, and other historical objects but often ventured into wider fields. It accepted Plains Indian and pre-Columbian artifacts from Central and South America; Luman Reed's extensive collection of paintings, many of them European; James Lenox's thirteen huge marble Nineveh sculptures; Dr. Henry Abbott's Egyptian collection (then the best in the country with 1,100 pieces including three large mummified bulls); and the 438 canvases of Thomas Jefferson Bryan's "Gallery of Christian Art." Not until the present century did the society begin to get rid of its extraneous holdings. Most of the other Eastern societies concentrated upon collecting libraries, publishing articles and books on state and local history, and holding meetings with lectures and special events. Through the years, however, many of them acquired historic houses, often as headquarters, gathered decorative art objects with which to furnish them, and sometimes were given comprehensive regional museum collections.

Wisconsin formed a private state historical society in 1846, two years before reaching statehood. For a time, it seemed likely to adopt the Eastern independent type of organization, and a strong faction tried to make it into a private club, the membership confined to those with a scholarly interest, or even to follow the Massachusetts and American Antiquarian restrictive models. But the arrival in Madison of Lyman Copeland Draper (1815–1891), the driving collector of manuscripts, newspapers, books, interviews, and other materials of the trans-Allegheny frontier, changed all that. He succeeded in obtaining a charter and constitution for the State Historical Society of Wisconsin in 1854 that called for a broad amateur membership statewide; but though anyone could join by paying dues of a dollar per year, the number of members remained small. Draper was the society's corresponding secretary, and with great ingenuity, tireless energy, and contagious enthusiasm, he used all kinds of promotional devices including honorary memberships and national and foreign exchanges to build an important historical research library, portrait gallery, and small cabinet of museum objects. The State Legislature in 1854 granted the society $500 with which to purchase books and other materials and, the next year, doubled that amount with $500 for Draper's salary. Wisconsin was the first state to make regular annual appropriations for its historical society and has continued that practice ever since.

Draper's main interest was the society's library, but in the museum field, he did build a creditable portrait gallery. He sent many American artists handsomely engraved certificates making them honorary members and requesting examples of their work. Robert M. Sully, of Richmond, Virginia, for example, contributed a copy of his portrait of Black Hawk, the Sauk chief; paintings of Black Hawk's son and of the glowering Winnebago medicine man, the Prophet; and a fanciful likeness of Pocahontas with flowers in her hair and pearls at her ears. Draper persuaded Sully to depart for Wisconsin to become the society's artist in residence, but on the way, in Buffalo, New York, the artist died during a drunken spree. Draper then secured Samuel M. Brookes and Thomas H. Stevenson, English born but living in Milwaukee, as official artists. He induced many governors and other political, industrial, and cultural leaders to present their likenesses and managed to finance portraits of several Indian chiefs. In 1886 the gallery contained 135 paintings, mainly portraits but some representations of Wisconsin towns, canals, and battlefields of the Black Hawk War. They constituted a documentary view of early Wisconsin and, on the practical side, were useful in securing legislative support from the leaders whose portraits graced the gallery. Other museum materials were less significant but included coins, medals, Indian antiquities (especially the Perkins Collection of rare copper implements), objects of pioneer life, and Civil War military equipment.

Draper thus was a great success as a historical society organizer and promoter. He built one of the leading historical libraries of the nation; obtained a small but influential statewide membership; and secured continuing appropriations from the state. Before he retired at the end of 1886 after thirty-three years of service, he cannily chose as his successor Reuben Gold Thwaites, a Madison newspaper editor, who was to become the most successful historical society director that the nation had known.[6]

## II

Reuben Gold Thwaites was born May 15, 1853, at Dorchester, Massachusetts, the son of George and Sarah (Bibbs) Thwaites, natives of Yorkshire, England, who had come to Massachusetts three years earlier. Reuben attended common school in Dorchester but at age thirteen moved with his parents to a farm in Omro near Oshkosh, Wisconsin. After working as a farmhand and going to public school, he taught elementary classes and systematically instructed himself in collegiate subjects. He also began to write for newspapers in the area and, as a staff member of the Oshkosh *Times*, in 1872 reported on the Democratic presidential convention in Baltimore. He became "a fire-eating Granger" and backed Joseph H. Osborn, his brother-in-law, who headed the Wisconsin State Grange from his farm near Oshkosh. Thwaites also began to become acquainted with the Indian tribes of Wisconsin and in 1876 wrote a piece for the *Times* on "Oshkosh, the last of the Menominee Sachems."

In 1874–1875 the young journalist became a special student at Yale University, taking post-graduate work in English literature, economic history, and international law. He admired greatly one of his instructors, William Graham Sumner. In 1876 Thwaites moved to Madison as city editor (later managing editor) of the Republican *Wisconsin State Journal* under the editorship of General David Atwood. As a reporter of legislative proceedings and political conventions he was well acquainted with the public men of the state. He supplied Eastern newspapers with Wisconsin news and later covered state legislative affairs for the Chicago *Tribune*. He made many friends and led an active social life. He became an early member of the exclusive Madison Literary Club and wrote an account of its first decade. He was an adjutant's clerk in the Lake City Guard, which he accompanied to Eau Claire in 1881 when Governor William E. Smith ordered it to help suppress the riotous conduct of mill hands and rivermen striking against the twelve-hour day.

In 1882 Thwaites was married to Jessie Inwood Turvill, also the scion of English immigrants. They had one son, Frederick, in 1883; he later taught geology at the University of Wisconsin and for a time was curator of its Geological Museum. The Thwaites' summer home, Turvillwood, was situated on Lake Monona, and Mrs. Thwaites was a cordial hostess who entertained their frequent visitors, including many Indians. She was a devoted botanist and gardener; later she and the son often accompanied Thwaites on his travels.

In 1884–1885, Thwaites visited New Mexico and Colorado and considered establishing a newspaper in that area. He suggested to his friend Frederick Jackson Turner, then a budding historian at the university, that he join him in the venture. But his career goal changed when Lyman Draper persuaded him to become assistant corresponding secretary of the State Historical Society, and in January 1887 he succeeded Draper as secretary (later superintendent).[7]

During his newspaper days, Thwaites had become a fluent writer and editor. He knew how to present the gist of complex matters and situations in clear, easily read prose and, faced with constant deadlines, to prepare articles and stories rapidly. He was punctilious about grammar and syntax, as Louise Kellogg said later: "never too busy to discuss the value of placing a comma correctly."[8] He also understood people and their motives and feelings. All those qualities made him an effective administrator and leader, so that he gave promise of taking the State Historical Society far in his quest to reach all the people of Wisconsin.

## III

When Lyman Draper retired, the Historical Society was housed in crowded, non-fireproof rooms in the State Capitol on Capitol Square. Its library of 118,666 titles contained mainly books on American history, bound newspapers, American patent reports, genealogy and heraldry, Shakespearian literature, and maps and atlases. It was adding about 2,500 titles yearly. The most numerous manuscript collection, which concerned the trans-Allegheny frontier, was Draper's personal property, available to researchers only with his permission. Draper also edited ten volumes of *Collections* of documents, articles, and interviews on Wisconsin history.

The society was financed by a combination of public and private money. Its General Fund of $5,000 yearly was appropriated by the State Legislature, which in addition paid the salaries of Draper and two assistants as well as expenses for printing, postage, express, and some binding and book purchasing. The private Binding Fund, accumulated from annual and life membership dues and sales of duplicates, came to about $17,000.[9]

"Energy, thy name is Thwaites," wrote Lucien S. Hanks, longtime curator and then-treasurer of the society; and the new corresponding secretary justified the description as he applied modern business practices throughout the society and proved himself a superb administrator. Thwaites added library materials systematically and paid close attention to exchanges with other institutions both in this country and abroad. He began a card catalogue of books and secured a better arrangement for newspapers. He sought Wisconsin manuscripts zealously, a field in which Draper had taken little interest, and visited historic spots around the state each year, obtaining Wisconsin materials and interviewing Indians, early traders, and settlers. He persuaded the Wisconsin Press Association to ask its members to send the society early imprints, examples of job printing, and newspapers. He encouraged Professor Turner to bring his advanced history class to a comfortable seminar room in the library; he also published in the *Proceedings* articles by graduate students. He cooperated with the university in collecting materials on foreign nationalities in the state, a process that he aided with personal visitation. Wisconsin, he thought, had a greater variety of those groups than any other American state—Germans, Scandinavians (Norwegians, Swedes, Finns, and Icelanders), Irish, British, Canadians, Bohemians, Dutch, French, Poles, and Belgians. He had the library collect Wisconsin authors and American labor history, the latter with the aid of Professor Richard T. Ely. By the end of Thwaite's administration, the library had tripled in size.[10]

Thwaites succeeded in gathering with great care a cadre of intelligent, capable, and industrious younger women to help him conduct the activities of the society. He often made their positions more exciting by involving them in editorial work for its publications. Thus the brilliant Annie Amelia Nunns, who began work in the library in 1899, was soon toiling long hours, often at night, on the seventy-three volumes of the *Jesuit Relations* and the thirty-two volumes of *Early Western Travels*; she became Thwaites's executive secretary and, upon his death, served as assistant superintendent under his three successors until she died in 1942. Mary S. Foster and Iva A. Welsh started work in the library in 1897 and retired forty-seven years later as, respectively, chief of the Reference Division and head cataloguer. Dr. Louise Phelps Kellogg began helping Thwaites as editor in 1902, was promoted to senior research assistant, and answered hundreds of questions yearly about society materials and Draper manuscripts as well as writing more than a dozen important books and countless articles on early Wisconsin and Midwest history. Her notable research achievements were recognized when she became the first woman to serve as president of the Mississippi Valley Historical Association and the first woman to receive an honorary doctorate from the University of Wisconsin. Thwaites's command of historical knowledge, good nature, and sense of humor caused such women to become devoted to him, and in fact made it difficult for his first two successors to elicit the same kind of loyalty.[11]

The art gallery and museum were starved for funds, most of which went to the library, and had to depend upon donations from members and patrons. The gallery continued to concentrate on Wisconsin, but the museum remained more eclectic. Since the university had natural history and geological collections, Thwaites thought that the society should confine its holdings to ethnology, archaeology, and history. But its accessions included a yucca plant from California, Chinese chopsticks, a horseshoe from Antwerp, a Filipino insurgent's uniform, a piece of the scaffold from which John Brown was hanged as well as a pair of iron firedogs from his birthplace, and other objects from Italy, Japan, Korea, and Mexico. Thwaites brought back from his travels in Britain bricks, flints, and pottery from the Roman remains of Verulamium near Silchester and a blackthorn shillelah and piece of the "Blarney stone" from Cork. Such widely gathered artifacts could possibly occasionally be justified in that the museum was serving university students. At the same time, valuable Wisconsin materials were accumulated, such as the silver ostensorium presented to the St. Francis Xavier Mission in De Pere in 1696 by Nicholas Perrot, the French commander in the West (deposited in the museum by Catholic Church authorities), Winnebago and Chippewa wigwams, a Winnebago dugout canoe, and a stove from the first state capitol. The society also was most proud to possess Daniel Boone's powder horn. And the museum was popular, attracting legislators, university faculty and students, numerous public school classes, and visitors seeing the sights of the capital city; they soon totaled 60,000 yearly.[12]

Thwaites's first great triumph was the obtaining of a new building for the society on the university campus, a splendid structure that still serves it well. Draper had tried without success to secure $50,000 for a new headquarters in 1881, and the legislature had killed a later attempt to erect such a building as a Civil War memorial. President Thomas C. Chamberlain of the university and Thwaites began discussing a joint structure in 1890; the latter was delighted because he thought that a building on the campus would portray "the Society as an educational institution," draw readers to the library, and attract more museum visitors when "placed near the collections in Science Hall." The society's

Board of Curators endorsed the idea unanimously, "provided the title of the site shall rest in the name of the Society as the trustee of the state." To help secure legislative backing, Thwaites obtained impressive testimonials to the great worth of the Historical Society's work from twenty-eight leading library and historical authorities throughout the country, including Woodrow Wilson and Theodore Roosevelt. The legislative act of 1895 provided that the university furnish the site, to which the society would hold title. The Building Commission spent more than a month visiting libraries in Washington, Philadelphia, Princeton, New York, Brooklyn, Newark, N. J., Southport, New Haven, Providence, Boston, Cambridge, Albany, Buffalo, Pittsburgh, and Allegheny, Pennsylvania. In October 1900 the completed, highly fire-resistant building was dedicated with speeches by Governor Edward Scofield, President Charles Kendall Adams of the university, and Secretary Thwaites. (The society was fortunate to have moved when it did, for the state capitol burned in 1904.)[13]

Though Thwaites considered the library more important than the museum, he recognized the latter's value as he wrote in 1891:

> To the world, the library is by far the most valuable; it is a great workshop for scholars, and they are the core of civilization; abroad, the society's library and its original investigations have alone given it prestige. The society, however, can do excellent missionary work among the masses, by making its museum more attractive, and by having especial regard to its possibilities as a factor in public education.[14]

And in 1903 he admitted: "[The museum] is the department of our work which chiefly appeals to the general public. Its importance as a factor in popular education is not to be over-estimated."[15]

The new building contained the society library in one wing and that of the university in the other. The art gallery and museum were on the top, fourth floor, illuminated from above by skylights. Separate halls contained ethnology, war history, framed photographs and engravings, bric-a-brac, and curiosities, while paintings were hung on the walls with sculptures below. The museum had only one attendant, the faithful Ceylon C. Lincoln who had been the society's janitor at the capitol. A northwest wing had been postponed by the state, and the society soon was telling the legislature how badly it needed more space. The state had to increase the society appropriation because of the added expense of the new building, even though the university paid half of the cost of public utilities, cleaning, and policing. The society's General Fund was raised to $15,000, and a separate state fund of $5,000 was added for library acquisitions.

Thwaites continued to have a difficult time with finances because the new appropriations did not quite meet the expenses incurred by moving into the new building. Beginning in 1907, however, the legislature added another $5,000 to the General Fund and from that time onward made other increases so that the society was less hard-pressed. By 1913 it was receiving $70,948 in state funds, and the private endowment had grown to $73,638. Upon Draper's death in 1891, his will left his manuscripts, books, homestead, and other property to the society. After the homestead was sold, the Draper Fund exceeded $11,000 and was used to bind the Draper manuscripts and for other expenses and publications about that collection.[16]

The library still received the lion's share of the funding, while the museum remained largely dependent upon gifts for accessions and special activities. It did, however, make some progress. President Robert L. McCormick donated two large, carefully researched paintings by Edwin Willard Deming of New York, portraying *Jean Nicolet's Landing in Wisconsin*, 1634, and *Braddock's Defeat*, 1775. Miss Ellen A. Stone of Lexington, Massachusetts, bestowed nearly two hundred colonial kitchen implements that had belonged to her great-grandfather, and Thwaites visited several extant colonial kitchens in the Boston area and chose one as a model for the society's reproduction. It proved so successful that he contemplated adding a log cabin of pioneer days. Dr. and Mrs. Charles Kendall Adams made a magnificent gift of books, pictures, and museum objects, and Mrs. Adams's personal jewels were sold to set up the Mary M. Adams Art Fund. But the museum collections remained general with separate rooms for Piranesi etchings and Arundel prints, a large display of Pueblo pottery from Arizona and New Mexico, a Japanese flute, and Eskimo artifacts. The museum walls were improved by installing planking covered with cloth. The Madison Art Association staged three special exhibitions in the museum during 1902–1903 with appropriate lectures and continued such offerings each year. Some of them displayed George Washington materials, Oriental handicrafts, European pottery, and Philippine weapons.[17]

The museum took an important step forward in 1908 with the appointment of Charles E. Brown as its chief. As secretary of the Wisconsin Archaeological Society and editor of its quarterly journal, he was to give one-third of his time to that society and two-thirds to the Historical Society. He at once began classifying and rearranging the collections, added Chippewa and other Indian materials, wrote an educational leaflet on the museum and a teachers' guide, and continued his energetic efforts to preserve and mark Indian mounds around the state. "Charlie" Brown got along well with people and was a popular speaker who enjoyed traveling. He turned over all the natural history specimens to the university and began to present many small special exhibits. Separate cases and screens were devoted to Wisconsin settlement, education, agriculture, religion, lumbering, mining, manufactures, commerce, and medicine. In 1911 the chief special exhibitions dealt with Increase A. Lapham, Wisconsin pioneer scientist; the tercentenary of the King James Bible; powder horns including, of course, Daniel Boone's; and Zionist colonies in Palestine. The next year, fifteen exhibitions lasted from one to three weeks; same of them concerned the centenary of Charles Dickens; Indian obsidian implements; and old-style valentines. The controversial Kensington Runestone, said to have been left in Minnesota in 1362 by traveling Norsemen, was shown for a single day. Educational programs with public school and university classes increased in number, as did special events such as an elaborate and picturesque Indian harvest dance with fifty university students and summer school pilgrimages around Lake Mendota inspecting Indian mounds.[18]

Thwaites and the society officers congratulated themselves on their wisdom in placing the museum in charge of such a competent expert, and in 1909 the society asked the legislature for a special annual appropriation of $3,500 to be used for better administration and growth of the museum. The request received considerable public backing and, two years later, an annual grant of $2,000 was approved with one of $1,500 for the Archaeological Society. The private Antiquarian Fund also was amended so that it could be used "in the general administration of the museum." A card catalogue of 9,000 entries covered museum objects. Some of the exhibitions were on fans, postage stamps, agriculture and horticulture, the centennial of Commodore Perry's victory on Lake Erie, and Japanese block prints.[19]

All the varied activity led to increased museum accessions (as many as 4,000 yearly) and to much larger attendance that reached 100,000 per annum. In 1911 the legislature agreed to an appropriation of $162,000 in three annual installments, with which to complete the northwest wing of the building; it, of course, would expand the museum on the fourth floor, but that project was not finished until the year after Thwaites's death. On October 22, 1913, the day before the annual meeting was to convene, Thwaites died suddenly. He had made his customary preparations for the meeting including his detailed Executive Committee report. The shocked board met only for a brief business session and adjourned until December 19 when a memorial service was held in the Assembly

Hall of the Capitol with Governor Francis F. McGovern presiding and Frederick Jackson Turner delivering his *Memorial Address*.[20]

## IV

Thwaites made many other innovative advances in the society's work. While they did not involve the museum directly, they caused more Wisconsin citizens as well as some national and international historical leaders to become aware of the society, its collections and progress. A Wisconsin archives act of 1907 began to bring state records to the society. Thwaites also backed historic preservation and recommended restoring the territorial capital at Belmont and marking historical spots throughout the state, a project that the Federated Women's Clubs were promoting. He instituted one of the most comprehensive publication programs yet undertaken by an American historical society. In trying to make the annual meetings of the society more stimulating, Thwaites experimented with a peripatetic two-day field convention at Green Bay in 1899, and later in Milwaukee and again in Green Bay. He secured a new law that encouraged the formation of local historical societies auxiliary to the State Society, the first two at Green Bay and Ripon and soon a total of fifteen in the state. He issued *Bulletins of Information* to encourage and instruct the local societies and museums, and they frequently invited Thwaites or Charlie Brown to speak at their meetings. Thwaites's philosophy of having the society serve the whole state fitted well with the Wisconsin Idea developed by the university, which held that it owed a duty to the state and that its faculty should provide support and impartial advice in solving state problems. His philosophy was compatible, too, with the Progressive Movement sweeping the country and blossoming in the state under the vigorous leadership of Robert M. La Follette.[21]

Not only did Thwaites travel extensively through the state collecting manuscripts, museum objects, and other materials and interviewing Indians and old timers. He made several lengthy canoe voyages in the region, once with his wife and ten-year-old son down the Monongahela to Pittsburgh and along the Ohio to Cairo, Illinois, on the Mississippi. He made two trips with his wife to England and Europe, visiting libraries and museums, improving the society's exchange arrangements, and arranging for the copying of Wisconsin materials in the archives in London and Paris. He later went to the Rocky Mountains to retrace part of the route of Lewis and Clark and to Berkeley, where he advised the University of California to acquire the Bancroft Library. Thwaites customarily attended the annual meetings held about the country by the American Library Association, of which he was president in 1899, and by the American Association of Museums, in which he took a leading part.[22]

Professor Turner and Thwaites worked closely together to advance the interests of both the society and the university. Turner continued to hold his advanced seminar at the society, of which he was an active board member, serving on important committees, often as chairman—Advisory, Library, Printing and Publication, among others. In 1893 the American Historical Association held its annual meeting in Chicago at the Art Institute as part of the Columbian Exposition. Both Thwaites and Turner read papers at one session, Thwaites on "Early Lead Mining in Illinois and Wisconsin" and Turner on "The Significance of the Frontier in American History," a seminal presentation famed in the annals of American historiography and still very much alive today.[23]

Professor Turner properly summed up Thwaites's services to the historical society world:

> What would the Historical Society be today but for the services of that skilled business administrator, that assiduous collector, that scientific editor: And not only the Wisconsin society, but many others . . . have been to school to him and carried his methods . . . to other states. . . . To a degree that can hardly be recognised, he has changed the conception of the [western] historical society.[24]

Thwaites and the Wisconsin example indeed encouraged many other states to form similar historical agencies and conduct broad-gauged programs—for instance, Iowa, Minnesota, Indiana, Kansas, and Ohio. They also participated in the national Conference of Historical Societies, in the formation of which Thwaites took a leading part in 1904. It met at the American Historical Association's annual winter meeting each year and in 1940 became the independent and influential American Association for State and Local History. The state societies also helped found the Mississippi Valley Historical Association (today the Organization of American Historians) in 1907, of which Thwaites became president five years later.[25]

One informal glance at Thwaites remains to be mentioned. When Dr. Milo M. Quaife succeeded him as superintendent in 1914, he had an amusing conversation with Bennie Butts, born a slave but whom Thwaites had hired years before as a messenger and now, an aged man, was in charge of a society washroom. "Doctor," he said, meaning Thwaites, "on his arrival in the library, always exchanged his shoes for a pair of slippers which he wore during the day," Bennie meanwhile cleaning and polishing the shoes. Quaife was too young and brash to agree to continue the practice, but it is pleasant to think of Thwaites energetically padding about his appointed rounds in his slippers.[26]

NOTES

1. For the independent historical societies, see Stephen T. Riley, *The Massachusetts Historical Society, 1791-1959* (Boston, The Society, 1959); R. W. G. Vail, *Knickerbocker Birthday: A Sesqui-Centennial History of the New-York Historical Society, 1804–1954* (New York: The Society, 1954); Cliffold K. Shipton, "The American Antiquarian Society," *William and Mary Quarterly* 2 (1945): 164–172; Shipton, "The Museum of the American Antiquarian Society," in Whitfield J. Bell and others, *A Cabinet of Curiosities: Five Episodes in the Evolution of American Museums* (Charlottesville: University Press of Virginia, 1967), 35–48; Julian P. Boyd, "State and Local Historical Societies in the United States," *American Historical Review* 40 (Oct. 1934): 10–37; Leslie W. Dunlap, *American Historical Societies, 1790–1860* (Philadelphia: Porcupine Press, 1974); Walter Muir Whitehill, *Independent Historical Societies: An Enquiry into Their Research and Publication Functions and Their Financial Future* (Boston: Boston Athenaeum, 1962).

2. Whitehill, *Independent Historical Societies*, 8.

3. Vail, *Knickerbocker Birthday*, 31, 33.

4. Shipton, "Museum of the American Antiquarian Society," 36; Whitehill, *Independent Historical Societies*, 68.

5. Shipton, "Museum of the American Antiquarian Society," 40–41.

6. The two chief works on Draper and Thwaites are William B. Hesseltine, *Pioneer's Mission: The Story of Lyman Copeland Draper* (Madison: State Historical Society of Wisconsin, 1954); Clifford L. Lord and Carl Ubbelhode, *Clio's Servant: A History of the State Historical Society of Wisconsin* (Madison: The Society, 1967). They are especially valuable because they use manuscript sources found at the Society. See also Edward P. Alexander, "An Art Gallery in Frontier Wisconsin," *Wisconsin Magazine of History* 29 (Mar. 1946): 281–300.

7. For Thwaites, see Hesseltine, *Pioneer's Mission*; Charles F. Lamb, "Sawdust Campaign," *Wisconsin Magazine of History* 22 (Sep. 1938): 12; Clifford L. Lord, *Keepers of the Past* (Chapel Hill: University of North Carolina Press, 1965), pp. 53–66; Lord, "Reuben Gold Thwaites," *Wisconsin Magazine of History* 47 (Autumn 1963): 3–11; Lord and Ubbelhode, *Clio's Servant*; Robert McCluggage, "Joseph H. Osborn, Grange Leader," *Wisconsin Magazine of History* 35 (Spring 1952): 12; Frederick Jackson Turner, *Reuben Gold Thwaites: A Memorial Address* (Madison: State Historical Society, 1914).

8. David Kinnett, "Miss Kellogg's Quiet Passion," *Wisconsin Magazine of History* 62 (Summer 1979): 277.

9. State Historical Society of Wisconsin, *Proceedings, 1887–1913*, 28 vols., cover Thwaites's administration. For Draper, see *Proceedings, 1887*: 10–13; *1902*: 10; State Historical Society of Wisconsin, *Collections, 1885–1888*, 10 vols.

10. *Proceedings, 1889*: 13–24, 26–28, 40, 47; *1890*: 50, 57–63; *1891 (Dec.)*: 70–71; *1893*: 34; *1894*: 33, 34; Lord and Ubbelhode, *Clio's Servant*, 84–100.

11. "Annie Amelia Nunns, 1868–1942," *Wisconsin Magazine of History* 25 (Mar. 1942): 261–63; "Louise Phelps Kellogg, 1862–1942," *Wisconsin Magazine of History* 26 (Sep. 1942): 5–7; "Mr. Brown, Miss Foster, Miss Welsh," *Wisconsin Magazine of History* 28 (Dec. 1944): 132–34; Kinnett, "Miss Kellogg's Quiet Passion," 267–99; Lord and Ubbelhode, *Clio's Servant*, 85–86.

12. *Proceedings, 1889*: 40–47; *1890*: 56–57; *1891 (Jan.)*: 52, 61–63, 68–70; *1892*: 68–72; *1895*: 49, *1897*: 43, *1898*: 31; *1900*: 77–78; *1903*: 72–75; *1904*: 88–91.

13. *Proceedings, 1889*: 48–50; *1894*: 73–84; *1895*: 54–60; *1896*: 29; *1897*: 7–11, 47, 50; *1898*: 7–10; *1899*: 24–25; *1900*: 32–34; Vernon Carstensen, "Adventure in Cooperation," *Wisconsin Magazine of History* 34 (Winter 1950): 95–99; Lord and Ubbelhode, *Clio's Servant*, 101–10, 122–26; Reuben Gold Thwaites, ed., *Exercises at the Dedication of Its New Building, October 19, 1900* ... (Madison: Democrat Printing Co., 1901); Jackson E. Towne, "President Adams and the University Library," *Wisconsin Magazine of History* 35 (Summer 1952): 257–61.

14. *Proceedings, 1891 (Dec.)*: 66.

15. *Proceedings, 1903*: 34.

16. *Proceedings, 1891 (Dec.)*: 31–37; *1893*: 35–36; *1896*: 19, 40–42; *1900*: 9–12, 29; *1901*: 18, 30–31; *1902*: 24–29; *1907*: 22–24; *1913*: 23–28; Lord and Ubbelhode, *Clio's Servant*, 178–179, 190–192.

17. *Proceedings, 1901*: 13, 18, 27–29, 89–90; *1903*: 35–36; *1904*: 37–40, 89–91; *1905*: 43–47; *1906*: 54–56; *1907*: 51–52; Lord and Ubbelhode, *Clio's Servant*, 179–180.

18. *Proceedings, 1908*: 41, 48–53; *1909*: 34–36; *1910*: 30–32; *1911*: 30–33; *1912*: 31–37; *1913*: 36–41; Lord and Ubbelhode, *Clio's Servant*, 181–187.

19. *Proceedings, 1909*: 34–36; *1910*: 30–33; *1911*: 13, 23; *1912*: 36; *1913*: 36–41.

20. *Proceedings, 1911*: 3–14, 42–43; *1913*: 11–12; *1914*: 45–46; Lord and Ubbelhode, *Clio's Servant*, 146–147, 197–198.

21. *Proceedings, 1899*: 5, 44, 52, 103–108; *1900*: 16, 26–27; *1901*: 20–21, 96; *1907*: 38–39, 102; Lord and Ubbelhode, *Clio's Servant*, 140, 142–145, 152–154, 167, 172–178.

22. *Proceedings, 1891 (Jan.)*: 32–33; *1897*: 46–47; Lord and Ubbelhode, *Clio's Servant*, 164; Reuben Gold Thwaites, *Historic Waterways: Six Hundred Miles of Canoeing down the Rock, Fox, and Wisconsin Rivers* (Chicago: A. C. McClurg, 1888); Thwaites, *Our Cycling Tour in England: From Canterbury to Dartmoor Forest, and Back by Way of Bath, Oxford and the Thames Valley* (Chicago: A. C.McClurg, 1892); Thwaites, *Afloat on the Ohio: An Historical Pilgrimage of a Thousand Miles in a Skiff, from Redstone to Cairo* (Chicago: May and Williams, 1897); Thwaites, *A Brief History of Rocky Mountain Exploration, with Especial Reference to the Expedition of Lewis and Clark* (New York: D. Appleton and Company, 1904); Thwaites, *The Bancroft Library: A Report Submitted to the President and Regents of the University of California . . .* (Berkeley: University of California, 1905).

23. *Proceedings, 1890*: 4; *1893*: 79–112; Ray Allen Billington, *Frederick Jackson Turner: Historian, Scholar, Teacher* (New York: Oxford University Press, 1973), 126–27.

24. Billington, *The Genesis of the Frontier Thesis: A Study in Historical Creativity* (San Marino, Cal.: Huntington Library, 1971), 214; Lord and Ubbelhode, *Clio's Servant*, 194–95.

25. *American Historical Review* 10 (Apr. 1903): 493–94; 11 (Apr. 1906): 502–05; Lord and Ubbelhode, *Clio's Servant*, 156–67.

26. Milo M. Quaife, "Some Memories of Forty Years," *Wisconsin Magazine of History* 38 (Summer 1955): 252.

## SELECT BIBLIOGRAPHY

Alexander, Edward P. "An Art Gallery in Frontier Wisconsin." *Wisconsin Magazine of History* 29 (Mar. 1946): 281–300.

*American Historical Review* 10 (Apr. 1903) and 11 (Apr. 1906).

"Annie Amelia Nunns, 1868–1942." *Wisconsin Magazine of History* 25 (Mar. 1942): 261–63

Billington, Ray Allen. *Frederick Jackson Turner: Historian, Scholar, Teacher*. New York: Oxford University Press, 1973.

_____. *The Genesis of the Frontier Thesis: A Study in Historical Creativity*. San Marino, Cal.: Huntington Library, 1971.

Boyd, Julian P. "State and Local Historical Societies in the United States." *American Historical Review* 40 (Oct. 1934): 10–37.

Carstensen, Vernon. "Adventure in Cooperation." *Wisconsin Magazine of History* 34 (Winter 1950): 95–99.

Dunlap, Leslie W. *American Historical Societies, 1790–1860*. Philadelphia: Porcupine Press, 1974.

Hesseltine, William B. *Pioneer's Mission: The Story of Lyman Copeland Draper*. Madison: State Historical Society of Wisconsin, 1954.

Kinnett, David. "Miss Kellogg's Quiet Passion." *Wisconsin Magazine of History* 62 (Summer 1979): 277.

Lamb, Charles F. "Sawdust Campaign." *Wisconsin Magazine of History* 22 (Sep. 1938): 12.

Lord, Clifford L. *Keepers of the Past*. Chapel Hill: University of North Carolina Press, 1965.

_____. "Reuben Gold Thwaites." *Wisconsin Magazine of History* 47 (Autumn 1963): 3–11.

Lord, Clifford L., and Carl Ubbelhode. *Clio's Servant: A History of the State Historical Society of Wisconsin*. Madison: The Society, 1967.

"Louise Phelps Kellogg, 1862–1942." *Wisconsin Magazine of History* 26 (Sep. 1942): 6–7.

McCluggage, Robert. "Joseph H. Osborn, Grange Leader." *Wisconsin Magazine of History* 35 (Spring 1952): 12.

"Mr. Brown, Miss Foster, Miss Welsh." *Wisconsin Magazine of History* 28 (Dec. 1944): 132–34.

Quaife, Milo M. "Some Memories of Forty Years." *Wisconsin Magazine of History* 38 (Summer 1955): 252.

Riley, Stephen T. *The Massachusetts Historical Society, 1791–1959*. Boston, The Society, 1959.

Shipton, Cliffold K. "The American Antiquarian Society." *William and Mary Quarterly* 2 (1945): 164–172.

_____. "The Museum of the American Antiquarian Society." In Whitfield J. Bell and others. *A Cabinet of Curiosities: Five Episodes in the Evolution of American Museums*. Charlottesville: University Press of Virginia, 1967.

State Historical Society of Wisconsin. *Proceedings*. 28 vols. (1887–1913).

Thwaites, Reuben Gold, ed. *Exercises at the Dedication of Its New Building, October 19, 1900* . . . Madison: Democrat Printing Co., 1901.

Thwaites, Reuben Gold. *A Brief History of Rocky Mountain Exploration, with Especial Reference to the Expedition of Lewis and Clark*. New York: D. Appleton and Company, 1904.

_____. *Afloat on the Ohio: An Historical Pilgrimage of a Thousand Miles in a Skiff, from Redstone to Cairo*. Chicago: May and Williams, 1897.

_____. *The Bancroft Library: A Report Submitted to the President and Regents of the University of California* . . . Berkeley: University of California, 1905).

_____. *Historic Waterways: Six Hundred Miles of Canoeing down the Rock, Fox, and Wisconsin Rivers*. Chicago: A. C. McClurg, 1888.

_____. *Our Cycling Tour in England: From Canterbury to Dartmoor Forest, and Back by Way of Bath, Oxford and the Thames Valley*. Chicago: A. C. McClurg, 1892.

Towne, Jackson E. "President Adams and the University Library." *Wisconsin Magazine of History* 35 (Summer 1952): 257–61.

Turner, Frederick Jackson. *Reuben Gold Thwaites: A Memorial Address*. Madison: State Historical Society, 1914.

Vail, R. W. G. *Knickerbocker Birthday: A Sesqui-Centennial History of the New-York Historical Society, 1804–1954*. New York: The Society, 1954.

Whitehill, Walter Muir. *Independent Historical Societies: An Enquiry into Their Research and Publication Functions and Their Financial Future*. Boston: Boston Athenaeum, 1962.

CHAPTER 6

# William Sumner Appleton *Preserves Important Sites Throughout New England*

## I

Sumner Appleton was in a discouraged mood during the early years of the twentieth century. Though he had enjoyed a Harvard education and European travel and led a full social life with deep interest in the arts, the theatre, music, and athletics, he was lonely and often depressed. He missed his three sisters who had married, and his real estate business venture had been unsuccessful. He had few financial worries since his father, upon his death in 1903, had left him a comfortable trust fund. But futility and diletantish lack of purpose characterized his life at the time.

Sumner had known Old World buildings and museums of distinction when, at age thirteen, he spent a year in Europe with his family and then, after graduation from Harvard in 1896, made the Grand Tour with a favorite tutor. His wide American travels included the Columbian Exposition of 1893 in Chicago, the mining camps of Nevada, San Francisco recovering from its earthquake, the charming town of Annapolis with its impressive ancient buildings, and photographing tours to record many of New England's surviving landmarks.

Sumner Appleton finally discovered a consuming purpose for his life when, in 1905 at age thirty-one, he served as secretary for the committee that succeeded in saving and restoring Boston's Paul Revere House. He then began to see the need for preserving from destruction the seventeenth-, eighteenth-, and early nineteenth-century buildings of historical and architectural distinction, not only of Boston but of all New England.[1]

At the end of 1909 and early the next year, Appleton met with Charles Knowles Bolton, an acknowledged cultural leader of Boston, and persuaded him to become president of a new historical preservation organization. On April 2, 1910, Appleton, Bolton, and sixteen carefully chosen men and women, first citizens of the community, incorporated the Society for the Preservation of New England Antiquities (SPNEA). Sumner, as corresponding secretary, was in the beginning the entire staff (he served for thirty-seven years without taking any salary and while making almost daily gifts of objects and funds to the society) in a small, crowded office in one half of a room. He at once began editing a *Bulletin* (it was later renamed *Old-Time New England*) to keep society members and other interested readers informed of the programs of historic preservation, not only in New England but in the whole country and abroad.

The first issue of the *Bulletin* (May 1910) contained Appleton's definition of the society's purpose, which ran:

> Our New England antiquities are fast disappearing because no society has made their preservation its exclusive object. That is the reason for the formation of this Society. . . . The situation requires aggressive action by a large and strong society, which shall cover the whole field and act instantly whenever needed to lead to the preservation of noteworthy buildings and historic sites. That is exactly what this Society has been formed to do.

The new organization would welcome members of other societies and those by residence, birth, or in any other way connected with New England and would seek to save blockhouses and garrison houses, early settlers' homes, seventeenth-century residences with their overhanging second stories, Georgian mansions, post-Revolutionary townhouses, taverns, structures with literary associations, battlefields, and old trails. And a new note was sounded: buildings "which are architecturally beautiful and unique" were as important as those of special historical interest. "It is proposed to preserve the most interesting of these buildings by obtaining control of them through gift, purchase, or otherwise, and then to restore them, and finally to let them to tenants under wise restrictions, unless local conditions suggest some other treatment." Society members would be permitted to visit the buildings at specified times. The society would also establish a museum, in which to keep parts of destroyed old buildings, decorative art objects and all kinds of historical materials that would show the cultural development of New England just as the Germanic Museum in Nuremberg and the National Museum at Munich were doing in Bavaria. Associate members of the society would pay dues of $2; active members, $5; and life members, $50. The endowment fund from life memberships would be used to purchase old houses. Thus, Appleton hoped "that the antiquities handed down from our ancestors shall be passed on unimpaired to our descendants."[2]

Historic preservation had begun in this country about 1850 with the purchase of the Jonathan Hasbrouck House, Washington's headquarters at Newburgh, New York, by the State of New York, and the rescue of Washington's plantation of Mount Vernon on the Potomac River by Ann Pamela Cunningham and the Mount Vernon Ladies' Association of the Union. Perhaps twenty or thirty other historic house museums had opened since then, and the appearance and rapid use of the automobile soon would activate many others. Alice Winchester was right, however, when she wrote of the society: "But it was new to organize such work on a broad basis, covering so large an area as the whole of New England, and it was new to direct its efforts to preservation not only of early buildings but of all that represented the past life of the area."[3]

Sumner Appleton's thirty-seven annual reports as corresponding secretary (he later added "and Real Estate Manager" to his title) were published in the *Bulletin* and *Old-Time New England*. He was always frank about the society's financial affairs; he listed its numerous needs and calculated the endowments necessary to meet them in the hope that members and other readers would supply gifts and bequests. He had thought optimistically that annual dues and the life membership endowment fund, plus local contributions, would permit the society to purchase two old buildings yearly and meet the cost of their repair and restoration. Obtaining 2,000 members who would pay dues of about $6,000 would provide maintenance funds, helped by operating most of the buildings as residences, some as museums with entrance fees, and a few as tearooms, antique shops, community centers, or some other kind of adaptive use. Those kinds of operations would allow most of the buildings to remain on the tax roll.[4]

After five years, however, the society had fewer than 1,500 members and only $8,450 in the life membership fund. Though it was helping community organizations such as historical societies, museums, family associations, and interested individuals so as to save at least one or two properties each year, it owned only three buildings, two of them heavily mortgaged. It had but two employees (Appleton and his capable secretary, Miss E. Florence Addison), who occupied two rooms in the fireproof building of the New England Historic

Genealogical Society, though Appleton felt that he needed two rooms for the museum collection, two for loan exhibitions, one for the library, and two for offices. In 1918, he reported that "the work of owning and maintaining a number of widely scattered old houses, and keeping them all as nearly as practicable in their original condition, is an experiment in this country. We have no sign posts to guide us and from the beginning have had to feel our way along." He had changed from thinking that his first duty was to repair and restore a building. Instead, he gave precedence to securing an endowment of at least $5,000 for each house so as to cover its ordinary upkeep.[5]

Appleton was much concerned also with the society's museum and library functions. Its museum should preserve not only architectural fragments and wallpapers but also furnishings, textiles, clothing, tools, dolls, toys, and other objects to show the area's cultural development. It should conduct frequent loan exhibitions; some of the early ones included a colonial parlor with furniture and furnishings; samplers; needlework; pictures; mourning jewelry; silhouettes; wax portraits and miniatures; and heraldry. So far as the library went, he thought only a few reference books were needed, but that photographs of New England buildings and social life, postcards, negatives, sketches, measured drawings, plans, and other visual materials should be collected aggressively. Appleton persuaded young Thomas T. Waterman, a rising architect, to visit houses with him and make measured drawings for the society's collection. (By the time of Appleton's death, the society's graphic holdings contained more than 600,000 items). Both museum and library required more space, while the former needed display cases and the latter, filing cabinets. The two operations were staffed by volunteers but obviously soon ought to have paid professional help.[6]

Appleton without success tried to promote an outdoor or open-air museum for New England. He admired the pioneer efforts in that field: Skansen at Stockholm, the Sandvig Collection at Lillehammer in Norway, and other European attempts with proper interior furnishings, suitable landscaping, and costumed interpreters and craft demonstrators. In his 1919 report, he outlined his plan thus:

> This would mean a group of six tiny villages covering New England's history up to date, each village with its meeting house situated on the village green or facing the village square and surrounded by the typical buildings of its period. . . . Probably few of these buildings would be of the first rank, for all such our Society must aim to keep on the original sites, but there are a host of lesser buildings of minor importance, still worth preserving, which would serve for the purpose of

> the outdoor museum. . . . Sooner or later such a museum will surely be started somewhere in New England and it would be pleasant indeed if it could be done under the auspices of our Society.

In his last annual report of 1946-1947, Appleton advocated also importing buildings from England to portray a village from which New England ones were derived.[7]

By its tenth anniversary in 1919, the society was well on its way. It owned seven historic buildings, including the Harrison Gray Otis House (1795) in Boston, which had become its headquarters. A distinct step forward took place when George Francis Dow joined the staff that year, to remain until his death in 1936. An indefatigable researcher and learned local historian, he supervised the museum, edited the magazine, and served as a font of historical knowledge. He was a pioneer in the preservation movement who, as curator and secretary of the Essex Institute at Salem, in 1907 had installed three period rooms of 1750–1800 based on careful research and then had enlarged the Institute's backyard to receive one of Salem's oldest buildings, the John Ward House (1684), as a kind of miniature outdoor museum. He also had restored the Parson Capen House (1683) for the Topsfield Historical Society and later would reconstruct two seventeenth-century rooms for the American Wing of the Metropolitan Museum of Art.[8]

To sum up, in ten years Appleton had made the society the strongest historic preservation organization in the whole country, and, with its new headquarters and the resourceful Dow on its staff, it was ready to expand its influence.

## II

William Sumner Appleton, Jr., was born at Boston on May 29, 1874, at the house his grandfather Nathan Appleton had built on Beacon Street. Nathan was a successful textile merchant and cotton manufacturer who left his son, William Sumner Appleton, Sr., comfortably fixed; he attended Harvard (A.B., A.M., and LL.B.), studying history and art. He was married to his cousin, Edith Stuart Appleton. The younger Sumner attended Miss Garland's School in Boston, St. Paul's in Concord, New Hampshire, and Hopkinson's School in Boston. His health was frail, and he was in a wheelchair recovering from diphtheria when he took his examination for Harvard. There, he studied French, history, fine arts, Latin, philosophy, economics, government, and English. He also attended the Saturday Evening Dancing Class, and he had a bet with a friend that made each of them pay five cents every time they used a swear word, though they made an exception for "To Hell with Yale." Sumner was an editor of the student magazine, the *Advocate*, but he suffered from weak eyes so that someone had to read to him to prepare for examinations. After graduation, he remained a staunch Harvard supporter, belonged to the Harvard clubs of Boston and New York, and always bought season tickets to the football games.

Upon his return from a Grand Tour of Europe, Sumner entered the real estate business in 1898 with Lombard Wilson but withdrew after three years when he almost suffered a nervous breakdown. While he was recovering, he spent summers at Moon Island on Squam Lake near Holderness, Hew Hampshire, where he played tennis, went canoeing, and swam at the beach. At home, he often invited young ladies to accompany him to cotillions, billiards, plays, or concerts (they referred to him as "Uncle Sumner"). He went calling on Sunday afternoons in frock coat and silk topper with cane. But he followed the example of his two Uncle Appletons and never married.

In 1905 Sumner Appleton met with a committee to save the Boston State House from damage by a subway and then began work with the Paul Revere Association. In 1906–1907 he took graduate courses at Harvard in botany, mining and metallurgy, and architecture. He began to visit Massachusetts historic sites systematically—at Salem, Newbury, Bedford, and Lexington. Then, starting work with the Preservation Society, he continued on that course for thirty-seven years until his death at Lawrence, Massachusetts, after a short illness on November 24, 1947.[9]

Everyone who knew Sumner Appleton agreed that he was modest, earnest, enthusiastic, democratic, wise, and patient. Edward J. Hipkiss, curator at the Museum of Fine Arts, declared: "To such a man wordy appraisal of his aims or his successes is pleasing, but he is a bit shy and puzzled about what others write or what they say in speeches. He gives his all in doing." Charles Knowles Bolton, who worked with him at the society for twenty-two years, recalled: "In all these years he has never lost his temper, but often when I, as President, said or did something which did not meet with his approval, a look of pain came over his face that only a Rembrandt or Franz Hals could have caught." His daily work routine was unconventional, and he sometimes became so absorbed in a problem that he lost track of time and might call a staff member or trustee in the middle of the night. Charles Messer Stow, the antiques editor of the New York *Sun*, knew Sumner well; he thought that "his greatness did not come from doing spectacular things blatantly. It came from doing quietly and modestly things of supreme importance to future generations." Stow joked that "he sometimes was dubbed parsimonious and many a bout with a disgruntled cab driver followed a nickel tip." His selfless but driving force for the Society for the Preservation of New England Antiquities was also well described as "by birth, instinct, preference and profession a New Englander."[12]

## III

Sumner Appleton's highest aim was that the society acquire and preserve buildings of great historical and architectural importance. The first step in the process was to be sure that a building was authentic. He used local historians and antiquarians to do thorough research on the building's history, often publishing their work in the *Bulletin* or *Old-Time New England*. He himself usually did the architectural research. He traveled constantly through New England examining structures that might be worth saving. He learned to strip sample sections of exteriors and interiors to discover what changes had taken place through the years, to remove wallpaper and interpret stenciling, and to scrape coats of paint so as to find the original colors. "Photograph, measure, and record" was a primary rule. He believed in preferably doing no restoration work or as little as absolutely necessary and in making sure that what was done was carefully marked and recorded. He described himself as "the most conservative restorer . . . and a building is in safe hands when I have charge of it." He also turned for advice to skilled antiquarian architects like Norman Morrison Isham or Joseph Everett Chandler. In 1940, Charles Knowles Bolton summed it up: "In all these thirty years Mr. Appleton has acquired enormous knowledge of building construction details." And any structure the society took had to meet his high standards.[13]

Once the society secured ownership of a building and repaired and restored it enough to insure its continuation, the next step was to discover some practical use that would contribute toward its maintenance. One device was to rent a building such as the Swett-Isley House (1670) in Newbury, the society's first acquisition (all houses cited here are in Massachusetts unless otherwise indicated), in this case for use as a tearoom. The second acquisition, the Samuel Fowler House (1810) in Danvers, would eventually revert to the society after the "life right" of a tenant expired, and for a time it served as the society's secondary museum. The third property, the Cooper-Frost-Austin House (1657) at Cambridge, was leased out at $50 a month for a tearoom and antique shop. The Quincy Memorial (1804) in Litchfield, Connecticut, and Bleakhouse (about

1796) in Peterborough, New Hampshire, are additional examples of the frequently used life-right arrangement. Another commonly employed approach, as at the Short House (1733) in Newbury, had a custodian with or without family in residence who collected an admission fee from all visitors except society members. The Sarah Orne Jewett Memorial (1774) at South Berwick, Maine, was operated as a museum in remembrance of that author; its adjoining Dr. Theodore Eastman Memorial (1851) served as a community center. The society not only used the Harrison Gray Otis House (1795) as its headquarters but also Elias Haskett Derby's Barn (1798) at Watertown for storage. The Spaulding Grist Mill (about 1840) and a Cooperage Shop (about 1825) at Townsend were both gifts of the Spaulding Fiber Company. The Peabody Family Burying Ground and Elias Smith Burying Ground (both 1775) at Middletown were maintained by a $10,000 endowment from the George August Peabody Estate.[14]

As Charles Hosmer has shown so well, Appleton could be tenacious as well as resourceful in saving a property. The Abraham Browne House (about 1663) in Watertown was in a ruinous state in 1915 and about to be torn down. Appleton failed to interest in its preservation Browne descendants, the Watertown Historical Society, a New York architect, or even his own trustees, who voted against allowing a special drive for $10,000 in its behalf. He then bought the house himself for $4,000 down. Finally, a small group of members raised money for its purchase and restoration, and the trustees accepted it in 1922. Appleton wrote his sister later that the Browne House

> is my own personal monument and the fact that it is now standing at all is simply because I got mad and decided that it shouldn't be pulled down, but I would hate to tell you how many thousands I had to risk paying myself had my efforts failed. At one time it seemed as though I would have to sell everything I owned.[15]

These examples indicate the wide variety of properties the society obtained and some of the ingenious ways of helping support them that Appleton developed. At the time of his death, the society owned fifty-six houses, about one-third of which were of the seventeenth century. Most of them were situated in Massachusetts, though Maine, New Hampshire, and Connecticut each had three, and Rhode Island, two. There was none in Vermont. Of the fifty-six properties, fifteen had come as gifts, twelve as bequests, four by ordinary purchase, and four by means of special drives.[16]

Appleton was nearly always willing to help other organizations secure historic properties when that appeared to be the preferable arrangement. Despite his reluctance to entrust a property to the Federal Government, he had the society in 1936 transfer its Richard Derby House (1762) at Salem to the National Park Service to become part of the Salem Maritime National Historic Site. The Laws House (about 1803) at Sharon, New Hampshire, was turned over to the Sharon Art Center. Appleton objected strongly in 1919 when the Metropolitan Museum of Art purchased and planned to move the Wentworth-Gardner House (1760) in whole or in part from Portsmouth, New Hampshire, to be incorporated into its American Wing. The museum heeded his protest and agreed to sell the property to the society, which administered it for about eight years but failed to raise the necessary payment and in 1940 permitted it and its neighboring Tobias Lear House (about 1740) to go to a local Portsmouth organization. Another example of cooperation occurred in 1935 when Appleton took a leading part in the five-day whirlwind drive that resulted in the acquisition of the Christopher Gore House (1805) in Waltham for $75,000; the society began by pledging $5,000, while the Massachusetts Society of Colonial Dames, the Trustees of Public Reservations, and the Massachusetts Society of Architects also made large contributions to the down payment. Appleton spoke frequently and enthusiastically before local groups and persuaded many community organizations to save houses; the society sometimes contributed funds in effecting such arrangements. Municipalities also occasionally helped, as when the mayor of Newport, Rhode Island, in 1916 arranged to preserve the Old Brick Market (1762).[17]

The society gave advice to preservation projects in many other places, such as Charleston, Baltimore, Philadelphia, Savannah, and several in Canada. Though it decided not to contribute when a New Jersey organization requested financial help, it publicized the matter in the hope that New Jersey might form its own preservation society. Appleton also recommended aid for many worthy projects including Mount Vernon and Westover in Virginia, the Brewton-Pringle House in Charleston, and Governor Keith's Graeme Park in Montgomery County, Pennsylvania.[18]

The venerable English Society for the Preservation of Public Buildings asked the SPNEA for funding help in 1924, a request refused on principle, though worthwhile British projects were described in *Old-Time New England* in the hope that they might attract gifts from individuals. The magazine regularly carried news of the British National Trust for Places of Historic Interest or Natural Beauty (1896), and the society was proud that that organization had been patterned after the Trustees of Public Reservations in Massachusetts (1891). The activities of other British organizations—for instance, the Society for the Preservation of

Commons, Footpaths, and Open Spaces—and appeals of churches for help with their repair and restoration were also publicized. During the First World War, the society, concerned about the possible destruction of European landmarks, sent resolutions to President Wilson urging him to seek their preservation and to offer safekeeping in this country of moveable art objects. It also approved the protest of the Society for the Preservation of Ancient Buildings against moving distinguished English houses such as Warwick Priory and Agecroft to America.[19]

Appleton favored making preservation assistance available throughout the nation. He would retain the front-line work of the patriotic-ancestral and local historical societies, but in 1919 proposed having four large regional organizations take the leadership—his own society, of course, along with the Association for the Preservation of Virginia Antiquities, the American Scenic and Historic Preservation Society of New York, and the Archaeological Institute of America. They should build up endowments that would enable them to purchase valuable architectural and historical properties and then deed them to local agencies, which would manage them. By 1926 he was urging the Archaeological Institute to adopt a different plan, which he described as follows:

> What is needed in this country is a fund of say five million dollars in the hands of a board of trustees having power to distribute its income up and down the whole country wherever most needed in order to preserve what is best. Probably the most efficacious way of using this would be to pay for the endowment of a property, provided local interest attended to the purchase. The endowment is generally the most expensive and difficult part of the undertaking and its application to the house could always be made dependent on its purchase within a certain definite time and its proper use by some local body.[20]

Appleton's national plans did not succeed. Probably no private organization could have carried them out on such a scale. Even the National Trust for Historic Preservation, chartered at Washington in 1949, for long had little success in securing properties of its own or subsidizing those of local agencies. The Historic Sites Act of 1935 did give the National Park Service authority to receive and maintain important historic structures and sites, and the expansion of the Federal Government's role since then has resulted in a stronger national system of historic preservation.

By far the greatest problem of the society was financial. At first, Appleton thought that a large membership would provide the necessary funds. By 1929, with constant appeals and energetic solicitation, 3,000 members had been obtained;

they brought in about $10,000 annually. The deepening economic depression, however, soon cut the membership in half. As early as 1913, the trustees had decided that special contributions above dues could be called for, and as many as three drives were held annually for carefully described projects. Often they sought only four or five thousand dollars, but larger sums were sometimes needed, as for the purchase of the Otis House headquarters ($22,725). In the late 1930s during the depression, such special drives were undersubscribed several times. After Helen F. Kimball gave $1,500 for an Emergency Fund in 1913 and Helen Collamore's bequest of $5,000 followed three years later for the upkeep of the society's real estate, gifts and bequests increased steadily. Minor sources of income included admission fees at the buildings and advertising (which had to have an antiquarian tone) in *Old-Time New England*. Appleton really made remarkable progress in obtaining funds in many ingenious ways. When he died in 1947, the society's real estate holdings were valued at $857,700 and its endowment at $507,800.[21]

Another pressing need of the society was space for its rapidly growing museum and library collections. Ten years after the society acquired the Otis House, the City of Boston decided to widen the street on which it faced. The society then bought four adjoining lots behind it and moved the Otis House forty feet back and thirty-five feet upward so as to occupy two of them. Two buildings on the other lots were joined to form a fireproof museum, library, and office complex. The society then began to create period rooms in the Otis House as well as holding special loan exhibitions there and in its other building. In 1932 furniture and other Washingtoniana were shown to commemorate the 200th anniversary of that hero's birth, and in the next year drawings and photographs of Colonial Williamsburg in Virginia. Appleton commented that "the group restoration of Williamsburg is so closely along the same lines of what we are doing in scattered units that the results are of greater interest to us, perhaps, than to any other single group in the country."[22]

The society enjoyed observing two important anniversaries. At its twenty-fifth in 1935, seven of the dozen survivors of the eighteen incorporators reenacted the first meeting of April 16, 1910, the ladies in the group donning costumes of that day. "The participants entered into the spirit of the occasion," the report of the meeting recorded, "with much zeal to the great entertainment of an audience that filled to overflowing the entire hall in the basement of Otis House." President William Crowninshield Endicott, an incorporator and treasurer for the first twenty years, said that "William Sumner Appleton is 'it,' to use a slang expression. His dream has been realized. Had it not been for him and his enthusiasm the Society would not have the standing that it has today."[23]

The thirtieth anniversary in 1940 was planned as a tribute to Appleton. Only four of the surviving seven incorporators could be present. Charles Knowles Bolton traced the society's history and Appleton's leading part in it and then moved that the room in which they were meeting at Otis House henceforth be known as Appleton Hall and that a committee be appointed to install a suitable tablet "memorializing Mr. Appleton's monumental service to the Society." The motion, of course, passed unanimously, and Appleton Hall later was elegantly furnished.[24]

Appleton provided wisely for the continuation of his efforts for the society. Bertram K. Little of Boston, who possessed great business ability, deep historical knowledge of New England, and, with his wife, Nina Fletcher Little, lively interest in collecting its surviving cultural objects, in 1932 became Appleton's chief assistant and virtual associate director as well as trustee and recording secretary. His fifteen years of experience in that role coupled with his sound scholarship allowed him to take over smoothly as director and corresponding secretary upon Appleton's death. For another twenty-three years, with devoted service he energetical carried the society's work to higher levels with many useful innovations.[25]

Sumner Appleton was a key figure in American historic preservation. He developed sound principles that have been accepted as standards in that field. He preached the preservation gospel up and down the land and even abroad—in visits to old buildings, speeches to preservation groups, trenchant articles in *Old-Time New England*, and a voluminous correspondence. He always stood ready to take architects, property owners, or publicists with him to visit historical and architectural treasures in order to make his points amid the three-dimensional evidence. And Appleton's services were well recognized. The Trustees of Public Reservations in 1944 gave him an award for Distinguished Service for Conservation with a handsome silver tray. In 1946 the American Scenic and Historic Preservation Society of New York bestowed upon him its George McAneny Medal in a moving ceremony. Later, the magazine *Antiques* devoted an entire issue to the society with real appreciation of Appleton's imaginative innovations and energetic efforts. As his friend Charles Messer Stowe told him: "You have met success and frustration with even hand, but victory for preservation has been so often on your side that historians of the nation revere you." And Charles Hosmer was right in regarding him as "the first full-time preservationist in twentieth-century America."[26]

## NOTES

1. The chief sources for this chapter are: "Special Issue: Society for the Preservation of New England Antiquities," *Antiques Magazine* 97 (May 1960), with articles by Alice Winchester, 464–65, Bertram K. Little, 466–68, and Abbott Lowell Cummings and Helen Comstock, 469–75; two superb treatments by Charles Hosmer, Jr.: *Presence of the Past: A History of the Preservation Movement in the United States Before Williamsburg* (New York: G. P. Putnam's Sons, 1965); *Preservation Comes of Age: From Williamsburg to the National Trust, 1926–1949*, 2 vols. (Charlottesville. Va.: University Press of Virginia, 1981); Bertram K. Little, "William Sumner Appleton," in Clifford L. Lord, *Keepers of the Past* (Chapel Hill: University of North Carolina Press, 1965), 215–22. Massachusetts Historical Society *Proceedings* 69 (Oct. 1947–May 1950): 70–80; *Old-Time New England* 30 (Apr. 1940): 106–110; 38 (Apr. 1948): 70–80; and Katherine H. Rich, "Beacon," *Old-Time New England* 66 (Jan.–June 1976): 42–60. Appleton's own sparse account is in *Who Was Who in America, 1945–1950* (Chicago: A. N. Marquis, 1950), 2: 29.

2. Society for the Preservation of New England Antiquities *Bulletin* 1 (May 1910): 4–7. See also Hosmer, *Presence of the Past*, 12, 238–44; Little in *Keepers of the Past*, 216–18.

3. Edward P. Alexander, *Museum Masters: Their Museums and Their Influence* (Nashville, Tenn.: American Association for State and Local History, 1983), 177–204; Hosmer, *Presence of the Past*, 35–37, 41–62; Winchester, "Special Issue: SPNEA," 466.

4. SPNEA *Bulletin* 3 (July 1912): 12–21.

5. Hosmer, *Presence of the Past*, 241, 242; Hosmer, *Preservation Comes of Age*, 1: 138–39; SPNEA *Bulletin* 6 (Apr. 1915): 18–22; 9 (Nov. 1918): 24–25.

6. William Sumner Appleton, "Destruction and Preservation of Old Buildings in New England," *Art and Archaeology* 8 (May–June 1919): 177–79; Cummings and Comstock, "Special Issue: SPNEA," 469–75; Hosmer, *Presence of the Past*, 241; Campbell Kaynor, "Thomas Tileston Waterman: Student of America's Colonial Architecture," *Winterthur Portfolio* 20 (Summer/Autumn 1985): 105–06; Little, "Special Issue: SPNEA," 422–25; SPNEA *Bulletin* 3 (Aug. 1913): 14; 6 (Apr. 1915): 18–22.

7. Laurence Vail Coleman, *Historic House Museums: With a Directory* (Washington, D.C.: American Association of Museums, 1933), 105, 133, 135; Hosmer, *Presence of the Past*, 246, 255–56; Hosmer, *Preservation Comes of Age*, 1: 161, 167–68; *Old-Time New England* 22 (July 1933): 3–13, 38 (Oct. 1947): 50; SPNEA *Bulletin* 10 (Oct. 1919): 23–24.

8. Coleman, *Historic House Museums*, 134; Hosmer, *Presence of the Past*, 213, 216, 250–51; Hosmer, *Preservation Comes of Age*, 1: 136; *Old-Time New England* 11 (July 1920): 40; (Apr. 1921): 187, SPNEA *Bulletin* 9 (Nov. 1918): 6–16; (Feb. 1919): 1–3.

9. Little, "Appleton," in Lord, *Keepers of the Past*, 215–222.

10. *Old-Time New England* 34 (Jan. 1944): 53.

11. *Old-Time New England* 30 (Apr. 1940): 107–10.

12. Hosmer, *Presence of the Past*, 257; *Old-Time New England* 38 (Apr. 1948): 75–77.

13. Hosmer, *Preservation Comes of Age*, 1: 133; Little, in *Keepers of the Past*, 220 and "Special Issue: SPNEA," 469; *Old-Time New England* 30 (Apr. 1940): 107–10; SPNEA *Bulletin* 3 (July 1912): 14–15; (Feb. 1913): 12–18, 20–24.

14. SPNEA *Bulletin* 2 (Aug. 1911): 9–13; (Mar. 1912), 1–9; 3 (July 1912): 1–7; 9 (Nov. 1918): 6–16; *Old-Time New England* 12 (Apr. 1922): 163–66; 19 (July 1928): ix; 22 (July 1931): 47–48; (Apr. l932): 192; 24 (July 1933): 17–25; 28 (July 1937): 25–26; Hosmer, *Presence of the Past*, 241–42, 246–50.

15. Hosmer, *Presence of the Past*, 246–50; *Old-Time New England* 13 (Apr. 1923): 181–82.

16. Little, "Special Issue: SPNEA," 466; *Old-Time New England* 32 (July 1941): 11–12; (Apr. 1942): 115; 33 (Apr. 1943): 44; 39 (Oct. 1948): 52–60.

17. Hosmer, *Presence of the Past*, 222–31; Hosmer, *Preservation Comes of Age*, 1: 143, 147–50, 201–06; *Old-Time New England* 27 (July 1936): 25; 28 (July 1937): 25–26; (Apr. 1938): 133–34, 146–47; 30 (July 1939): 34; (Apr. 1940): 137; 40 (Apr. 1950): 219–26; SPNEA *Bulletin* 6 (Jan. 1916): 2–11.

18. Appleton, "Old Buildings in New England," 179–81, 183; Hosmer, *Presence of the Past*, 252–55; *Old-Time New England* 11 (Apr. 1921): 182; 12 (Apr. 1922): 181–82; 24 (July 1933): 30–31.

19. Hosmer, *Presence of the Past*, 255–56; Little, in *Keepers Of the Past*, 220; *Old-Time New England* 15 (Oct. 1924): 91–92; 16 (Apr. 1926): 173–74; 18 (July 1927): 48; (Jan. 1928): 141–43; 21 (Oct. 1930): 85–87; SPNEA *Bulletin* 5 (Dec. 1914): 19.

20. Edward P. Alexander, "Sixty Years of Historic Preservation: The Society for the Preservation of New England Antiquities," *Old-Time New England* 61 (Summer 1970): 14–19; Appleton, "Old Buildings of New England," 179–83; Hosmer, *Presence of the Past*, 273–97.

21. Hosmer, *Presence of the Past*, 244–45; *Old-Time New England* 12 (Apr. 1922): 187; 15 (July 1924): 44–45; 27 (July 1937): 25–26; 28 (Apr. 1938): 153; 29 (Apr. 1929): 149; 39 (July 1948): 28; SPNEA *Bulletin* 3 (Feb. 1913): 11; 4 (Aug. 1913): 15; 7 (Dec. 1916): 2; 8 (Mar. 1917): 1–16; 9 (Nov. 1918): 25.

22. Hosmer, *Presence of the Past*, 251; *Old-Time New England* 17 (Oct. 1926): 90–96; 18 (Oct. 1927): 95–96; 22 (Apr. 1932): 152–61; 23 (Jan. 1933): 127; 24 (July 1933): 30–31; 27 (Apr. 1937): 155–57.

23. *Old-Time New England* 26 (July 1935): 32–33.

24. *Old-Time New England* 30 (Apr. 1940): 107–10.

25. Hosmer, *Presence of the Past*, 257; Hosmer, *Preservation Comes of Age*, 1: 179–82; *Old-Time New England* 23 (July 1932): iii; 39 (July 1948): 12–14; (Oct. 1948): 52–60; 61 (July–Sep. 1970); 14–25.

26. Hosmer, *Preservation Comes of Age*, 1: 133; *Old-Time New England* 34 (June 1944): 49–53; 38 (Apr. 1948): 73–77; "Special Issue: SPNEA," 464–502.

## SELECT BIBLIOGRAPHY

Alexander, Edward P. *Museum Masters: Their Museums and Their Influence*. Nashville, Tenn.: American Association for State and Local History, 1983.

Appleton, William Sumner. "Destruction and Preservation of Old Buildings in New England." *Art and Archaeology* 8 (May–June 1919): 177–79.

Coleman, Laurence Vail. *Historic House Museums: With a Directory*. Washington, D.C.: American Association of Museums, 1933.

Hosmer, Charles, Jr. *Presence of the Past: A History of the Preservation Movement in the United States Before Williamsburg*. New York: G. P. Putnam's Sons, 1965.

_____. *Preservation Comes of Age: From Williamsburg to the National Trust, 1926–1949*. 2 vols. Charlottesville. Va.: University Press of Virginia, 1981.

Kaynor, Campbell. "Thomas Tileston Waterman: Student of America's Colonial Architecture." *Winterthur Portfolio* 20 (Summer/Autumn 1985): 105–06.

Little, Bertram K. "William Sumner Appleton." In Clifford L. Lord. *Keepers of the Past*. Chapel Hill: University of North Carolina Press, 1965.

Massachusetts Historical Society *Proceedings* 69 (Oct. 1947–May 1950).

*Old-Time New England*. Vols. 11–66 (1920–1976).
Rich, Katherine H. "Beacon." *Old-Time New England* 66 (Jan.–June 1976): 42–60.
"Special Issue: Society for the Preservation of New England Antiquities." *Antiques Magazine* 97 (May 1960).
SPNEA *Bulletin*. Vols. 1–10 (1910–1919).

# CHAPTER 7

# Frank Friedman Oppenheimer *Uses Visitors as Part of Museum Experiments*

## I

While he was teaching physics at the University of Colorado in Boulder beginning in 1950, Frank Oppenheimer began to conceive a new kind of museum of science and technology. He and his associate, Malcom Correll, assembled in a large attic space a "Library of Experiments," which they used in enthusiastic and exciting teaching and then left in the hallways for their undergraduate students to operate, study, and enjoy. The library eventually contained some eighty experiments, all of them requiring hands-on participation from their viewers, not the mere pushing of buttons or turning of switches but instead the activation of the experiment, the involvement of the participant's sensory perception—sight, hearing, smell, or touch—and varied efforts to find the limitations of the experience. The students used the exhibits in their own individual ways, often with what Oppenheimer called "playfulness." "Turn the dials, manipulate, change the controls, do it yourself" were the phrases associated with the participatory exhibits, and their users often remarked, "How nice to be in a museum where touching is encouraged."[1]

In 1965 Oppenheimer received a Guggenheim fellowship that allowed him to spend the next year at University College in London, during which he visited the leading European museums of science and technology. In London the Science Museum at South Kensington impressed him with its hands-on experiments, its Children's Room, and the traveling shows of interactive exhibits it sent about

Britain. In Paris he admired the college students who acted as demonstrators at the Palais de la Découverte. And the Deutsches Museum in Munich, undoubtedly then the best museum of science and industry in the world, elicited his praise for its numerous experiments, for letting technicians and craftsmen work visibly among its exhibits, and for its training programs for schoolteachers during summers and school terms, even though he criticized what he considered the museum's rigid overcom-partmentalization of physics. Oppenheimer was an avid visitor of museums throughout his life and always ready later to apply useful practices that he observed to his own operation. Thus he mentioned receiving help with his project from the Corcoran Gallery, National Gallery, and the Smithsonian's National Museum of Natural History in Washington, the Franklin Institution in Philadelphia, Ontario Science Center in Toronto, Chicago Museum of Science and Industry, State Art Museum in Copenhagen, a small historic house in Vermont, and the Steinhart Aquarium in San Francisco.[2]

Oppenheimer took a leave of absence from the University of Colorado in 1969 in order to set up a museum of hands-on exhibits at the old Palace of Fine Arts (which he renamed the Palace of Arts and Science) in San Francisco; it opened its doors to the public that September. The Palace, with a cavernous hall of 86,000 square feet—1,000 feet long, 40 feet high, and 120 feet wide—had been built for the Panama-Pacific Exhibition of 1915 that honored the completion of the Panama Canal. A semicircular classical beaux-arts building with pink Corinthian columns, it was designed by Bernard Ralph Maybeck and was adjacent to the City Marina on a tree-lined approach to Golden Gate Bridge. Since that exhibition had closed, at various times the palace had housed eighteen tennis courts, an Army motor pool, two fire departments, a warehouse for overseas shipments, and a storage depot for telephone directories. The city now paid for its extensive renovation and rented it to the museum for one dollar per year. Oppenheimer disliked the word "museum" because he thought it had a passive connotation for many people, and he thus coined the name "Exploratorium." The Corcoran Gallery helped him obtain the show, "Cybernetic Serendipity," which the British Institute of Contemporary Arts in London had prepared, for the opening, for which he also secured a model from the Stanford Linear Acceleration Center. But the heart of the new Exploratorium consisted of interactive, dynamic, and entertaining experiments (which soon numbered 300) scattered about the huge space and before long attracting 300,000 visitors yearly.[3]

## II

The Exploratorium's main purpose was not the collection of objects but instead the teaching of the principles of science and technology by means of interactive, hands-on experiments, similar to those Oppenheimer had developed at the University of Colorado. The "Enchanted Tree" at rest was plain looking, but a sound-sensitive microcomputer caused it to light up in varied colors whenever anyone clapped, whistled, or shouted before it. That experiment showed how sound energy was converted into electric energy and then into light energy. The "Distorted Room" appeared rectangular at first glance but had a slanting floor; a person moving across it, viewed from a slit on one side, appeared to change from a giant into a dwarf. Thus the visitor learned something about visual perception and perspective. One of the most popular demonstrations was the dissection of a cow's eye with a sharp razor. Visitors at first were repelled by the experiment but then awed when the demonstator extracted the clear round transparent lens and passed it around to be looked through. A "Catenary Arch" could be built with a set of wooden blocks in the same shape in reverse of a suspended chain. If one clapped hands in front of the "Echo Tube," the sound came back like a ricocheting bullet; and "Everyone Is You and Me" made the viewer's and a companion's faces merge into a single joint image. The "Shadow Box" had strobe lights that caused a phosphorescent rear screen to retain momentarily shadow images in sharp relief when children leaped, danced, and somersaulted in front of it; and a walk-in "Kaleidoscope" transformed the reflections of three youngsters into a crowd of images. A "Pedal Generator" required fast pedaling to keep three electric lights bright; the "Momentum Machine" whirled one about dizzily; and the "Vidium" (oscilloscope) produced colors and patterns when a visitor spoke or sang into a microphone. Then there were lasers, stroboscopes, holography, computer poetry, space craft models, a large gyroscope, and a cathode ray tube. These were only samples of the hundreds of experiments that kept children as young as three or four as well as adults engrossed and amused. Each exhibit had two cards beside it; one described the scientific phenomenon, and the other told how to bring the experiment to life.[4]

Oppenheimer since childhood had been interested in art and art museums. He came to believe that both art and science were needed to describe and understand the world of nature. Thus he defined the Exploratorium as a museum of science, art, and human perception and enlisted artists on his staff as well as scientists. In 1973 he obtained grants to finance a year-long artist-in-residence program, and it became a permanent educational feature of the museum. Several spectacular exhibits were created by various artists. The "Sun Painting" by Robert Miller consisted of a revolving mirror that directed sunlight from a hole in the roof onto a series of prisms and mirrors which broke it into a mixture of subtle hues and nuances of pure color. The "Tactile Dome" developed by August Coppola became a favorite exhibit. It was a geodesic dome thirty feet in diameter, totally dark on the inside; a visitor climbed, crawled, and slid on the stomach along walls, floors, and ceilings while experiencing hot and cold temperatures, rough and smooth surfaces, tight and open spaces, rope networks, close-fitting tubes, and the textures of corduroy, fur, vinyl, and birdseeds. An "Aeolian Harp" by Douglas Hollis was placed on the roof over an entrance to the museum; it was activated by the wind and produced different sounds from soft humming to complex harmonics caused by the wind's turbulence. Thus Oppenheimer acquired interactive exhibits for understandings of both art and science.[5]

The new museum was governed by the Palace of Arts and Science Foundation of twenty-three members, with eight scientists (three of them Nobel laureates) and the remainder leaders from business, labor, civic life, and the arts. Its president was the head of the Homestead Mining Company; the two vice-presidents were connected with the University of California; the treasurer had retired from the Owens Illinois Glass Company; and the secretary was secretary-treasurer of the International Longshoremen's and Warehousemen's Union. The finances came from federal, state, county, city, private foundation, corporate, and individual grants, as well as from some 260 members. At first, both admission and parking were free of charge, but one could make a donation by dropping a coin in a box, thus activating a sound and light display, so pleasing that many viewers dropped another coin in order to see it again. The Exploratorium was open from 1 to 5 p.m., Wednesdays through Fridays, 7 to 9:30 p.m. on Wednesday evenings, and from noon to 5 p.m. on weekends. Mornings were reserved for school children who constituted the predominant audience during the week, while adults formed the majority on weekends. A 1978 survey found that 26,000 came in scheduled school groups from kindergarten through college, with more than 50 percent of them from grades 5–6. In the yearly total of 300,000 visitors, 50 percent were over 21 years of age; 25 percent were under 10; 30 percent came from San Francisco, with 40 percent from other parts of the Bay Area and 30 percent from outside the region.[6]

The experiments at the Exploratorium usually were built in its carpentry, machine, and electronic shops, and the artists, technicians, and craftsmen working in them were visible to the public at one end of the great hall. Ideas for new exhibits were always welcomed, and industries, federal agencies, artists and scientists from throughout the country, and visiting students made suggestions. The exhibits had a home-made look and were done rather crudely when they were first placed on the floor. The public's reaction to them was closely observed, and then they were revised in more permanent form. They might be tested again and, if necessary retested until they satisfied the staff.[7]

The Exploratorium had no regular guards or guides but instead "Explainers" in distinctive red jackets. They were patterned after the demonstrators of the Palais de la Découverte, but most of them were high school students paid $2.25 per hour. Ten of them worked full time (twenty hours) during the week, and another ten part-time for eight hours per day on weekends. They consisted of an equal number of young men and young women, and more than half of them were orientals, blacks, or Hispanics. Applicants were interviewed by the museum staff, chosen because of their ability to communicate, trained in an eight-hour orientation session, and then kept up to snuff with two half-hour lectures on weekends. The explainers kept an eye on the exhibits so that the museum experienced no vandalism. They roamed about the floor answering questions from the visitors and assisting them with the experiments. Another half-dozen high school students were hired each summer to help construct and repair exhibits.[8]

Oppenheimer started a School in the Exploratorium (SITE) for upper grade and junior high teachers of the San Francisco and Marin County public schools. It was modeled on the Deutsches Museum's schools for teachers and aimed to acquaint them with scientific phenomena and to stimulate their perceptual awareness. In the school year 1974/1975, 600 of them attended all-day sessions once a week for five weeks or eight weekly two-hour periods. They used hands-on methods; for example, in studying vision, they used the cow's eye dissection and experimented with lenses, prisms, magnifying glasses, light angles, and filters. Oppenheimer had artists speak to them and even a poet who discussed the musical textures of words. After the course, they could use a lending library of props and portable exhibits in their classrooms and encourage students to invent their own experiments. The parents of students often became enthusiastic about the course, and in one instance they raised money to permit another class to participate in the program.[9]

A Medical Technology Series in 1979 attracted attendance of 50,000 in six months. The program was planned with local physicians and medical researchers and used volunteer health technicians to help the participants interact with the equipment. Monthly programs were devoted to "Speech and Hearing," "Vision," "The Heart-Lungs," "Movement and the Body," "Imaging the Body: From X-Rays to Ultrasound," and "The Technology of Treatment: Cancer Therapy." Those attending could lie on the X-ray table and watch their own EKGs. In the appropriate months they could take hearing tests, preschool and adult vision tests, lung volume and stress tests, and foot examinations. Equipment was demonstrated and explained by medical researchers, and volunteer health professionals encouraged visitor interaction, answered questions, and analyzed the devices. Questionnaires at the end of the course showed that the participants had come out of general curiosity or because they or a relative were ill, and their reactions were generally most enthusiastic. The Exploratorium encouraged other museums to offer similar courses.[10]

A Dissemination Program supported by the Kellogg Foundation for five years provided internships of two to five weeks to 125 museum professionals (81 from the United States and 44 from other countries) to enable them to study the Exploratorium exhibits and adapt them for their own museums. A Conference on Science and the Media attracted representatives from television, newspapers, magazines, book publishing, and libraries, as well as scientists from museums and universities. Another Conference on the Elements of Coed Design was equally successful. The Exploratorium issued three *Cookbooks* that explained in detail the preparation and duplication of 201 exhibits; thus it shared its expertise with science centers and other types of museums. Many academic faculty members attended such activities and returned to their campuses and communities to institute Exploratorium practices.[11]

All in all, Oppenheimer succeeded in starting a new kind of museum that continued to make innovations and soon built up an enthusiastic following; it became known nationally and internationally as the progressive and trail-breaking leader of the science and technology museum field.

## III

Frank Friedman Oppenheimer was born in New York City on August 14, 1912, the son of Julius and Ella (Friedman) Oppenheimer. As he grew up there, he made frequent visits to the American Museum of Natural History, the Metropolitan Museum of Art, and later the Museum of Modern Art. He attended Johns Hopkins University at Baltimore, where he received a B.S. in 1933. He then began research on particles in the Cavendish Laboratory at Cambridge University in England and also visited the Institute di Arceti in Italy. He returned to the United States to continue nuclear studies at the California Institute of Technology in Pasadena and received his Ph.D. there in 1939. He was a research associate at Stanford for two years and then began work with Ernest O. Lawrence at the Radiation Laboratory of the University of California at Berkeley on the electromagnetic separation of uranium isotopes. He moved on to the Los Alamos, New Mexico, Weapons Laboratory late in 1943; his older brother Robert, another atomic physicist, was in charge there. As part of the Manhattan Project, Frank supervised the instrumentation of the first successful nuclear explosion at the Trinity test site. He often said jokingly that he was "the uncle of the atomic bomb."[12]

Oppenheimer was married to Jacquenette Yvonne ("Jackie") Quant in 1936. They both were dismayed by the economic depression of the 1930s and were seeking "an answer to the problems of unemployment and want in the wealthiest and most productive country in the world." Thus they joined the Communist Party in 1937 but became disillusioned and left it three and one-half years later. Their strong social conscience remained, however, and Frank in 1945 became a leader in the Association of Los Alamos Scientists (ALAS) formed "to promote the attainment and use of scientific and technological advances in the best interests of humanity." It later became the National Federation of American Scientists. They feared for the future of the world in face of the enormous destructive force of nuclear weaponry and attempted to institute some kind of civilian or international control. Though they failed, Oppenheimer never stopped trying. In 1965 he wrote a guest editorial in the *Saturday Review* commenting on the book entitled *Brighter Than a Thousand Suns* and arguing that nuclear weapons made future wars inconceivable, that the armament race was unconscionable, and that an immediate solution must be found to allow the settlement of world problems without resort to war.[13]

In 1947 Oppenheimer left the Manhattan Project to become assistant professor of physics at the University of Minnesota. There he did landmark research on cosmic rays, chasing hydrogen balloons across the Minnesota countryside and later through the Caribbean. The balloons ascended some twenty miles and enabled him to become a co-discoverer of the heavy nuclei component of cosmic rays. In 1949, however, his career in physics was cut short when he was called before the Un-American Activities Committee of the United States House of Representatives. He admitted there his former membership in the Communist Party and talked freely about his actions, but he courageously refused to identify other party members (many of them his friends) "because that might be used to impugn the loyalty of others, whom I know nothing against." His work at the Oak Ridge and Los Alamos laboratories counted in his favor, for General Leslie R. Groves, the head of those operations, had written a letter of praise for his efforts, and the committee did not hold him in contempt. But he was forced to resign his post at Minnesota, and no other university or institute dared hire him. He attended the Denver International Cosmic Ray Symposium at Idaho Springs in the same year, and his paper there "received one of the few spontaneous bursts of applause." Frank's brother Robert in 1954 was declared a security risk by the Atomic Energy Commission because of his attempts to control atomic weaponry, though he remained director of the Institute for Advanced Study at Princeton with the full backing of its trustees.[14]

Oppenheimer decided in 1949 to move with his wife and two children (Judi, 9, and Mike, 6) to a cattle ranch of 380 acres situated near Pagosa Springs, high in the Blanco Basin of Colorado. A good craftsman (carpenter, plumber, and mechanic), he became a successful rancher. He also was elected to head the local Cattle Ranchers' Association. He remarked that he "never had the slightest trouble from anyone about the Communist thing." In 1957 Oppenheimer began to teach science to a class in the county elementary school at Pagosa Springs. He was an innovative teacher who "really cared about getting his students excited" over learning; he even conducted some classes in a local junkyard. Robert H. Johnson, the Jefferson County superintendent of schools, was impressed by his work and asked him to teach a special physics class made up of twenty-six top ranking seniors from the eight high schools of the county. Again he enjoyed great success and went on to administer a University of Colorado summer institute for teachers of physics. Though he kept serving as a consultant to the county schools, he soon moved in 1959 to Boulder (his daughter Judi was entering her sophomore year there), where he became professor of physics at the university and developed the library of experiments which was the predecessor of the Exploratorium. He became more and more interested in education and in 1969 began giving his chief attention to his new conception of a museum.[15]

Thus after brilliant careers as an atomic and cosmic rays researcher and as an outstanding teacher of science from elementary and high school through college and university, he devoted the remaining seventeen years of his life to a new kind of teaching museum. His wife Jackie was a full partner in that activity and became head of the museum's graphic department, where she excelled in making the language of science intelligible to the general public. And Oppenheimer's original contributions in his varied fields brought him considerable fame. In 1973 he delivered the Robert A. Millikan lectures before the American Association of Physics Teachers; in 1979 he received the Kirkwood Award for Distinguished Service from the California Institute of Technology and soon similar honors from the University of Colorado and the American Association of Museums. He was also the subject of a Nova television program sponsored by the Smithsonian Institution. He died at his home in Sausalito, California, on February 3, 1985. But his Exploratorium continues to keep alive his fresh and forceful ideas about education and museums.[16]

## IV

Frank Oppenheimer was not only a keen observer but a deep thinker, ever probing below the surface of phenomena trying to discover their true meaning. It is thus rewarding to examine his speeches and writings in sequence in order to understand the development of his ideas. That process also allows one better to define the Exploratorium which is indeed the culmination of a long intellectual search. Oppenheimer first came to the attention of the museum world when he attended the Smithsonian Institution's Conference on Museums and Education held in 1966 at the University of Vermont in Burlington. In a formal address on science and technology museums, he asserted that they made people aware of the wholeness of our culture and that science and technology were as important components of that culture as art and history. Though such science museums were expensive and had no sure recipe for success to follow (the Deutsches Museum, however, was a good model), a medium-sized city of 100,000 or more could develop one by accumulating a core of demonstration apparatus, models, and reproductions of significant experiments. The Science Museum in Paris, the University of Colorado's demonstration laboratory, and the London Science Museum's traveling exhibits were all worth examination. Science museums appealed to passive visitors or wanderers as well as to school classes with docents, to children and adults, and to community educational programs and correspondence school courses. Local industries could help set up exhibitions and encourage their personnel to use them. Perhaps Americans, surrounded by so much science and technology on all sides, needed fewer such museums, but they were especially important for developing countries which ought to support strongly the acquisition of laboratory equipment and the institution of teacher training courses.[17]

In the discussion period at the conference, Oppenheimer held the audience spellbound with a remarkable extemporaneous passage. Though he said that he was a non-museum person, he considered museums terribly important because they filled holes in one's experience and provided synthesis for objects of great variety. Both art and science made one aware of one's surroundings and changed "the way one looks at oneself and the rest of the world." Both of them were concerned increasingly with the inaccessible and trying to find new techniques to reach it.[18]

Dr. Albert Eide Parr, the former director of the American Museum of Natural History who had retired to become a senior scientist there and was speaking and writing many articles on the significance of museums, was attending the conference and was deeply impressed by Oppenheimer's remarks. The two men had much in common. Oppenheimer as a boy of four or five had learned to ride a bicycle, though his legs were too short to reach the pedals all the way round. He then was delighted to teach the other children of the neighborhood to ride. Parr had grown up in Norway and, as a boy of the same age, had taken a trip across the bay to buy fish for his family. He remembered how much he had learned in wandering about the stores, civic buildings, fire station, and museum that he passed and from the adult conversations that he overheard on the way. He regretted that many of the homes of children were in the suburbs far removed from city centers and that the automobile had made such treks too dangerous for children to walk there. Parr thought that Oppenheimer's vision of the museum offered some substitute for learning through experience; he visited him when he was setting up the Exploratorium and, from his own broad background, helped make it a powerful teaching force.[19]

Parr encouraged Oppenheimer to explain his ideas for the Exploratorium that he was about to open, and he did so in a 1968 article in the American Museum of Natural History's professional museum magazine, *Curator*. First of all, people needed to understand the science and technology so important in their world. While books, magazine articles, television, motion pictures, and general science courses in the schools offered some help, they lacked props, that is, apparatus that people could handle; trying to explore science and technology without props was like telling a person how to swim without going near the water. Oppenheimer then outlined a possible form for an exploratorium or science center in five main sections. The first would deal with hearing: musical instruments; everyday sounds and noises; the physics of sound—vibration, oscillation, resonance, interference, and reflection; the physiology of the ear; and industrial techniques such as speakers, microphones, acoustics, hearing aids, telephone, radio, and sonar. Next would come vision with the physics of light; the eye; pigment manufacturing; television; photography; infrared and ultraviolet lighting; and lasers. The third section on taste and smell would consider food; perfume; the chemistry involved; and food and cosmetic industries. The fourth would examine clothing and housing; perceptions of hot, cold, and roughness; the physics of heat; and fibers and building materials. And last would come control of the body in dancing, athletics, and bicycle riding; muscles and nerves; and semicircular canals.

Such a museum could start by saving and using science fair exhibits; securing apparatus shown in educational television science programs; placing in a central location laboratory equipment developed by schools and colleges; and obtaining objects from industry and scientific organizations. He summed up the objective of such a museum as follows:

> A museum should not be a substitute for a school or classroom but it should be a place where people come both to teach and to learn. Visitors should be able to find it refreshing and stimulating. Above all it should be honest and then convey the understanding that science and technology have a role which is deeply rooted in human values and aspirations.[20]

For the remainder of his Exploratorium career, Oppenheimer expanded his ideas on museums and museum education. He used many different approaches in defining the Exploratorium. Once he said: "I intended a kind of woods of natural phenomena that were organized and selected in some way so that people could take many constructive paths. This is not a museum, it's a curriculum."[21] He insisted that "the whole point of education is to transmit culture, and museums can play an increasingly important role in the process. It is a mistake to think that preserving culture is distinct from transmitting it through education."[22] And the Exploratorium never needed an education director; the entire museum was devoted to education. One commentator found Oppenheimer "a gentle yet forceful man with a mission: to make the understanding and appreciation of science a source of enrichment in people's lives."[23]

The methods used by the Exploratorium are best described by the experiments and the way they worked. Still, some generalizations are possible. Oppenheimer thought that exhibit materials

> should give the viewer the opportunity to explore and manipulate them. Individual exhibits . . . must be of value at a variety of levels which range from rela-

> tively superficial sightseeing through to a broad and deep understanding. The exhibit must provide a multiplicity of interacting threads and pathways which visitors can select.[24]

Nor was sightseeing or one-shot wandering about the exhibits bad; one must remember that sightseeing provided exceptional stimulation and insights for a Marco Polo or a Darwin. Again, Oppenheimer stated that "only a limited amount of understanding comes from watching something behave; one must also watch what happens as one varies the parameters that alter the behavior." Even more important was "the flexibility that allows exhibits to be used for play." Many times he emphasized that playfulness should be encouraged, and he pointed out how much both animals and children learned through play.[25]

Oppenheimer was especially interested in the contrasting educational practices of schools and museums. He thought that too much was expected of the schools and listed ten things that they were supposed to accomplish: make learning appear worthwhile; teach skills; cultivate values; transmit culture; produce creative individuals; develop physical and mental fitness through athletics; make the most of both gifted and challenged students; keep young people off the streets and out of their parents' hair; eliminate prejudice; and certify students for employment or further education.[26] Good teachers must set up environments and situations conducive to learning and help get students unstuck when they could not understand something. But most classroom programs were two-dimensional and used lectures, blackboards, television programs, and motion pictures. Museums, on the other hand, provided "a reversible, deflectable, three-dimensional form of education." Visiting students were free from learning tensions; no one ever flunked a museum, and one museum was not a prerequisite for another. But museums often had not understood their educational purpose; their exhibits had not paid attention to touch or kinasthesia; and the public had regarded them as merely a leisure-time activity. The Exploratorium's rationale, however, was "developing a core of participating exhibits and demonstrations that elucidate the mechanisms of human sensory perception involved in sight, hearing, touch, etc." It was "to provide a learning environment outside the classroom situation where individuals may develop an understanding of human sensory perception." And it was most important that the museum and academic worlds work together toward that end.[27]

Thus Oppenheimer contributed to the museum education field. His participatory Exploratorium was soundly established and bringing new liveliness and zest into science centers and even to their art and history cousins. Some of his ideas were too advanced for the present time. For example, he thought that cities ought to establish Museum Districts just as they had School Districts. He also suggested Library Districts, Recreation and Park Districts, and Educational Television Districts. But he was always hopeful that "if people spend a little more of their lives in a museum, it will change what happens in the classroom."[28]

Frank Oppenheimer's Exploratorium has continued influential. Dr. Robert L. White, formerly professor of electrical engineering at Stanford University, succeeded him as director and still considered the Exploratorium's mission "to make the world around us understandable and fun." Its exhibits soon numbered 750, and its annual attendance grew to 500,000. Its sway has been worldwide, and similar science exhibits and museums are now found in New York, Paris, Hong Kong, Oklahoma City, Helsinki, Atlanta, Beijing, San Diego, Stockholm, Milwaukee, Barcelona, Ann Arbor, Osaka, Phoenix, Toronto, Singapore, and elsewhere.

The exhibit growth and storage needs of the original Exploratorium in San Francisco, however, demanded much new space; the floor area was doubled and a separate 750-car parking garage erected. Also, a sounder financial underpinning evolved. Oppenheimer had had to depend mainly on sporadic government and foundation grants and earned income, but later substantial yearly coporate and individual support was obtained to provide steadier funding. And a less personal, more conventional management organization and style was adopted. But Oppenheimer's inspired vision and innovative practices were still in use, and they continued to produce valuable changes, not only in the science field but in the whole museum world.[29]

## NOTES

1. An excellent full treatment of the museum subject is Hilde Hein, *The Exploratorium: The Museum as Laboratory* (Washington, D.C.: Smithsonian Institution Press, 1990). Other sources for this chapter are American Association of Museums, *Museums for a New Century* (Washington, D.C.: AAM, 1984); K. C. Cole, "The Art of Discovery in San Francisco—Exploratorium," *Saturday Review* 55 (Oct. 14, 1972): 40–43; Victor J. Danilov, "The Exploratorium of San Francisco Twenty Years Later," *Museum* 163 (1989): 155–59; Judy Diamond, Terry Vergason, and Gaile Ramey, "Exploratorium's Medical Technology Series," *Curator* 22 (Dec. 1979): 281–98; Kenneth W. Ford, "The Robert A. Millikan Award, 1973," *American Journal of Physics* 41 (Dec. 1973): 1309–10; Marvin Grosswirth, "San Francisco's Exploratorium Makes You Part of the Action: Its Exhibits Give New Meaning to the Concept of the Hands-on Visitor," *Science Digest* 7 (June 1980): 60–64; Sherwood Davidson Kohn, "It's OK to Touch at the New-Style Hands-on Exhibits," *Smithsonian* 9 (Sept. 1978): 78–83; Eric Larrabee, ed., *Museums and Education* (Washington, D.C.: Smithsonian Institution Press, 1968); Mary Ellen Munley, *Catalysts for Change: The Kellogg Projects in Museum Education*

(Washington, D.C.: Kellogg Projects, 1986), 7–20; Barbara Y. Newsom and Adele Z. Silver, eds., *The Art Museum as Educator* (Berkeley: University of California Press, 1978), 299–305, 440–42, 697–98; Frank Oppenheimer, "Aesthetics and the 'Right Answer'," *Humanist* 39 (Mar./Apr. 1979): 18–26; Oppenheimer, "The Exploratorium: A Playful Museum Combines Perception and Art in Science Education," *American Journal of Physics* 40 (July 1972): 978–84; Oppenheimer, "A Rationale for a Science Museum," *Curator* 11 (Sept. 1968): 206–09; Oppenheimer, "Schools Are Not for Sightseeing" and "Some Special Features of the Exploratorium," in Katherine J. Goldman, ed., *Opportunities for Extending Museum Contributions to Pre-College Science Education* (Washington, D.C.: Smithsonian Institution, 1970), 7–11, 115–18; Oppenheimer, "A Study of Perception as a Part of Teaching Physics," *American Journal of Physics* 42 (July 1974): 531–37; Oppenheimer, "Teaching and Learning," *American Journal of Physics* 41 (Dec. 1973): 1310–13; Paul Preuss et al, "Education with an Edge: An Introduction to the Educational Programs at the Exploratorium," *Physics Teacher* 21 (Nov. 1983): 514–19; Al Richmond, "Doctor Oppenheimer's Exploratorium," *Nation* 211 (July 6, 1970): 6–9; Evelyn Shaw, "The Exploratorium," *Curator* 15 (1972): 39–52; Kenneth Starr and Oppenheimer, "Exploratorium and Culture: Oppenheimer Receives Distinguished Service Award," *Museum News* 61 (Nov./Dec. 1982): 36–45.

2. Hein, *Exploratorium*, 4–5; Oppenheimer, "Schools Are Not for Sightseeing," 7–11; Starr and Oppenheimer, "Exploratorium and Culture," 43–45.

3. Hein, *Exploratorium*, 1, 32–39; Newsom and Silver, eds., *Art Museum as Educator*, 697–98; Oppenheimer, "Aesthetics and the 'Right Answer'," 22; Oppenheimer, "Exploratorium: Playful Museum," 978–84; Richmond, "Doctor Oppenheimer's Exploratorium," 6–9; Shaw, "Exploratorium," 39–40.

4. Hein, *Exploratorium*, 71–123, illustrations after 146, 147–70. See also Cole, "Art of Discovery," 40–43; Grosswirth, "San Francisco's Exploratorium," 61; "How Do Lasers Work? What Is Eye Logic? Exploratorium," *Sunset* 154 (Feb. 1974): 40; Munley, *Catalysts for Change*, 10; Newsom and Silver, eds., *Art Museum as Educator*, 299–300; Oppenheimer, "Aesthetics and the 'Right Answer'," 24–26; Preuss et al, "Education with an Edge," 518; Shaw, "Exploratorium," 46, 48–49.

5. Hein, *Exploratorium*, 147–70.

6. Grosswirth, "San Francisco's Exploratorium," 63; Hein, *Exploratorium*, 20–21; Newsom and Silver, eds., *Art Musewn as Educator*, 697–98; Richmond, "Doctor Oppenheimer's Exploratorium," 6–9; "San Francisco Museum Stresses Involvement," *Physics Today* 24 (June 1971): 62.

7. Hein, *Exploratorium*, 45–70; Oppenheimer, "Exploratorium: Playful Museum," 978–79; Shaw, "Exploratorium," 48.

8. Hein, *Exploratorium*, 135–39; Newsom and Silver, eds., *Art Museum as Educator*, 440–42.

9. Hein, *Exploratorium*, 129–35; Newsom and Silver, eds., *Art Museum as Educator*, 299–305; Preuss et al, "Education with an Edge," 518.

10. Diamond et al, "Exploratorium's Medical Technology Series," 281–98.

11. American Association of Museums, *Museums for a New Century*, 94; Raymond Bruman, *Exploratorium Cookbook I* (San Francisco: Exploratorium, 1975); Ron Hipschmann, *Exploratorium Cookbook II, III* (San Francisco: Exploratorium, 1981, 1987); Danilov, "Exploratorium Twenty Years Later," 158; Hein, *Exploratorium*, 187–88, 210–11; Munley, *Catalysts for Change*, 7–20.

12. Ford, "Millikan Lecture Award," 1309–10; Grosswirth, "San Francisco's Exploratorium," 60; David Hawkins, "Frank Oppenheimer (obituary)," *Physics Today* 38 (Nov. 1985): 122; Hein, *Exploratorium*, 7; *Who Was Who in America* (Chicago: A. N. Marquis Company, 1985), 8 (1982–1985): 308.

13. Hein, *Exploratorium*, 9, 11; "An Ex-Red Oppenheimer," *Newsweek* 33 (June 27, 1949): 25–26; Frank Oppenheimer, "The Mathematics of Destruction," *Saturday Review* 48 (Jan. 16. 1965): 20; Alice Kimball Smith, *A Peril and a Hope: The Scientists' Movement in America, 1945–47* (Chicago: University of Chicago Press, 1965), 115.

14. "Condon and Oppenheimer at International Cosmic Ray Meeting," *Science News Letter* 56 (July 9, 1949): 21; "Ex-Red Oppenheimer," 25–26; Ford, "Millikan Lecture Award," 1309–10; Hawkins, "Frank Oppenheimer," 122–24; Hein, *Exploratorium*, 11; "Investigation of the Brothers," *Time* 53 (June 27, 1949): 14–15.

15. Ford, "Millikan Lecture Award," 1309–10; Hawkins, "Frank Oppenheimer," 122–24; Hein, *Exploratorium*, 11–14; "Return from Exile," *Newsweek* 54 (Sept. 14, 1959): 72.

16. Ford, "Millikan Lecture Award," 1309–10; Hein, *Exploratorium*, 62–63; Oppenheimer, "Study of Perception," 531–37; Starr and Oppenheimer, "Exploratorium and Culture," 36–45.

17. Labaree, ed., *Museums and Education*, 167–68.

18. Ibid., 207, 213–16.

19. Oppenheimer, "Teaching and Learning," 1312; A. E. Parr, "The Child in the City: Urbanity and the Urban Scene," *Landscape* 16 (Spring 1967); Starr and Oppenheimer, "Exploratorium and Culture," 40–41.

20. Oppenheimer, "Rationale for Science Museum," 206–09.

21. Kohn, "It's OK to Touch," 81.

22. Grosswirth, "San Francisco's Exploratorium," 61; American Association of Museums, *Museums for a New Century*, 57.

23. Ford, "Millikan Lecture Award," 1309; Starr and Oppenheimer, "Exploratorium and Culture," 38.

24. Shaw, "Exploratorium," 42–43.

25. Newsom and Silver, eds., *Art Museum as Educator*, 268–69, 300; Oppenheimer, "Aesthetics and the 'Right Answer'," 25; Oppenheimer, "Exploratorium: A Playful Museum," 979–83; Oppenheimer, "Schools Are Not for Sightseeing," 9.

26. Frank Oppenheimer, "The Exploratorium and Other Ways of Teaching Physics," *Physics Today* 28 (Sep. 1975): 9.

27. Newsom and Silver, eds., *Art Museum as Educator*, 698; Oppenheimer, "Some Special Features of the Exploratorium," 115; Oppenheimer, "Schools Are Not for Sightseeing," 7–11; Oppenheimer, "Teaching and Learning," 1311; Starr and Oppenheimer, "Exploratorium and Culture," 45.

28. Newsom and Silver, eds., *Art Museum as Educator*, 304; Oppenheimer, "Exploratorium and Other Ways of Teaching Physics," 11.

29. Danilov, "Exploratorium Twenty Years Later," 158–59.

## SELECT BIBLIOGRAPHY

American Association of Museums. *Museums for a New Century*. Washington, D.C.: AAM, 1984.

*American Women: The Official Who's Who among the Women of the Nation*. Los Angeles: Richard Blank, 1935.

Bruman, Raymond. *Exploratorium Cookbook I*. San Francisco: Exploratorium, 1975.

Cole, K. C. "The Art of Discovery in San Francisco—Exploratorium." *Saturday Review* 55 (Oct. 14, 1972): 40–43.

"Condon and Oppenheimer at International Cosmic Ray Meeting." *Science News Letter* 56 (July 9, 1949): 21.

Danilov, Victor J. "The Exploratorium of San Francisco Twenty Years Later." *Museum* 163 (1989): 155–59.

Diamond, Judy, Terry Vergason, and Gaile Ramey. "Exploratorium's Medical Technology Series." *Curator* 22 (Dec. 1979): 281–98.

Ford, Kenneth W. "The Robert A. Millikan Award, 1973." *American Journal of Physics* 41 (Dec. 1973): 1309–10.

Grosswirth, Marvin. "San Francisco's Exploratorium Makes You Part of the Action: Its Exhibits Give New Meaning to the Concept of the Hands-on Visitor." *Science Digest* 7 (June 1980): 60–64.

Hein, Hilde. *The Exploratorium: The Museum as Laboratory*. Washington, D.C.: Smithsonian Institution Press, 1990.

Hipschmann, Ron. *Exploratorium Cookbook II, III*. San Francisco: Exploratorium, 1981, 1987.

"How Do Lasers Work? What Is Eye Logic? Exploratorium." *Sunset* 154 (Feb. 1974): 40.

"Investigation of the Brothers." *Time* 53 (June 27, 1949): 14–15.

Kohn, Sherwood Davidson. "It's OK to Touch at the New-Style Hands-on Exhibits." *Smithsonian* 9 (Sept. 1978): 78–83.

Larrabee, Eric, ed. *Museums and Education*. Washington, D.C.: Smithsonian Institution Press, 1968.

Munley, Mary Ellen. *Catalysts for Change: The Kellogg Projects in Museum Education*. Washington, D.C.: Kellogg Projects, 1986.

Newsom, Barbara Y., and Adele Z. Silver, eds. *The Art Museum as Educator*. Berkeley: University of California Press, 1978.

Oppenheimer, Frank. "Aesthetics and the 'Right Answer'." *Humanist* 39 (Mar./Apr. 1979): 18–26.

_____. "The Exploratorium and Other Ways of Teaching Physics." *Physics Today* 28 (Sep. 1975): 9.

_____. "The Exploratorium: A Playful Museum Combines Perception and Art in Science Education." *American Journal of Physics* 40 (July 1972): 978–84.

_____. "The Mathematics of Destruction." *Saturday Review* 48 (Jan. 16. 1965): 20.

_____. "A Rationale for a Science Museum." *Curator* 11 (Sept. 1968): 206–09.

_____. "Schools Are Not for Sightseeing" and "Some Special Features of the Exploratorium." In *Opportunities for Extending Museum Contributions to Pre-College Science Education*. Edited by Katherine J. Goldman. Washington, D.C.: Smithsonian Institution, 1970.

_____. "A Study of Perception as a Part of Teaching Physics." *American Journal of Physics* 42 (July 1974): 531–37.

_____. "Teaching and Learning." *American Journal of Physics* 41 (Dec. 1973): 1310–13.

Parr, A. E. "The Child in the City: Urbanity and the Urban Scene." *Landscape* 16 (Spring 1967).

Preuss, Paul, et al. "Education with an Edge: An Introduction to the Educational Programs at the Exploratorium." *Physics Teacher* 21 (Nov. 1983): 514–519.

"Return from Exile." *Newsweek* 54 (Sept. 14, 1959): 72.

Richmond, Al. "Doctor Oppenheimer's Exploratorium." *Nation* 211 (July 6, 1970): 6–9.

"San Francisco Museum Stresses Involvement." *Physics Today* 24 (June 1971): 62.

Shaw, Evelyn. "The Exploratorium." *Curator* 15 (1972): 39–52.

Smith, Alice Kimball. *A Peril and a Hope: The Scientists' Movement in America, 1945–47*. Chicago: University of Chicago Press, 1965.

Starr, Kenneth, and Frank Oppenheimer. "Exploratorium and Culture: Oppenheimer Receives Distinguished Service Award." *Museum News* 61 (Nov./Dec. 1982): 36–45.

# CHAPTER 8

# Anna Billings Gallup *Popularizes the First Children's Museum*

## I

IN 1899 PROFESSOR WILLIAM HENRY GOODYEAR, curator of fine arts for the Brooklyn Institute of Arts and Sciences, returned from a European trip during which he had been greatly impressed by the natural history exhibits which were attracting many young people at the Manchester Museum in England. He suggested to Franklin William Hooper, director of the institute, that they set up a children's museum for natural history in the old Adams House, which the institute formerly had used for a warehouse, in beautiful little Bedford (today Brower) Park. Hooper liked the idea, and the city leased them the old building at a nominal rental; it was remodeled, redecorated, and provided with electric lights. On December 16, 1899, the Brooklyn Children's Museum opened its doors, the first children's museum in this country and in the world.

The new museum planned to treat every branch of natural history, attempt to "delight and instruct the children who visit it," and "stimulate their powers of observation and reflection." It hoped to be a "wonder house for children" and would aim

> through its collections, library, curator, and assistants . . . to bring the child or young person, whether attending school or not, into direct relation with the most important subjects that appeal to the interest of their daily life, in their school work, in their reading, in their games and rambles in the fields, and in the industries which are carried on about them.

The museum at first had only two exhibit rooms, but they soon expanded to six on the first floor. The Model Room contained charts, colored cartoons, and natural history specimens purchased from Émile Deyrolle of Paris for about $92; along with such unusual items as a papier maché silkworm (five feet long) and a snail (three and a half feet) that could be taken apart. The Animal Room had models of a mastodon as well as some of today's creatures; the Botanical Room featured forty-two giant dissectible flowers; and in the Anatomical Room were enlarged models of the human heart and human ear that also could be separated into sections. A Lecture Room with forty seats and lantern slide projector was presided over by the first curator, Dr. Richard Ellsworth Call, a trained and enthusiastic science teacher who arranged and labeled the exhibits and conducted the lectures. On the second floor of the building was a library, at first containing only 300 volumes on natural history, and the curator's office; and in a tower on the roof were meteorological instruments.[1]

## II

The Children's Museum began to expand as an educational instutution when Anna Billings Gallup joined the staff in May 1902 as assistant curator. She had been born on November 9, 1872, in Ledyard, Connecticut, the daughter of Christopher M. and Hannah Eliza (Lamb) Gallup, and took pride in being a maternal descendant of Elder William Brewster of the Plymouth Colony. After attending public school in Ledyard and the Norwich Free Academy, she enrolled in 1889 in the Connecticut State Normal School at New Britain, from which she was graduated four years later. She then taught biology for four years at the Hampton (Virginia) Normal and Agricultural Institute. She stopped teaching to enter the Massachusetts Institute of Technology, from which she received a Sc.B. degree in 1901. She then instructed in biology for another year at the Rhode Island State Normal School in Providence before coming to the Children's Museum. She was thirty years old, an imaginative, energetic, and persuasive science teacher.[2] Carolyn Spencer has given the following description of her:

> Behind all this activity stands a tall, dark-eyed, pleasant-faced woman, with a soft musical voice and a ready smile. Ever ready to give a helping hand to a boy or girl, to encourage, to cheer, and to stimulate interest, Miss Anna Billings Gallup is the guiding star of the Brooklyn Children's Museum.[3]

She at once began to give half-hour illustrated talks to children from second grade through grammar school on botanical subjects, such as "Little Fall Wanderers" (maple seeds and the like). But she soon started to learn how to use museum objects for instruction. She devised short labels in simple language and large, readable type and saw that the table desk museum cases were cut down to the right height for youngsters, with labels on hinged boards that hung from the cases so that the children could lift them to easy reading distance. She made a bird calendar, listing under each month birds to be found in the neighboring Prospect Park, and also did labels for plants and trees there. She mounted and labeled pressed plants for a herbarium, conducted meetings of the Nature Study and Humboldt clubs, and led walks in the parks. She liked to take her charges through the museum rooms, unlocking cases as they went along so that the children could handle objects and pet live animals.

Gallup said later that the museum was "in the van of progressive education" and

> in a word, the Children's Museum *way of learning things* is pure fun. This *way* is the magic key that opens one door of knowledge after another, it is the magic wand that gives each branch of learning a potential of joy, it is the magnet that draws the crowd, the engineer that keeps them busy with efficiency of action.[4]

The following summer, Gallup spent her vacation studying and collecting in the Marine Biological Laboratory in Bermuda as a member of a New York and Harvard University group, bringing back corals, lizards, sponges, fishes, mollusks, seaweeds, and a Great Surinam Toad. Her talks then concerned not only zoology but sounds, high and low tones, musical instruments, the human voice and ear, the barometer, air pressure, and frictional electricity. In 1904 she was promoted to curator, and Mary Day Lee, trained in physics and chemistry, became assistant curator. She guided some of the boys who were experimenting with astronomy and wireless telegraphy, and took a share in the lecture program. Agnes E. Bowen soon held a similar position for history.

The museum collection was expanding to include arts, technology, geography, and history. In 1903 Gallup had toured Europe for four months, visiting many museums; Dr. F. A. Brower, a curator of the British Museum and member of the editorial staff of the British Museums Association's *Museums Journal*, helped her plan the trip.[5] Upon her return, she added talks on the Alps, Russia, Italy, Holland, London, and Paris. The next year, she saw to it that her sixth graders studied the Andes, the Amazon, Argentina, Chile, Japan, China, and Korea, while the seventh graders considered San Francisco, Chicago, New Orleans, and Boston, and those in the eighth grade, pyramids, temples, statues, and sphynxes. Meanwhile, the younger students heard about warblers, hummingbirds, Baltimore orioles, and scarlet tanagers, or ants, hornets, spiders, and butterflies. She also gave practical talks such as "The Care of Aquariums" and called in a scientist to explain "How to Collect and Preserve Insects." She presented seasonal lectures that included "How Christmas Began and Is Celebrated in Other Lands," "Thanksgiving in the Colonies," and discussions of Lincoln and Washington on national holidays.

Gallup took great interest in the live animal collection. The toad was joined by "Bunny," which wandered in of its own accord; "Fluff," a tame owl; "King Cole," a crow; "General and Mrs. Green," frogs; "Petie" and "Dickie," two white rats; "Plato," a spider monkey from South America that observed its first anniversary at the museum with a feast of peanut brittle and malaga grapes; and numerous snakes and insects, as well as fish in the museum aquarium. Bees were kept in an observation hive and a colony of ants in a glass case. One boy had formed an astronomical group that used two telescopes on the roof. Some fifteen other boys built a wireless telegraph station to communicate with their homes and other operators within a hundred-mile radius, and eventually with Paris and Honolulu. Austin M. Curtis and Lloyd Espinchied were leaders of that group. The boys also replaced fuses, repaired apparatus, and installed a telephone system for the museum.

## III

Classroom teachers found that some of their pupils had begun to take deep interest in studying science and asked them where they had acquired their developing knowledge. One nine-year old answered quickly: "In the Children's Museum and I expect to become a great scientist."[6] The teachers started bringing their classes from kindergarten through high school to the museum; in 1906, for example, there were 561 class visits from 125 schools, and 17,351 students came to lectures. For 1910 the total yearly attendance was 187,612.

The museum furnished a docent, a young college graduate, to welcome all young visitors; find out the child's chief interest, whether birds, insects, minerals, or geography; and serve as guide with informal questions and oral tests as they proceeded. The docent sometimes used competitive museum games, distributing cards of graded questions to be answered by closely inspecting objects and their labels and doing research in the library; the youngster answering the most questions correctly in some twenty minutes would be declared the winner. Jigsaw puzzles were also at hand to be assembled. Eventually, the Brooklyn Board of Education assigned four regular teachers for full-time service at the museum. On weekends and holidays, students often spent the day there, eating lunch in the park nearby. Gallup was especially proud of the museum's after-school activities. They included a laboratory with minerals and experiments in physics and chemistry. In the "busy bee room," the younger children studied specimens under magnifying glasses and microscopes. Eight subject matter courses lasted several weeks and led to credits and engraved silver medals. The students pressed and labeled plants for their herbariums, classified minerals, and mounted insects. The after-school scholars formed ten clubs that dealt with bees, carpentry, crafts, junior and senior sciences, the LDH Guild (literature, dramatics, history), microscopes, photography, Pick and Hammer (woodworking tools), and stamps. There was a popular Children's Museum League, where the youngsters held discussions and gave lectures on nature subjects; they paid ten cents for a button and life membership. The museum also served as headquarters for Girl Scout and Boy Scout nature programs.[7] Gallup thought that after-school work

> attracts children to active pastime of the highest educational value. It challenges their minds with real things, subjects of beauty and great interest. . . . But best of all it develops the child's latent powers, gives him experiences that cause him to respect his own work, offers him standards of values and enters him into a consciousness of the worth of his own efforts.[8]

Several of the students who came to the museum regularly in later life showed good results from their devotion. One, after graduating from a university, saved the wheat crop of Indiana from a plague. Another became professor of plant breeding at Cornell University. Three of those who worked on the telegraph secured positions as operators an oceangoing steamships that journeyed to the South, Puerto Rico, and Europe. Of these, Austin Curtis secured a permanent position in South America, gathered an impressive collection of butterflies and moths in Brazil and Argentina, which he presented to the museum, and sent it the spider monkey "Plato" from Colombia, while Lloyd Espenschied was a prominent researcher for radio systems, and his son, Lloyd, Jr., came to the museum frequently.[9]

Gallup was actually the executive head of the museum from the time she became curator, though it was under the supervision of the Brooklyn Institute of Arts and Sciences and its director. After about twenty-two years of service, she seems to have become curator-in-chief at her own suggestion. The story goes that one of her budget requests had been turned down by a city board, and to soften the blow, those in charge said that she might have the one thing she wanted most, whereupon she chose the title, curator-in-chief. It remained in use at the museum for more than forty years but was finally changed to director when the Children's Museum became independent and had its own board, long after Gallup's retirement.[10]

Through the years the museum was always expanding its facilities and activities. The lecture room was enlarged to 100 seats and received improved slide and motion picture projectors. Educational films were shown daily except on the crowded Sundays and holidays. The library occupied several rooms and contained 8,000 volumes. The astronomy section added a planetarium to its telescopes on the roof. Disabled children were welcomed and taken on "please touch" tours. The history rooms procured models such as Henry Hudson's "Half Moon" and Robert Fulton's "Clermont," as well as dioramas of political and military historical events, doll houses, and dolls dressed in the costumes of many nations. A journal was started and enlarged to include news of the Brooklyn Institute; it went to the schools, libraries, and museums of the city. A loan collection of some 5,000 items with stuffed birds, butterflies, minerals, costumed dolls, and 30,000 mounted pictures was distributed by its own truck to schools, libraries, churches, clubs, and other community groups. Individual children could take home for study birds, insects, and many specimens carefully mounted in boxes. By 1929 the loan service was making one million contacts each year. Prize contests on birds, trees, history, minerals, and aquatic life were held; in 1917 they attracted entries from eighty children in thirty schools. A year later, the museum began participating in an Americanization program that helped immigrant families become American citizens.[11]

## IV

Gallup did her part in arousing interest and sometimes obtaining financial support for the museum. She spoke to mothers' clubs in Brooklyn; the New York State Science Teachers meeting at Cornell University; the Alumni Association of M.I.T. at Boston; 1,000 public school teachers, principals, and superintendents at five Teachers' Institutes; the State Library Association; and scores of other groups. She worried about funds for the museum, for the city paid only salaries and limited running expenses. She pointed out again and again the need for a larger lecture room; though its capacity had been expanded it was still much too small. In 1919 she gave her talk on Lincoln six times to a total of 721 children, while Lee repeated hers on Washington seven times to 973 students. The children endured long waiting lines and often could not get into the lecture room. One principal called to complain that twenty of his students had to miss a presentation. Gallup was disappointed several times, as in 1915 when the city failed to provide a new fireproof building with an auditorium to seat at least 500.[12]

Gallup made a great step forward in 1916 when she enlisted Helen Butterfield (Mrs. John J.) Schoonhoven in forming the Women's Auxiliary of the Children's Museum. Schoonhoven asserted then: "Our quest is for an intelligent understanding of a great objective, and a constant adherence to an enduring idea in education." The auxiliary gave tea parties for teachers and principals; sponsored an annual bridge tournament that included such luminaries as Edna St. Vincent Millay and Hendrik van Loon; and raised money in other ingenious ways. It brought many new programs into action. Schoonhoven built a strong organization of 2,500 able and active women—headed by Ida Willets (Mrs. I. Sherwood) Coffin as president—and a strong, forceful Executive Board. Membership, social aid and Americanization committees and a thriving speakers' bureau were soon consolidated into an Education Committee of fifteen members. The auxiliary persuaded women's clubs, civic groups, school executives and teachers, and many individual donors to finance its activities. In 1917 various community women's clubs began purchasing ten models or dioramas created by Dwight Franklin for the geography room. They included Eskimos harpooning a whale; Lapps encamped beside their reindeer herd; penguins, seals, and gulls in the desolate, frigid Antarctic; an aboriginal Australian kangaroo hunt; Carib Indians stalking monkeys in Brazil; Bedouins with their camels at an oasis in the Sahara; and Masai attacking a lion invader of their village in British East Africa. Later, twenty-five dioramas added to the world history room included several models of the pursuits of primitive man, Phoenician traders, Marco Polo, the Magna Carta, Prince Henry the Navigator, Columbus, Gutenberg, George Washington, and the Wright Brothers operating their flying machine at Kitty Hawk. The public schoolteachers of New York City raised money for another group of thirty diaramas, many of them chosen by Professor Dixon Ryan Fox of the History Department of Columbia University; they soon began appearing in the American history room.[13]

The auxiliary gave the museum $10,000 in 1920 for a Franklin W. Hooper Loan Collection Fund to honor his role in founding the first children's museum, and on that occasion Gallup spoke of the museum "as an open door for children to a knowledge of the wonderful things of the world." Other contributions helped finance a part-time science curator, numerous summer field trips (as many as thirty-six one year), the film library, and a car to transport museum lecturers to the schools, as well as helping build an endowment fund, which in 1930 reached $12,000.[14]

One of the most important services of the auxiliary was persuading the city to spend nearly $500,000 to purchase a neighboring lot and modernize its Victorian house so as to help the museum meet its pressing space needs. The new building contained the enlarged library, a more spacious auditorium, the loan collection, and rooms for general community meetings and for the Boy Scouts. An auxiliary member soon contributed $8,000 for an elevator to serve the three-story structure.[15]

On June 4, 1929, the Women's Auxiliary carried out a notable observance of its annual Children's Day. Eleanor (Mrs. Franklin D.) Roosevelt, then the First Lady of the State of New York, met with some 500 children in Bedford Park, they carrying balloons in various bright colors inscribed, "Visit the Brooklyn Children's Museum." She then spoke to the auxiliary members in the newly acquired neighboring building and expressed her deep admiration of the museum's work. It was one of the auxiliary's red-letter days.[16]

In her thirty-five years of service, Gallup made the Brooklyn Children's Museum into a potent educational force. She successfully opposed a plan to move the museum to the Brooklyn Institute's main building, insisting that the children must feel their institution belonged only to them. She summed up her conviction on this point thus:

> A museum can do the greatest good and furnish the most effective help to the boys and girls who love it as an institution, who take pride in its work for them and with them, and who delight in their association with it. To inspire children with this love and pride in the institution, they must feel that it is created, and now exists for them, and that in all of its plans it puts the child first. The child must feel that the whole plant is for him, that the best is offered to him because of faith in his power to use it, that he has access to all departments, and that he is always a welcome visitor, and never an intruder.[17]

In another place she said: "Knowledge itself all children love. It is the labor of organizing knowledge that they find distasteful. Inject happiness into the process of learning and you turn the child's work into educational play." And Gallup had a basic principle on how to arrange effective exhibits and activities.

It was simply: "Follow the child around." Thus she insisted that, at the museum, "No new program was accepted until the children had pronounced it full of promise." This emphasis caused one youngster to advise an adult friend: "Perhaps if you have a child with you, you can get into the lecture room."[18]

Gallup, always a magnetic speaker, passionately promoted children's museums and outlined "How Any Town Can Get One." Educators in a community first should secure trustees and a salary for a carefully chosen director and find an unused suitable space in the town. Children then would pour in, be delighted, bring their parents, and obtain the support and pride of the grown-up community. The success of the Brooklyn institution caused several other museums to begin working with children—the Children's Room at the Smithsonian Institution, the American Museum of Natural History, the National Museum of Wales in Cardiff, and others in St. Johnsbury (Vermont), Stepney Borough in London, Milwaukee, Charleston, San Francisco, Cleveland, Berlin, Australia, and New Zealand. Other such American museums (twenty-two of them by the 1930s) sprang up in Boston, Detroit, Indianapolis (now the largest in the world), Fort Worth, Corpus Christi, Little Rock, Jacksonville, Portland (Oregon), Seattle, and Troy in Rensselaer County, New York. Much later, in the 1980s, an Association of Youth Museums was organized, which soon had more than 200 members.[19]

By the time Gallup retired in 1937, the Children's Museum's yearly attendance had reached 600,000. She was known throughout the nation and abroad. A charter member present at the formation of the American Association of Museums in 1906, she regularly attended and often spoke at its annual meetings. In 1937 she persuaded that body to establish a Children's Museum Section; often Schoonhoven and a delegation of auxiliary members accompanied Gallup to its meetings. As early as 1909, the Hudson-Fulton Celebration had given her an award, and in 1930 the National Institute of Social Sciences presented its gold medal in recognition of "her distinguished service to humanity as curator-in-chief for more than a quarter century." The British *Museums Journal*, which always followed her career closely, recorded her deeply felt thanks to the institute, especially for its "public recognition of a life-giving idea" and her hope that it would "send Children's Museum service to higher levels and extend it to widening circles of children." The *Journal* commented that "our readers will rejoice in this honor bestowed on one who has been an inspiration and example to the whole museum world."[20]

Museum workers from all over America came to see Gallup and the Children's Museum, many of them hoping to establish one of their own. Museum studies courses also visited; Laura M. Bragg of the Charleston Museum brought the class she was teaching at Columbia University, and the apprentices from the Newark Museum's training program came twice. Museum people of foreign countries corresponded and often appeared at the museum from Brazil, Colombia, India, Australia, New Zealand, and elsewhere.[21] In 1955, the year before her death, she received the William Hornaday Memorial award for service and leadership in the junior museum field. That same year, she was invited to attend the Indianapolis Children's Museum's thirtieth birthday party. She did not feel up to making the journey but sent her regrets, saying: "I am glad our children's museums are creeping up into big money. It took many years for human thought to realize what we were talking about when we wanted for the country a new kind of museum."[22]

The Brooklyn Children's Museum has continued along the path that Gallup outlined and still provides vigorous leadership in its field. In 1969 its two old Victorian mansions could no longer meet city housing standards and had to be razed. The museum moved to a new location temporarily in a former poolhall and automobile showroom in Crown Heights and became known as "MUSE." Its varied and exciting programs continued to attract enthusiastic youngsters for twelve hours a day. In 1976 under Lloyd Hezekiah, a Trinidad-born but Brooklyn-educated director, the Children's Museum left MUSE, which continued as a neighborhood African-American museum, and returned to its former site in Bedford Park but to a new, innovative $3.5-million building. The structure lies forty feet underground with the entrance at the top through a former subway kiosk. A "people tube" runs 180 feet through the hill with a flowing stream in the center. Its auditorium seats 250. Major exhibits have concerned *The Mystery of Things,* their shape, form, color, and material; *Night Journeys,* an exploration of sleep and dreams; *Animals Eat,* which examines their food chain and environmental habitat; *The Boneyard,* containing human and animal skeletons; *Under Your Feet,* on geology and animal and insect life underground; and *Collection Connections in the Children's Resource Library.* The last exhibit allows children to conduct individual investigations using not only reading, audio-visual materials, and computers, but also object study boxes that include coins and butterflies, or deal with such topics as Plains Indians, Africa, and Jewish traditions.[23] Anna Billings Gallup surely would have rejoiced to see her dream of a new building so ingeniously carried out and put to such imaginative uses.

## NOTES

1. The direct quotations are found in "The Children's Museum of the Brooklyn Institute," *Scientific American* 82 (May 12, 1900): 296–97. Other accounts of the museum are Peter Farb, "An Island of Nature," *National Parent-Teacher* 54 (Apr. 1960): 10–12; Anna Billings Gallup, "A Children's Museum and How Any Town Can Get One," National Education Association *Addresses and Proceedings* 64 (1926): 951–53; Gallup, Address Before the Congressional Club, Washington, D.C., Feb. 7, 1930; Gallup, Radio Broadcast on Children's Museums, Education and Fun, Brooklyn Children's Museum, Oct. 20, 1937 (transcript); Gallup, "A Museum for Children," National Institute of Social Sciences *Journal* 3 (1917): 107–09; William Henry Goodyear to Franklin W. Hooper, Jan. 17, 1899, Brooklyn Children's Museum MSS.; Herbert and Marjorie Katz, *Museums U.S.A.: A History and Guide* (Garden City, N.Y.: Doubleday, 1963), 209–12; Philip Mershon, *The Brooklyn Children's Museum: The Story of a Pioneer* (Brooklyn: Brooklyn Children's Museum, 1959); Gabrielle V. Pohle, "The Children's Museum as Collector," *Museum News* 85 (Nov./Dec. 1979): 32–37; Smithsonian Institution, *Women's Changing Roles in Museums: Conference Proceedings* (Washington: Smithsonian Institution, 1986), especially Melinda Young Frye, "Women Pioneers in the Public Museum Movement," 11–17, and Jean M. Weber, "Images of Women in Museums," 20–26.

2. *American Women: The Official Who's Who among the Women of the Nation* (Los Angeles: Richard Blank, 1935), 1; Mershon, *Children's Museum*, 4; *Who Was Who in America* (Chicago: A. N. Marquis, 1935), 3: 310; *Who's Who in America* (Chicago, A. N. Marquis, 1940), 1: 21; *Who's Who in the East* (Washington: Mayflower, 1930), 797–98; Barbara Fletcher Zucker, *Children's Museums, Zoos, and Discovery Rooms: An International Reference Guide* (New York: Greenwood, 1987), 153–56.

3. Carolyn Spencer, "Miss Gallup, Curator of Children's Museum, Introduces Youngsters to Wonders of Nature," unidentified, undated newspaper clipping, Brooklyn Children's Museum Scrapbook.

4. Gallup, Radio Broadcast, 1937, p. 1.

5. The periodical reports of the Children's Museum during Miss Gallup's service are found in *Children's Museum Bulletin* 1–18 (Oct. 1902–Mar. 1904); *Children's Museum News* 1–8 (Apr. 1904–Mar. 1905); *Museum News* (Apr. 1905–May 1913); *Children's Museum News*, vols. 1–24 (Oct. 1913–May 1937). This footnote covers *Children's Museum News* 12 (Oct. 1924): 136.

6. Gallup, Radio Broadcast, 1937, p. 1; *Children's Museum News* 10 (Feb. 1923): 37.

7. "A Children's Museum," *Scientific American* 112 (Mar. 13, 1915): 250; Laurence Vail Coleman, *The Museum In America: A Critical Study*, 3 vols. (Washington: American Association of Museums, 1939), 2: 253; Miriam S. Draper, "The Children's Museum in Brooklyn," *Library Journal* 35 (Apr. 1910): 154; Anna Billings Gallup, "The Children's Museum as Educator," *Popular Science Monthly* 72 (Apr. 1908): 371–79; Gallup, Congressional Club, 1930, pp. 3, 6; Gallup, "A Museum for Children," 109; Catharine Kneeland, "Museum for Children," *Hygeia* 17 (Aug. 1939): 743; Mershon, *Children's Museum*, 3, 8; *Museums Journal* 30 (Aug. 1930): 65; (June 1931): 291; Sydney Reid, "Children's Wonder House," *Independent* 72 (Jan. 4, 1912): 30–36.

8. Brooklyn Institute *Museum News* 3 (Oct. 1907): 13; 5 (Jan. 1910): 55–57; (May 1910): 119; Anna B. Gallup, "Brooklyn Children's Museum," *School and Society* 32 (Dec. 27, 1930): 865–66.

9. *Children's Museum News* 10 (Feb. 1923): 37; 12 (Oct. 1924): 121; Draper, "Children's Museum," 153–54; Gallup, "A Children's Musuem," 952–53; Gallup, "Children's Museum as Educator," 371–79.

10. Mershon, *Children's Museum*, 4, 9.

11. Brooklyn Institute *Museum News* 2 (Feb. 1907): 84–85; 3 (Feb. 1908): 88; 4 (Feb. 1917): 102–03; 5 (Oct. 1917); 6 (Jan. 1918): 30; 7 (Feb. 1920): 25–29; *Children's Museum News* 10 (Feb. 1923): 37; 12 (Oct. 1924): 121; Rose Mary Daly, "Films for Fledglings," *Saturday Review of Literature* 32 (Nov. 19, 1949): 58; Draper, "Children's Museum," 153–54; Gallup, Congressional Club, 1930, p. 5; Gallup, "Brooklyn Children's Museum," 865–66; Katz and Katz, *Museums U.S.A.*, 210–11; Mershon, *Children's Museum*, 4, 9–10; "Museums and Visual Instruction: World History Series of Models," *Elementary School Journal* 30 (June 1930): 722; Zucker, *Children's Museums*, 151–56.

12. Auxiliary of Brooklyn Children's Museum, *25th Anniversary* (Brooklyn, 1941), 16 pp.; "Brooklyn Children's Museum Proposed New Building," *School and Society* 41 (Feb. 16, 1935): 226; Brooklyn Institute *Museum News* 3 (Feb. 1908): 89; 4 (Oct. 1916): 71; (Dec. 1916): 88; 5 (Feb./Mar. 1918): 36–38; 7 (Feb. 1920): 18–20; Draper, "Children's Museum," 153; Anna B. Gallup, "The Work of the Children's Museum," American Association of Museums *Proceedings* 1 (1907): 144–47; Gallup, Congressional Club, 1930, p. 5; Mershon, *Children's Museum*, 7–8; "Museums and Visual Instruction," 722; *Museums Journal* 14 (May 1915): 357–58; New York *Times*, Dec. 4, 1939, 201; Reid, "Children's Museum House," 35–36.

13. *Children's Museum News* 11 (Mar. 1924): 100; 14 (Oct./Dec. 1928): 66–68; 18 (Oct. 1930): 6; 20 (Jan. 1933): 29, (Mar. 1933): 36; 21 (Apr. 1934): 11, 24; 22 (Mar. 1935): 1–7.

14. *Children's Museum News* 7 (Feb. 1920): 18–20; 18 (Feb. 1931): 38.

15. Brooklyn Children's Museum, *The Geographical Models* (Brooklyn, 1917), 16 pp.; Children's Museum Auxiliary, *25th Anniversary*, 16 pp.; *Children's Museum News* 11 (Feb./Mar. 1924): 98; 12 (Oct. 1924): 124–25; (Oct./Dec. 1928): 70; 18 (Nov. 1930): 12; Mershon, *Children's Museum*, p. 10.

16. *Children's Museum News* 17 (Oct. 1929): 77.

17. Gallup, "A Children's Museum," p. 951.

18. Anna Billings Gallup, "Memories and Satisfactions," *Children's Museum News* 27 (Dec. 1939/Jan. 1940); Eleanor M. Moore, *Youth in Museums* (Philadelphia, University of Pennsylvania Press, 1941), 8, 51–54, 56.

19. Draper, "Children's Museum," 150; Gallup, "A Children's Museum," 953; Gallup, "Children's Museum as Educator," 379; "Growth of Children's Museums," *Hobbies* 53 (Mar. 1948): 26; Sherwood Davidson Kohn, "It's OK to Touch at the New-Style Hands-on Exhibits," *Smithsonian* 9 (Sep. 1978): 81–83; Kneeland, "Museums for Children," 743; Nancy Kriplen, *Keep an Eye on That Mummy: A History of the Children's Museum of Indianapolis* (Indianapolis: The Museum, 1982); Pohle, "Children's Museum as Collector," 32–37; Reid, "The Children's Wonder House," 36; "Youth Museums Number," *History News* 44 (Nov./Dec. 1989).

20. Children's Museum News 10 (May 1923): 61–63; 12 (Oct. 1924): 121; 13 (Oct. 1925), 294; 14 (Oct. 1926): 4; 16 (Oct. 1930); 18 (Apr. 1931): 54; 24 (May 1937); Frye, "Women Pioneers," 13–15; Mershon, *Children's Museum*, 10; *Museums Journal* 30 (July 1930): 25; *Who Was Who*, 3: 310.

21. *Children's Museum News* 7 (Oct. 1919): 6, (Nov. 1919): 12; 10 (Nov./Dec. 1922): 16, (Feb. 1923): 37; 13 (Mar./Apr. 1926): 229; 14 (Oct. 1926): 4, (Feb./Mar. 1927): 36.

22. Gallup, "Children's Museums," 951–53; Kriplen, *Keep an Eye on That Mummy*, 94.

23. Ellen Perry Berkeley, "MUSE: Bedford-Lincoln Neighborhood Museum, Brooklyn," *Architectural Forum* 129 (Sep. 1968); Kohn, "It's OK to Touch," 81–83; Pohle, "Children's Museum as Collector," 32–37; Zucker, *Children's Museums*, 152–53. Ms. Nancy Paine, the Children's Museum's Curator of Collections, kindly has supplied the up-to-date information in addition to reading and making helpful suggestions on this chapter.

## SELECT BIBLIOGRAPHY


Auxiliary of Brooklyn Children's Museum. *25th Anniversary*. Brooklyn, 1941.

Berkeley, Ellen Perry. "MUSE: Bedford-Lincoln Neighborhood Museum, Brooklyn." *Architectural Forum* 129 (Sep. 1968).

Brooklyn Children's Museum. *The Geographical Models*. Brooklyn, 1917.

"Brooklyn Children's Museum Proposed New Building." *School and Society* 41 (Feb. 16, 1935): 226.

"A Children's Museum." *Scientific American* 112 (Mar. 13, 1915): 250.

*Children's Museum Bulletin*. Vols. 1–18 (Oct. 1902–Mar. 1904).

*Children's Museum News*. Vols. 1–24 (Oct. 1913–May 1937).

"The Children's Museum of the Brooklyn Institute." *Scientific American* 82 (May 12, 1900): 296–97.

Coleman, Laurence Vail. *The Museum In America: A Critical Study*. 3 vols. Washington: American Association of Museums, 1939.

Daly, Rose Mary. "Films for Fledglings." *Saturday Review of Literature* 32 (Nov. 19, 1949): 58.

Draper, Miriam S. "The Children's Museum in Brooklyn." *Library Journal* 35 (Apr. 1910): 154.

Farb, Peter. "An Island of Nature." *National Parent-Teacher* 54 (Apr. 1960): 10–12.

Gallup, Anna Billings. "A Children's Museum and How Any Town Can Get One." National Education Association *Addresses and Proceedings* 64 (1926): 951–53.

_____. Address Before the Congressional Club, Washington, D.C., Feb. 7, 1930.

_____. "Brooklyn Children's Museum." *School and Society* 32 (Dec. 27, 1930): 865–66.

_____. "The Children's Museum as Educator." *Popular Science Monthly* 72 (Apr. 1908): 371–79.

_____. "A Museum for Children." National Institute of Social Sciences *Journal* 3 (1917): 107–09.

_____. Radio Broadcast on Children's Museums, Education and Fun, Brooklyn Children's Museum, Oct. 20, 1937 (transcript).

_____. "The Work of the Children's Museum." American Association of Museums *Proceedings* 1 (1907): 144–47.

Goodyear, William Henry, to Franklin W. Hooper, Jan. 17, 1899. Brooklyn Children's Museum MSS.

"Growth of Children's Museums." *Hobbies* 53 (Mar. 1948): 26.

Katz, Herbert and Marjorie. *Museums U.S.A.: A History and Guide*. Garden City, N.Y.: Doubleday, 1963.

Kneeland, Catharine. "Museum for Children." *Hygeia* 17 (Aug. 1939): 743.

Kohn, Sherwood Davidson. "It's OK to Touch at the New-Style Hands-on Exhibits." *Smithsonian* 9 (Sep. 1978): 81–83.

Kriplen, Nancy. *Keep an Eye on That Mummy: A History of the Children's Museum of Indianapolis*. Indianapolis: The Museum, 1982.

Mershon, Philip. *The Brooklyn Children's Museum: The Story of a Pioneer*. Brooklyn: Brooklyn Children's Museum, 1959.

Moore, Eleanor M. *Youth in Museums*. Philadelphia, University of Pennsylvania Press, 1941.

"Museums and Visual Instruction: World History Series of Models." *Elementary School Journal* 30 (June 1930): 722.

Pohle, Gabrielle V. "The Children's Museum as Collector." *Museum News* 85 (Nov./Dec. 1979): 32–37.

Reid, Sydney. "Children's Wonder House." *Independent* 72 (Jan. 4, 1912): 30–36.

Smithsonian Institution. *Women's Changing Roles in Museums: Conference Proceedings*. Washington: Smithsonian Institution, 1986.

Zucker, Barbara Fletcher. *Children's Museums, Zoos, and Discovery Rooms: An International Reference Guide*. New York: Greenwood, 1987.

# CHAPTER 9

# John Robert Kinard *Expands the Neighborhood Museum*

## I

"THIS PLACE," SAID JOHN R. KINARD, the director of the Anacostia Neighborhood Museum in Washington, D.C., "has brought people who wouldn't otherwise be caught dead in a museum." Its exhibitions often might be based on "requests found in the suggestion box, giving local residents a real feeling of 'this is our place'." At the museum, neighbors could "meet to discuss local problems and try to find ways of improving them," and its exhibits and programs expressed every aspect of the Anacostia experience—psychological, spiritual, social, and political. Thus such a museum could meet the practical needs of its community, while attracting a significant number of neighborhood people at all levels.[1] And finally, Kinard asserted, such a museum should concern the common people:

> Our country and its museums have scandalously never told us the truth about Western society. Because presentations were written about the middle-class white Americans by middle-class white Americans who study and write about what interests them, their presentations on our society represent the life of celebration, of achievement and conquest. This is not of interest to most Americans, for our lives are lived striving to achieve self-identity, and to make something out of everyday life.[2]

The Anacostia Neighborhood Museum was the result of a dream of Dr. S. Dillon Ripley, the always innovative secretary of the Smithsonian Institution. In

1966 he began considering the establishment of an experimental community "storefront" or neighborhood museum as a branch of the Smithsonian. A group of citizens known as the Greater Anacostia Peoples, Inc., in a predominantly black area of Washington east of the Anacostia River with a population of some 257,000, persuaded the Smithsonian to establish the branch in Anacostia. More than ninety local citizens met as a Neighborhood Advisory Committee, and the Smithsonian sent Charles Blitzer, then director of its office of Education and Training, and Mrs. Caryl Marsh, a consultant to the city's Recreation and Parks Department who had worked on neighborhood social problems, to help them as well as technicians to convert the run-down, abandoned Carver movie theatre on a main street, Nichols (now Martin Luther King, Jr.) Avenue, into a museum. A committee consisting of Stanley J. Anderson, Almore M. Dale, Mrs. Marian Conover Hope, and Alton Jones were leaders in the movement.[3]

Mrs. Hope, seeking a director for the new museum, had John R. Kinard, a friend of her son's, go to see Blitzer, who was impressed by that vigorous and decisive thirty-year-old black community worker. Blitzer sent him to Dillon Ripley who surprised him with the greeting, "Thanks for taking the job." Kinard knew nothing about museums, but he later recalled: "I thought what the hell. Everybody ought to take a leap once in their lives—just jump and not know where they'll land."[4]

On September 15, 1967, the Anacostia Neighborhood Museum staged a gala opening attended by about four thousand community citizens and residents of the entire metropolitan area, featuring an 84-piece band, two jazz combos, and an enthusiastic block party with energetic youngsters and adults serving refreshments. Exhibits borrowed from the Smithsonian's National Museum of Natural History, National Museum of American History, and National Zoo included an 1895 store of early Anacostia with a post office; metal toys, butter churn, ice cream maker, coffee grinder, and water pump; as well as live monkeys, a large green parrot, other birds, and a black snake. A group of young local artists known as the Trail Blazers painted a mural of primitive life in Africa on a nearby fence, and the lot across from the museum contained a dinosaur, Uncle Beasley, on which children delighted to climb. A projector with slides was available in the museum, and show boxes of small natural history exhibits with bird and animal skins, shells, and fossils could be examined. The community accepted the new institution as its own and maintained it carefully. No unpleasantness took place there during the Washington race riots of that period, and no losses occurred from vandalism. The museum was estimated to cost $125,000–150,000 per year, covered at first by Smithsonian private funds and foundation grants. When that figure proved too small, the local community raised $7,000 to match a grant, with indivudual contributions ranging from five cents to one dollar. A local businessman also provided a bus to take children downtown to the Smithsonian for Saturday morning classes.

## II

John Robert Edward Kinard was born in Washington on November 22, 1936, the son of Robert Francis and Jessie Beulah (Covington) Kinard. After graduation from Springarn High School in 1955 and a year and a half at Howard University, he went to Salisbury, North Carolina, studying history and graduating there with a B.A. degree from Livingstone College in 1960 and a Bachelor of Divinity degree from Hood Theological Seminary in 1963. While in college, he spent one summer in Tanzania with Operation Crossroads Africa helping build a dining room and dormitory for students. Upon the urging of Dr. James Robinson, founder of Crossroads, Kinard returned to Africa as a paid staff member with American and Canadian volunteers, working with local students in Tanzania, Kenya, and Zanzibar on self-help programs, and he was made coordinator of all Crossroads projects from Cairo to Zimbabwe. In 1964 he came back to Washington, serving as a counselor of the Neighborhood Youth Corps, organizer with the Southeast Neighborhood House, and analyst of social programs in counties on the Eastern Shore of Maryland.

On November 14, 1964, Kinard was married to Marjorie Anne Williams, who had been a classmate at Livingstone, and the couple went on to have three daughters—Sarah, Joy, and Hope. In 1966 he became assistant pastor of the John Wesley African Methodist Episcopal Zion Church in northwest Washington. He served on many local educational and cultural boards and committees that included the Washington Performing Arts Society and the Corcoran Museum of Art. The *Washington Magazine* in 1974 selected him as a "Washingtonian of the Year."[5] Tragically, John R. Kinard died at age fifty-two on August 5, 1989, after a lengthy illness of myelofibrosis, a disease of the bone marrow. As Dr. Robert McC. Adams, then the Smithsonian head, put it, Kinard was "the founding director and guiding light of the Anacostia Neighborhood Museum . . . one is tempted to say *his* museum" for twenty-two years. And, according to the British expert Kenneth Hudson, he "developed the Anacostia Museum into one of the small number of museums of influence in the world."[6]

## III

The chief teaching device of the Anacostia Neighborhood Museum was the special exhibition. An early one prepared in conjunction with the Museum's Youth Advisory Council of about twenty teenagers and with the assistance of Smithsonian curators and exhibition experts was devoted to *This Thing Called Jazz*; it was accompanied by lectures and discussions, jazz performances, and gospel singing. Another show on *Frederick Douglass, the Sage of Anacostia, 1817?–1895* portrayed that pioneer black leader and his world; it was sent about the United States by the Smithsonian Institution Traveling Exhibit Service (SITES). The Junior League of Washington gave the museum a grant that established a Mobile Division with a bright blue van, serviced by an educator, which carried somewhat abbreviated exhibitions, speakers, learning kits, and books to schools, libraries, playgrounds, churches, hospitals, and other community organizations. Outstanding shows treated *Black Patriots of the American Revolution* with 7,000 booklets on the subject sent to the schools; *Toward Freedom: The Civil Rights Movement since 1954*; and the fascinating *Lorton Reformatory: Beyond Time*, presented with the active involvement of inmates at that correctional institution and including an original play and concerts by its band and gospel choir. Perhaps most sensational of all was *The Rat: Man's Invited Affliction* with live rats running about in one showcase and much advice to the viewers on how to rid their homes of that pest. The exhibition traveled on to the Buffalo Science Museum, where it was equally successful. These are a few examples of the more than thirty-five major exhibitions presented in the first eight years of the museum's existence.[7]

The displays continued throughout Kinard's administration. Some later ones included *Blacks in the Westward Movement* (five copies distributed in thirty states by SITES); *Black Women: Achievement Against the Odds*; *The Anacostia Story: 1608–1930*; *Out of Africa: From West African Kingdoms to Colonization*; *Portraits in Black: Outstanding Negroes of American Origin*; *The Renaissance: Black Arts of the 20s*; *Black Wings: The American Black in Aviation* (borrowed from the Smithsonian's Air and Space Museum and redesigned); *The Real McCoy: Afro-American Invention and Innovation, 1619–1930*; and *Climbing Jacob's Ladder: The Rise of the Black Church in Eastern American Cities, 1740–1877*.[8]

These exhibitions attracted heavy attendance from the Washington area; visitors also came from all over the country and from abroad to see them and to consult with Kinard. Numerous smaller educational programs made the museum a bustling community center, for Kinard regarded his charge as a combination museum, cultural arts center, meeting place for neighborhood groups, and skill training center for youngsters. Education chief Zora B. Martin, later Zora Martin-Felton, worked with Kinard and the museum from its beginning; she conceived and developed a successful grant proposal for the Mobile Division and conceptualized and served as curator for the rat exhibit. She early recruited a black Santa Claus at Christmastime and with a community committee developed a kit for the African-American Kwanzaa Celebration. An Annual Festival of the Arts in Anacostia produced skits, plays, concerts, and dance programs. Other yearly exhibits displayed paintings and sculptures by the District of Columbia Art Association or featured student art shows.

A local opinion poll showed that citizens thought the neighborhood's chief problems were crime, drugs, housing, unemployment, and education, and the museum staged exhibits and programs focusing on those issues. Do-it-yourself corners were set up for the plastic arts and other crafts. An exhibit design and production laboratory sought to train Anacostia young people for museum work; in 1976 it accepted 10 trainees, chosen from 100 applicants. A Children's Room in the exhibit area provided an opportunity to develop experimental programs and offered demonstrations in making soap, butter, ice cream, taffy, and candles. Puppet theaters accompanied some exhibitions. The community helped send three Youth Advisory Council members to Africa and others to Puerto Rico, the Bahamas, and Haiti.[9]

The last exhibition in the renovated movie theater took place in 1985–1986, and early the next year the museum moved to Fort Stanton Park, where the Design and Production Department had had quarters since 1976. The new site also contained an exhibition hall, multipurpose room, and office space, while the wooded park outside had picnic tables and benches. At the age of twenty, the Anacostia Neighborhood Museum changed its name and became simply the Anacostia Museum. It had evolved from a strictly local institution to a museum recognized nationally and internationally for its treatment of African-American history, art, and culture as well as for its strong civil rights advocacy. It continued to attract heavy community participation with Lunch Bag Forums of lectures, concerts, and dramatic presentations, as well as a popular Family Day. Special events also helped interpret its exhibitions; for example, a four-day workshop instructed teachers on the history of the black church, and a seminar on "Conservation for the Lay Person" drew church historians, archivists, and others. A computerized inventory of the permanent collections was also completed.[10]

## IV

Kinard's experience at Anacostia gave him many definite ideas about museums. First of all, he was sure that the old kind of museum with its emphasis on collection, conservation, research, and even interpretation and display was not enough. Instead, a museum always should stress social change and public service; its exhibits and educational programs ought to enable a community better to understand and work toward solving its current problems. A museum must not be a place for the entombment of relics, but rather, as Neil Harris had said, should be devoted to "reaching a large lay audience, capturing its attention, increasing its knowledge, and shaping its sense of possibility."[11] In a speech to the International Council of Museums (ICOM), Kinard stated that a museum should deal with "the everyday life of everyday men and women," instead of with "the rich and princely playthings and the best of the past."[12]

He was never satisfied with the accomplishments of the Anacostia Museum; so much remained to be done. Museums ought to understand the needs, problems, and inspirations of those who did not visit them. Kinard told the Museum Educators of the American Association of Museums (AAM) in 1977:

> We have left undone the greatest portion of our public responsibility, and that is to evaluate ourselves against those who don't visit museums. For that testimony—provocative, sobering and critical—may be what we need to make our finest contribution to the times of which we are a part, and the future.[13]

This point of view was emphasized in the museum's "Revised Mission Statement" of 1981 which ran:

> The Anacostia Neighborhood Museum should continue to be a neighborhood institution which, while it may focus especially upon the history and culture of Anacostia as a local community and collect objects related to that focus, shall above all be a center for experimentation in the ways museums can reach and involve segments of the population they are not reaching.[14]

Kinard was somewhat unhappy about part of this statement which had emanated from a committee Secretary Ripley had appointed to study the museum. He felt that the wording tended to limit the museum too much to the neighborhood when, in actuality, it was already reaching a national and international audience with its emphasis on the African-American heritage and the whole field of civil rights. Different exhibitions were devoted to those subjects throughout the years, such as *This is Africa*; *Africa: Three Out of Many:—Ethiopia, Ghana, Nigeria*; and others. Such programs had made the museum evolve from a strictly local institution, and they were often dramatized by participatory special events; for example, *An Afternoon of Ghanaian Culture* included drumming, dancing, a fashion display of African clothing, and an "African Food Fair", as well as the usual lectures, films, and teacher seminars.[15]

Kinard showed his unwavering faith in the broader aspects of the museum's work in his Foreword to Louise Daniel Hutchinson's *Out of Africa: From West African Kingdoms to Colonization* (1979):

> For out of Africa and cascading down the corridors of time have come earthshaking ideas, beautiful things, resources, riches, and people. Collectively, they have made wealthy all nations of the earth, for centuries past, and until this very day. If in fact the protest marches, freedom rides, sit-ins, kneel-ins, and pray-ins of the 1960s are to be more than a shallow victory, the black American must understand his history and heritage if he is to reshape his future. . . . As Arthur Schomburg has noted: "For the African American, a group tradition must provide compensation for prejudice. History must store what slavery took away. For it is the special damage of slavery that the present generation must repair."[16]

Kinard's fertile ideas, charismatic personality, and hard, slogging work were much appreciated by his associates. Zora Martin-Felton, who had worked so closely with him since the opening of the museum, said that "John did whatever he had to at the museum, from creating exhibitions to running the vacuum cleaner. He has touched all our lives in a profound manner."[17] Adolphus Ealey, curator of the Barnett-Aden Gallery, thanked Kinard for his concern and assistance with an exhibition on that art museum and described him as "this friend and man of all seasons."[18] Louise Hutchinson, who wrote a history of Anacostia, admired "the constant support and encouragement of one man who continues to open doors and provide opportunities for the growth and development of his staff."[19] And Ralph Burgand, director of New York State and Community Relations, at a Seminar on Neighborhood Museums concluded:

> I think our problem is to create more John Kinards, someone who understands that there are voices in the community. . . . John, if you went from door to door, which is the last thing, somebody would speak to you before they would speak to me.[20]

Kinard had great influence on the American museum movement. He attended and spoke frequently at the national meetings of the AAM and served as its vice-president in 1981–1982. He was a member of the board of the AAM's Northeastern Museums Conference (today the Mid-Atlantic Association of Museums). He took a leading part in forming the African American Museums Association in Detroit in 1978 and was its treasurer in 1982–1983. He visited numerous museums and museum conferences throughout the country, always impressive with his outgoing personality and moving oratory. As a result, museum leaders from all over the land came to him for advice and inspiration.[21] "John Kinard was among those who changed the face of American museums," said Tom Freudenheim, the Smithsonian assistant secretary for museums. "He not only directed a creative and dynamic program . . . but . . . the Anacostia Museum served as a model for a growing number of African American museums around the country—indeed for other ethnically oriented museums as well." Leonard Jeffries of the Black Studies Department of the City College of New York described Kinard "as a teacher, preacher, and soldier in the war against racism."[22]

Kinard was also well known internationally. In 1971 he spoke at the regular triennial meeting of ICOM in Paris and later attended a conference sponsored by the Ditchley Foundation in England. He met ICOM's venerable, highly respected secretary, Georges Henri Rivière, and the two became fast friends. Rivière came from France to Washington to explore a neighborhood museum first hand, and both men were interested in the new ecomuseums that tried to bring museums and their communities together to solve local problems. The movement began in Canada in the 1970s and soon spread through France, Mexico, Spain, and Portugal. Kinard wrote another important article for ICOM in 1985 on "The Neighborhood Museum as a Catalyst for Change."[23] He was called upon to address many museum meetings in Europe, Africa, and the Caribbean. A fascinating instance was his speech on "Museums as Instruments for Social Change" at the annual conference of the Southern African Museums Association at Pietermaritzburg, South Africa, in 1987, at which he dared to criticize openly the racism which white South Africans were displaying. After his talk, a white national administrator declared it "one of the most stringent and worst attacks on white South Africans that he had ever heard." Whereupon, some seventy (one-third) of the delegates walked out of the conference to show their disapproval of the administrator's harangue and their support of Kinard. John later joked about the incident that he had been "the fox let into the chicken coop."[24]

In July 1989 during Kinard's final illness when he was in great pain and had lost 60 pounds, he gave an interview to a Washington *Post* reporter. The resulting article was entitled "Lion of the Anacostia Museum: Director John

Kinard and His Lifetime Mission of Conscience," in which he showed himself indignant with the Smithsonian and with Ripley's successor as secretary, Robert McC. Adams, because they were not providing the Anacostia Museum with enough resources to carry out his program and to obtain an adequate, much larger headquarters at Poplar Point on the bank of the Anacostia River. Kinard also backed the erection of a new comprehensive National Museum of African American History on the Washington Mall. He bluntly blamed the neglect of these projects upon "racism" and called Secretary Adams a "closet racist" who mistreated and slighted blacks. Adams responded that the Smithsonian was making progress achieving changes in these areas but admitted that "John had a point of view that needs to be expressed within the institution" and that he as secretary had "certainly never tried to get him to tone down." Former Secretary Ripley wrote ruefully: "Here was a man who needed every ounce of support and encouragement which we could give; I am only sorry that such support and encouragement could not be more bountiful."

Kinard on his part said that "Adams will tolerate views that he doesn't like or agree with, without being punitive—at least in my regard. . . . But that doesn't mean that anything gets done." He was also disturbed by Adams's costly plan to move the main part of the Museum of the American Indian from New York to a Washington site near the Mall.

Kinard ended his interview with the Washington *Post* as follows:

> I wasn't chosen for this position. I didn't seek it out. The job found me . . . I believe it's the will of God that I'm here. I'm a servant, and I follow. So when I shuffle off this mortal coil, if it can be said of me that "he was a good servant," that will be enough. I just play my role, and when I'm gone, somebody else will come along and pick up where I leave off. Just to be a good servant is all I aspire to.[25]

In that July also, a young woman from the Smithsonian called on Kinard to interview him for an oral history. She intended to have several more sessions with him, but he died before they could be held.[26]

Finally, though I know it is somewhat risky to do so, I'd like to end on a personal note. I had met John Kinard at various AAM functions and in about 1970 I invited him to come to Colonial Williamsburg and bring with him Zora Martin and several other key staff members to discuss with our principal directors how we were treating the subjects of blacks and slavery in eighteenth-century Williamsburg. I was dissatisfied with out interpretation of those topics, especially since blacks constituted more than 50 percent of Williamsburg's colonial population. Well, John and his group were shocked by our neglect and told us so frankly. Zora in 1971 wrote a highly critical account of what they saw. Great numbers of black school children were visiting us, but she thought the introductory film, of which we were so proud, showed only "happy, well-fed, well-clothed blacks working in the fields or around the large plantation house" but "nothing to indicate that they were dissatisfied with their status." Most black employees visible about the project worked at manual labor, often as waiters, waitresses, busboys, or gardeners; there were no black docents or interpreters. And the white hostesses who took visitors about made small mention of slavery or blacks. Zora concluded: "A visit to Williamsburg reinforces the antiquated belief of minimal black participation and smiling faces."[27]

When I retired at Colonial Williamsburg in 1972, I came to the University of Delaware to teach in a Museum Studies program. During some six years I had an enrollment of about 360, chiefly graduate students, and I invited John to come each year to speak to my classes on "Neighborhood Museums." I was always amused that, though he devoted a moderate amount of time to museums, his chief interest obviously was the civil rights movement; still, I thought it well for the students to hear that subject discussed from an African-American viewpoint. Sometimes John brought along an associate, and on one occasion a young black student about to graduate from high school, and the class engaged in some spirited discussions.[28]

The best single word to describe John Kinard is "charismatic," and his wide knowledge, boundless energy, good humor, and imaginative speaking made him a great hit. It was a real disaster for the museum world that he had to die so young.

## NOTES

1. "Museums: Opening Eyes in the Ghettos," *Time* (June 21, 1968): 78; *Anacostia Neighborhood Museum, Smithsonian Institution, Sept. 15, 1972 [Fifth Anniversary]* (Washington: Smithsonian Institution, 1972), 1–2; John Kinard in *Smithsonian Year: Annual Report of the Smithsonian Institution, 1969*: 565. I am most grateful to Zora Martin-Felton and Gail S. Lowe of the Anacostia Museum and my daughter, Mary Sheron Alexander, for reading this chapter and making helpful suggestions for its improvement. I also had insightful interviews with Charles Blitzer and Stephen E. Weil.

2. John Kinard, "The Visitor Versus the Museum," in *The Visitor and the Museum*, edited by Linda Draper (Seattle: Museum Educators of the American Association of Museums, 1977), 4.

3. *Smithsonian Year, 1969*: 6–12; *1988*: 6–11; *Anacostia Neighborhood Museum, Smithsonian Institution, 1966–1967* (Washington: Smithsonian Institution, 1977), ii, 1–3; John R. Kinard and Esther Nighbert, "The Anacostia Museum," International Council of Museums, *Museum*

24, no. 2 (1972): 108; Caryl Marsh, "A Neighborhood Museum that Works," *Museum News* 47 (Oct. 1968): 14–16; Zora Martin-Felton and Gail S. Lowe, *A Different Drummer: John Kinard and the Anacostia Museum, 1967–1989* (Washington: Anacostia Museum, 1989), 17–19.

4. Martin-Felton and Lowe, *Different Drummer*, 20–21; Washington *Post* (July 19, 1989): D10.

5. *Anacostia Neighborhood Museum [Fifth Anniversary]*, 9, 43; *John R. E. Kinard, 1936–1989: A Memorial Tribute* (Washington: Smithsonian Institution, National Museum of Natural History, 1989), 4 pp.; John R. Kinard, "The Neighborhood Museum as a Catalyst for Social Change," *Museum* 148 (1985): 217; "John R. Kinard" (obituary), New York *Times* (Aug. 7, 1989)II: 6; Martin-Felton and Lowe, *Different Drummer*, 1–4, 7–12, 21–22, 26–27, 28–30, 69–70; *Museums: Their New Audience: A Report to the Department of Housing and Urban Development* (Washington: American Association of Museums, 1972), 111; "Oral History Project: Interview with John R. Kinard, Director, Anacostia Museum, July, 1989" (Archives and Special Collections of the Smithsonian Institution), 41 pp.; "Tribute for John Kinard," *The Torch, Smithsonian Institution Monthly Newspaper* 89 (Sept. 9, 1989): 8; Michael Welzenbach, "Lion of the Anacostia Museum: Director John Kinard and His Lifetime Mission of Conscience," Washington *Post* (July 19, 1989): Di, D10–11; *Who's Who in the South and Southwest, 1973–1974* (Chicago: Marquis Who's Who, 1974), 403.

6. *Smithsonian Year, 1989*: 31, 101; Kenneth Hudson, *Museums of Influence* (Cambridge: Cambridge University Press, 1987), 170–81; Martin-Felton and Lowe, *Different Drummer*, 51–56, 59.

7. *Smithsonian Year, 1969*: 565–67; *1970*: 108–09; *1971*: 103–04; *1972*: 19, 119; *1973*: 14, 158–60; *1974*: 219–21; *1975*: 251–55; Kinard and Nighbert, "Anacostia Neighborhood Museum," 102–09; Marsh, "Neighborhood Museum," 14–15; Martin-Felton and Lowe, *Different Drummer*, 23–28.

8. *Smithsonian Year, 1975*: 251–53; *1976*: 248–50; *1977*: 160–69; *1978*: 210–13; *1979*: 268–70; *1980*: 265–66; *1981*: 251–53; *1982*: 270–72; *1984*: 179–80; *1985*: 102; *1986*: 20; *1987*: 102; *1988*: 98; *1989*: 100–02; Martin-Felton and Lowe, *Different Drummer*, 27–28, 36–38.

9. *Smithsonian Year, 1969*: 565–67; *1972*: 19; *1973*: 158–60; *1979*: 268–70; *1980*: 265–66; *The Torch* 80: 8; Martin-Felton and Lowe, *Different Drummer*, 23–24, 56–57.

10. *Smithsonian Year, 1985*: 27; *1986*: 20; *1987*: 102; *1988*: 98; Martin-Felton and Lowe, *Different Drummer*, 32–33, 37.

11. Kinard, "Neighborhood Museum as Catalyst," 217–21; Neil Harris, "Museums, Merchandizing, and Popular Taste: The Struggle for Influence," in *Material Culture and the Study of American Life*, edited by Ian M. O. Quimby (New York: W. W. Norton, 1976), 142.

12. John Kinard, "To Meet the Needs of Today's Audience," *Museum News* 50 (May 1972): 15–16.

13. Kinard, "Visitor Versus Museum," 44.

14. *Smithsonian Year, 1981*: 283.

15. *Smithsonian Year, 1987*: 102; Martin-Felton and Lowe, *Different Drummer*, 33.

16. Louise Daniel Hutchinson, *Out of Africa: From West African Kingdoms to Colonization* (Washington: Smithsonian Institution Press, 1979), 11–12.

17. *The Torch* 80: 8.

18. Anacostia Neighborhood Museum, *The Barnett-Aden Collection* (Washington: Smithsonian Institution Press, 1979), 13.

19. Louise Daniel Hutchinson, *The Anacostia Story* (Washington: Smithsonian Institution Press, 1977), xv.

20. Emily Denis Harvey and Bernard Friedberg, eds., *A Museum for the People: A Report of Proceedings at the Seminar on Neighborhood Museums, Held November 21, 22, 23, 1968* (New York: Arno Press, 1971), 31.

21. *The Torch* 89: 8.

22. Ibid.: 1, 8; Martin-Felton and Lowe, *Different Drummer*, 41–50.

23. Kinard, "Neighborhood Museum as Catalyst," 217–23; Kinard, "To Meet the Needs of Today's Audience," 15–16.

24. *The Torch* 89: 1; Martin-Felton and Lowe, *Different Drummer*, 12–14; the fox and chicken coop remark was made to my daughter, Mary Sheron Alexander.

25. Washington *Post* (July 19, 1989): D1, D10–11.

26. See note 5 above for this oral history.

27. Zora Martin, "Colonial Williamsburg—A Black Perspective," in *Museum Education Anthology* (Washington: Museum Education Roundtable, 1984), 83–85. In 1983 she returned to Colonial Williamsburg and reported racial interpretation considerably improved. Zora Martin-Felton, "And Afterward, 1983," in *Museum Education Anthology*, 85–86.

28. Martin-Felton and Lowe, *Different Drummer*, 72–74.

## SELECT BIBLIOGRAPHY

Anacostia Neighborhood Museum. *The Barnett-Aden Collection*. Washington: Smithsonian Institution Press, 1979.

*Anacostia Neighborhood Museum, Smithsonian Institution, 1966–1967*. Washington: Smithsonian Institution, 1977.

*Anacostia Neighborhood Museum, Smithsonian Institution, Sept. 15, 1972 [Fifth Anniversary]*. Washington: Smithsonian Institution, 1972.

Harris, Neil. "Museums, Merchandizing, and Popular Taste: The Struggle for Influence." In *Material Culture and the Study of American Life*. Edited by Ian M. O. Quimby. New York: W. W. Norton, 1976.

Harvey, Emily Denis, and Bernard Friedberg, eds. *A Museum for the People: A Report of Proceedings at the Seminar on Neighborhood Museums, Held November 21, 22, 23, 1968*. New York: Arno Press, 1971.

Hudson, Kenneth. *Museums of Influence*. Cambridge: Cambridge University Press, 1987.

Hutchinson, Louise Daniel. *The Anacostia Story*. Washington: Smithsonian Institution Press, 1977.

_____. *Out of Africa: From West African Kingdoms to Colonization*. Washington: Smithsonian Institution Press, 1979.

*John R. E. Kinard, 1936–1989: A Memorial Tribute*. Washington: Smithsonian Institution, National Museum of Natural History, 1989.

Kinard, John R. "The Neighborhood Museum as a Catalyst for Social Change," *Museum* 148 (1985): 217.

_____. "To Meet the Needs of Today's Audience." *Museum News* 50 (May 1972): 15–16.

_____. "The Visitor Versus the Museum." In *The Visitor and the Museum*. Edited by Linda Draper. Seattle: Museum Educators of the American Association of Museums, 1977.

Kinard, John R., and Esther Nighbert. "The Anacostia Museum." International Council of Museums, *Museum* 24, no. 2 (1972): 108.

Marsh, Caryl. "A Neighborhood Museum that Works." *Museum News* 47 (Oct. 1968): 14–16.

Martin, Zora. "Colonial Williamsburg—A Black Perspective." In *Museum Education Anthology*. Washington: Museum Education Roundtable, 1984.
Martin-Felton, Zora, and Gail S. Lowe. *A Different Drummer: John Kinard and the Anacostia Museum, 1967–1989*. Washington: Anacostia Museum, 1989.
"Museums: Opening Eyes in the Ghettos." *Time* (June 21, 1968): 78.
*Museums: Their New Audience: A Report to the Department of Housing and Urban Development*. Washington: American Association of Museums, 1972.
"Oral History Project: Interview with John R. Kinard, Director, Anacostia Museum, July, 1989." Archives and Special Collections of the Smithsonian Institution.
"Tribute for John Kinard." *The Torch, Smithsonian Institution Monthly Newspaper* 89 (Sept. 9, 1989): 8.
Welzenbach, Michael. "Lion of the Anacostia Museum: Director John Kinard and His Lifetime Mission of Conscience." Washington *Post* (July 19, 1989).

# CHAPTER 10

# Katherine Coffey *Attracts the Community into a General Museum*

## I

KATHERINE COFFEY, AGED TWENTY-FIVE, left her position as executive secretary of the Alumnae Association of Barnard College in 1925 to become staff assistant at the Newark Museum in New Jersey. In her new post she had the opportunity to work closely with John Cotton Dana, the museum's founder and one of the most progressive and innovative museum directors in the country. She began to help him plan the construction of the new building that Louis Bamberger, charter trustee and officer who owned Newark's leading department store, was giving to the museum. Dana appreciated "the reliable skill of Coffey" and found her both capable and easy to work with. As soon as the handsome new headquarters with its large, walled garden at the rear was opened in March 1926, Coffey assumed many tasks in the design and installation of special exhibits of art, history, and natural science, as well as the conduct of other educational activities; they attracted families throughout the city—blue collar workers and their employers, those with immigrant backgrounds, and the well-to-do. Coffey also directed the museum's new pioneering training program, which taught about nine young college graduates yearly and had them work as apprentices in the various departments of the museum.[1]

Coffey found the Newark Museum an exciting place in which to work. Dana had been trained in the law and took delight in argumentation and controversy. He recruited several capable women to help him with the museum. Beatrice

Winser, his assistant librarian and museum director, was a strong and skilled administrator who looked after the everyday affairs, assisted by Margaret Gates and Alice W. Kendall. Louisa Connolly, an experienced educator, visited sixty-five museums around the country to report on their educational programs and advise the Newark Museum in that field; she also taught in the Training Program. Thus Coffey was fortunate to work with an energetic boss who stirred her imagination and stimulated her to put forth her utmost effort and, at the same time, to become a member of a talented team that cooperatively carried out sound programs.[2]

## II

Katherine Coffey was born in New York City, May 15, 1900, the daughter of John J. and Mary (Wallace) Coffey. She attended Barnard College at Columbia University and was graduated with an A.B. degree in 1922. (She received an M.A. in 1953 from Rutgers University and honorary doctorates later from Rutgers and Seton Hall.) As an undergraduate, she took an active part in college life, was chairman of the Freshman Greek Games Committee, president of the Sophomore Class, and vice-president of the Undergraduate Association. She then served in 1923–1924 in the responsible position of executive secretary with the alumnae association.

At the Newark Museum, upon Dana's death in 1929, Beatrice Winser was made librarian and museum director in his place, and two years later, Coffey was promoted to curator in charge of exhibitions, educational programs, and museum training. She received a fellowship from the Oberlander Trust of the Carl Schurz Foundation in 1936 and visited Europe to study museums there. Later, during World War II, she did canteen work overseas with the Eighty-sixth Division of Engineers. When Winser stepped down in 1947, Alice Kendall succeeded her with Coffey as assistant director, and upon Kendall's retirement two years later, Coffey became director, remaining in that post until her retirement in 1968. Coffey did much extra-curricular museum work during her directorship. She was a member of the Council of the American Association of Museums, 1953–1956, and president of the Northeast Museums Conference (today the Mid-Atlantic Association of Museums) for two years. She was the organizer and first chairman of the Museum Council of New Jersey and an elected member of the Association of Art Museum Directors. She belonged to an important AAM committee that persuaded the Smithsonian to take over the museum of the Cooper Union in New York as the Cooper-Hewitt National Museum of Design.[3]

Six months before her retirement, Samuel C. Miller, formerly assistant director of the Albright-Knox Gallery in Buffalo, had become her understudy, and he succeeded to the directorship. She was then elected a trustee of the museum, and the Katherine Coffey Endowment Fund of $100,000 was established in her honor. She lived in New York City during her retirement but remained active as a consultant of the New Jersey Historical Society and was a member of the new Accreditation Commission of the American Association of Museums. She died suddenly on April 4, 1972.[4]

## III

To understand Coffey's contributions to the Newark Museum, we need to examine the three fields in which she took major responsibility—special exhibitions, educational activities, and museum training. The museum offered a total of some 150 major exhibitions during her service between 1926 and 1968, an average of about three and a half yearly. In addition, there were many smaller shows. While she had the leading role in staging the exhibitions, the curators, who numbered between six and seven, usually wrote the catalogues, for which, aided by assistants, they did much of the research. William H. Gertz, Jr., curator of painting and sculpture, was the author of many of them.[5]

The museum was much interested in promoting the cause of contemporary art. Some of the chief exhibitions during Coffey's time treated *Paintings and Sculptures by Living Artists* (1926); *Modern American Watercolors* (1930, 1948); *Color Photography* (1940); *Contemporary American Negro Art* (1944) with the work of thirty leading painters and sculptors; *Contemporary Prints* (1946); *Changing Tastes in Painting and Sculpture, 1795–1946*; and *Abstract Art from 1910 to Today* (1956).

The museum paid much attention to New Jersey artists. A show of their work was held every three years from 1952 through 1968. Other displays introduced some comparatively unknown state artists in *Native Talent* (1948); examined *Modern Architecture in New Jersey* (1955); and exhibited 110 works from a staff-compiled list of over 1,000 *Early New Jersey Artists, 1783–1920* (1957). An elaborate celebration of New Jersey's three centuries (1966) comprised eight exhibitions.

The museum was proud when it persuaded Holger Cahill to organize the first exhibition in the country of *American Primitive Painting* (1930), which was circulated to museums in Chicago, Toledo, and Rochester, New York. The next year, the museum presented the pioneer show of *American Folk Sculpture* with ship figureheads, cigar store Indians, weathervanes, and bird and animal carvings.

Dana began the practice of exhibiting the products of New Jersey industries in an effort to persuade their managers, workers, and the whole community to take pride in their achievements as well as to attract them to the museum. Shows in that area during Coffey's day included *Nothing Takes the Place of Leather* (1926); *Jewelry Made in Newark* (1929); *Aviation: A Newark Industry* (1932), featuring the Newark Airport; *Modern Miracles: Chemistry Changes the World* (1934), stressing the fact that New Jersey ranked second in the United States in chemical industries; *War and Peace: The Industrial Front in the Newark Area* (1945), in which fifty-six firms participated; and *Newark in World Trade* (1949).

The museum appealed to consumers as well as to local firms by pointing out that low-priced goods could be well designed. *Inexpensive Articles of Good Design* (1928, 1929) contained objects that cost between ten and fifty cents procured from local five-and-ten-cent and department stores. *Christmas Gift Suggestions of Good Design* (1950) showed goods valued from ten cents to ten dollars; that exhibit was often repeated and after 1956 contained works for sale by New Jersey artists and craftsmen.

The museum did many exhibitions of art from all over the world. Its own collection of Tibetan art is one of the best in the country and was displayed in *Tibetan Life and Culture* (1949). *Primitive African Art* (1928) was followed much later by *Art in the Life of Africa* (1954), which examined the tribal concept of art as religion. Two shows treated *Art in Judaism* (1957) and *Art in Buddhism* (1958). *Japanese Prints and Their Influence* (1953) was followed by *Arts of Japan* (1954), while *Islands of the Pacific* (1939) concerned Oceania, as did *Arts of the South Sea Islands* (1967). *Theatres of War* (1943) used the museum's ethnological and oriental collections to picture the Pacific areas in which American troops were fighting. Focusing on India and Iran were *20th Century Indian Art* (1956) and *Paintings of Persia and Mughal India*. *Three Southern Neighbors—Ecuador, Peru, Bolivia* (1941) was a Latin American "good neighbor" exhibition. And several shows covered British, Italian, and Spanish art.

The museum's science collections were used in *The Geology of New Jersey* (1951); *The Physical Sciences* (1960) on the mysteries of light, electricity, magnetism, and sound with visitor-operated, "hands-on" displays; and *The Natural Sciences* (1968) showing New Jersey birds, fossils, and minerals. The museum emphasized the advance of technology with *From Shank's Mare to 16 Cylinders*

(1930) on the rise of the automobile; *Atomic Energy* (1948); *Approaching Mars* (1956); and *Satellite Science* (1958).

The special exhibitions were by far the most popular attractions of the museum. They drew heavy attendance, not only new visitors especially interested in the fields covered but a steady, large number of repeat visitors. The shows utilized the museum's growing collections, in addition to borrowing occasionally from other museums.

Coffey, both as staff member and then director, had much to do with the development of the museum's other educational activities.[6] The exhibitions were always accompanied by programs of lectures, demonstrations, discussions or workshops that attracted much community participation. Special tours were instituted for the blind that allowed them to handle ceramics and baskets. The opening of the new building resulted in the establishment of a Department of Education that worked more intimately with the schools in tailoring museum class visits to the schools' curriculums. The museum also dispatched exhibits to the schools, and its Lending Department grew to contain 10,000 objects. Staff members also went to the schools, clubs, and other community organizations to lecture or participate in varied activities. The museum's Reference Library was open to both the public and the staff, and it exchanged publications with other institutions throughout the country. Teachers came to the museum to take credit courses in using museum objects offered by the local State Teachers' College with the backing of the Newark Board of Education.

The museum had early organized a Junior Museum with its own exhibits and classes in drawing, painting, modeling, and crafts, and a Museum Club with a life membership charge of a mere ten cents that encouraged youngsters to collect stamps, coins, natural history specimens, and other objects. Those activities led to much after-school and weekend student participation. A Junior Museum Council, made up of representatives from the numerous junior clubs, staged an annual pageant, which was eventually replaced by an exhibition of its year's work.

The economic depression of the 1930s reduced the city appropriation for the museum markedly, but the staff kept its regular activities afloat and began to offer adults, many of them unemployed, Sunday afternoon classes in sketching, modeling, and nature study. Staff members volunteered to supervise the program without pay, and visiting lecturers frequently participated. Those classes developed into the Newark Nature Club, the Newark Science Workshop, and the Arts Workshop for Adults with courses in weaving, painting, ceramics, sculpture, and the like. In 1933, too, the museum began to present concerts, given monthly from November through March.

In 1953, a new Spitz Planetarium, the gift of Mr. and Mrs. Leonard Dreyfus opened with regular astronomical shows; the couple gave $50,000 for its upkeep and in 1960 added an Optical Observatory. In 1977 the museum acquired the John H. Ballantine House next door and added a four-story extension in the rear, into which moved the Junior Museum, Lending Department, Arts Workshop for Adults, and Reference Library. The house itself later was restored with period rooms furnished with New Jersey decorative arts. Two other additions were the old Newark Schoolhouse of 1784, properly furnished and in 1939 placed in the museum's spacious garden, and the Newark Fire Museum, installed in 1967 in the former Ballantine Carriage House and also moved to the garden.

Members who joined the museum—numbering 2,173 by 1969— received many privileges, including lectures, special events, film showings, and family trips. A monthly *News Notes* was mailed to them as well as a quarterly entitled *The Museum*, which contained articles on the collections and local history. In 1950 a Members' Room was opened, and they were invited to borrow paintings and prints for their homes and offices. The whole community was encouraged to use the study collections and consultation service; and circulating exhibits of paintings and prints went to educational institutions.

In listing the museum's activities in her 1959 report, Coffey pointed out

> We are fortunate that the direction given the Museum by its founders allows for flexibility that makes it possible for us to meet the demands of changing times, and the needs of the community. The Museum is not static in its collections, programs or activities; only in the integrity does it remain unchanged.[7]

The changing times to which Coffey referred were illustrated in the makeup of Newark's population. When the museum was founded in 1909, Newark contained about twenty European nationalities including German, Irish, Italian Russian, Polish, Lithuanian, and Hungarian, but few blacks (only about 2.8 percent of the population). During the First World War, blacks began to migrate to the city despite the fact that only menial jobs were open to them, and after the Second World War, they moved from the South in droves so that by the time Coffey retired, they constituted nearly 60 percent of the population. White flight to the suburbs that included many of the upward-bound European nationalities was helping make Newark a black city. The blacks suffered shameful segregation lived in appalling slums, and were subject to much crime, venereal disease tuberculosis, infant mortality, lead poisoning, and drug abuse. One of every four was on some type of government relief, and unemployment for young men, aged sixteen to twenty-five, reached 40 percent.

In July 1967 after the police killed a black man engaged in a crime, black discontent erupted into five days of rioting, and downtown stores and other places were looted and burned. The Governor ordered in the State Police and the National Guard, and order was restored with the use of truncheons and guns; it was found that twenty-three blacks had died in the melee. But the museum, despite its location in the central city, was untouched during the disturbances. In attempting to serve the whole community, it had welcomed many black visitors. It had held four important exhibitions on black culture, one of which displayed the work of thirty black painters and sculptors, while the other three treated African art as part of the black heritage.[8]

The next crucial test of the museum came in February 1969, just after Coffey's retirement, when the Newark City Council voted unanimously to discontinue on April 1 the appropriations for both the Public Library (about $12 million) and the museum (nearly $800,000). The action took place during the museum's African Festival which included an ambitious exhibition of *African Art* and smaller shows on *Photos of People of Africa* and on prints, paintings, and collages by local artists who called themselves "Black Motion." The festival included motion pictures, a fashion show, and music, dancing, and drumming; it attracted members of both the black and white communities as well as United Nations representatives of African countries, many of them in their native costumes.

When an all-day hearing was held on the plan to stop the appropriations, more than 400 citizens from all parts of the community jammed the council chamber to oppose the motion. The Council of Racial Equality (CORE), National Association for the Advancement of Colored People (NAACP), Urban Coalition of Newark, New Jersey Library Association, university and college spokespersons, and many others strongly, sometimes passionately, supported the museum and library, and demonstrators journeyed to the state capital at Trenton to implore Governor Richard J. Hughes and the State Legislature to increase the state appropriation. (The council's real motive for dropping the appropriations was based on the hope of obtaining greater state and county support.) As a result of the continuing agitation, the City Council rescinded the February vote, the state increased its museum support to about one-third of the total, and one county appropriated $50,000. Since that time, the museum has continued to offer its community-supported programs, and the blacks who succeeded in electing Kenneth

Gibson, a black engineer, mayor in 1970 and taking over the city government, have steadily supported the museum.[9]

## IV

On February 5, 1925, Dana had announced that the museum would offer a "School for Museum Workers," beginning that fall. It would last for nine months, enroll not more than twelve college graduates, and be devoted to the management of museums. Formal teaching would take place for about ten hours each week, but the students also would do actual work in the different museum departments and act as interpreters or docents for its special exhibitions. The program was successful from the start, and nine bright young women were graduated in the spring, all but one of them going to work in museums.

Coffey, as supervisor of the training course, did a great deal of work selecting the students, supervising their programs, and helping them find jobs. The students considered her exacting but fair.[10] In the second year, another nine pupils were graduated, all but one taking museum positions. In the fifth year, eight of fifty applicants were accepted; they came from seven states and six colleges. By 1942, when the course was interrupted because of the war, 108 young women and men had been trained, and most of them were working in museums in the United States or Canada. In 1961 Coffey announced that the program would resume.[11]

The Newark Museum training course was one of the two most important ones in the country at that time; the other one, taught by Paul Joseph Sachs at Harvard's Fogg Art Museum, was devoted to art museums. Museum studies courses soon began to multiply elsewhere, but Henry Watson Kent, secretary of the Metropolitan Museum of Art and Dana's close friend, thought that many of them made the mistake of trying to give instruction in art history or other subject matter. He insisted that a good course in museum studies should teach museum management or economy and leave subject instruction to colleges and universities. And Newark followed that practical principle.[12]

Coffey made a clear statement of her museum philosophy when she wrote an article in *Museum News* during a controversial discussion of the place of research, education, and public service in museum work.[13] She began by praising the late George Brown Goode of the Smithsonian's United States National Museum, who defined a museum as "an institution for the preservation of those objects which best illustrate the phenomena of nature and the works of man, the utilization of these for the increase of knowledge and for the culture and enlightenment of the people."[14] She also approved his quotation from Sir Henry Cole, the founder of what became the Victoria and Albert Museum in London, which ran:

> If you wish your schools of science and art to be effective, your health, the air, your food to be wholesome, your life to be long, your manufactures to improve, your trade to increase and your people to be civilized, you must have museums of science and art to illustrate the principles of life, health, nature, art, and beauty.[15]

Coffey insisted not only that a museum's purpose was to collect and preserve objects but that its chief functions were research, exhibition, and education. Museums founded around great collections of science and art, usually in large cities, had a dual responsibility for both sound subject matter research and the enlightenment of the swarms of visitors they attracted. Smaller museums could do less subject matter research but devote themselves mainly to education and public service; even then, however, they needed to do sound educational research. University museums had to have less concern for education of the general public, while for the scholars and students that they served, subject-matter research was all important.

Coffey concluded that the purpose of each individual museum ought to be abundantly clear to both its trustees and staff, and that the professionalization of the museum staff was highly desirable. Curators should be interested not only in their collections and connoisseurship but also in education, and educators ought to understand the subject matter so important to the curators. The director should be a well-trained professional who comprehended the overall purpose and functions of the museum and knew how to inspire both curators and educators to work together harmoniously for the common good of the museum. Striving vigorously to carry out these ideals enabled Coffey to insure that the Newark Museum remain a powerful community source of education and culture.

Katherine Coffey served the Newark Museum for some forty-three years, nearly twenty of them as director. One of the few women museum heads in the country, she was well known and highly respected for work in her own museum and for her outside activities. The Mid-Atlantic Association of Museums, which she had served so well as president, in 1972 established the prestigious Katherine Coffey Award, given annually to a man or woman "for distinguished accomplishment in the museum profession." Thus her name and contributions are preserved justly in the annals of American museum history.

## NOTES

1. For Coffey, see Katherine Coffey, "Operation of the Individual Museum," *Museum News* 40 (Oct. 1961): 26–29; *Museologist*, 125 (Oct. 1972); *Museum News* 50 (June 1972): 60; Newark Museum *News Notes* (May 1972): 1–2; *Who's Who in America* (Chicago: A. N. Marquis, 1956) 28 (1954–1955): 513. The direct quotation is in Frank Kingdon, *John Cotton Dana: A Life* (Newark, N.J.: Public Library and Museum, 1940), 161–62.

2. Kingdon, *Dana*, 161–62.

3. *Museum News* 40 (Oct. 1961): 16; 42 (Jan. 1964): 37–38; 44 (Nov. 1965): 6; 47 (Sept. 1968): 6; 50 (June 1977): 60.

4. *Museum News* 47 (Sept. 1968): 6; (May 1969): 27.

5. This section on exhibitions is based on *A Survey: 50 Years of the Newark Museum* (Newark, N.J.: Newark Museum Association, 1959); *The Newark Museum, Collections and Exhibitions, 1959–1968: Survey 60* (Newark, N.J.: Newark Museum, 1969); *Art Digest* 18 (Apr. 15, 1944): 20; *Museum News* 38 (1960–1961) and 47 (1967–1968) with frequent mentions and especially 38 (Feb. 1960): 4; 42 (Mar. 1964): 37, 44. For Gertz, see *A Survey: 50 Years*, 29–32; *Museum News* 45 (Sept. 1966): 49.

6. The educational activities are described in Katherine Coffey, "Service," *A Survey: 50 Years*, 23–25; *The Newark Museum: A Chronicle of the Founding Years, 1909–1934* (Newark, N.J.: Newark Museum Association, 1934), 14–15, 20, 26, 31–34, 36–38; Newark Museum, *A Museum in Action: Presenting the Museum's Activities* (Newark, N.J.: Newark Museum, 1944); *Museum News* 42 (Mar. 1964): 37.

7. *A Survey: 50 Years*, 25.

8. Daniel Gaby, "Newark: The Promise of Survival," *Nation* 219 (Dec. 14, 1974): 619–22; Tom Hayden, *Rebellion in Newark: Official Violence and Ghetto Response* (New York: Vintage Books, 1967); Kenneth T. and Barbara B. Jackson, "The Black Experience in Newark: The Growth of the Ghetto, 1870–1970," in *New Jersey since 1960: New Findings and Interpretations*, edited by William C. Wright (Trenton: New Jersey Historical Commission, 1972), 36–56; Ron Perambo, *No Cause for Indictment: An Autopsy of Newark* (New York: Holt, Rinehart and Winston, 1972); Clement A. Price, "The Beleagured City as Promised Land: Blacks in Newark, 1917–1947," in *Urban New Jersey since 1970*, edited by William C. Wright (Trenton: New Jersey Historical Commission, 1975), 10–45; Ralph Whitehead, "Behind the Violence in Newark: Anatomy of a Riot," *Commonwealth* 86 (Aug. 11, 1967): 492–94.

9. Samuel C. Miller, "An African Festival at the Newark Museum," *Museum News* 47 (May 1969): 25–27; "Crisis in Newark," *Library Journal* 94 (Mar. 15, 1969): 1081; "Newark City Council Votes to Drop Library," *Library Journal* 94 (Mar. 15, 1969): 1083; "Newark City Council Rescinds Library Budget Slash," *Library Journal* 94 (Apr. 1, 1969): 1403–04; Russell Lynes, "After Hours: How to Make Politics from Art and Vice Versa," *Harper's Magazine* 239 (Aug. 1969): 21–24; *Museum News* 47 (Apr. 1969): 3; "Victory from the Jaws of Defeat: A Tribute to the Newark Public Library," *Wilson Library Bulletin* 45 (Apr. 1969): 740–47.

10. Session on "The Legacy of John Cotton Dana," at which Elizabeth Dusenberry, a former Newark museum apprentice, spoke. Mid-Atlantic Association of Museums *1990 Annual Meeting* (Oct. 31, 1990), 18.

11. *American Museum of Art* 20 (Dec. 1929): 710; 21 (Dec. 1930): 726–29; *Museum News* 39 (June 1961): 7; (Oct. 1961): 4; Newark Museum, *A Museum* 1 (May 1925): 42–43; (Sept.-Dec. 1925): 67; 2 (Jan. 1927): 117.

12. Henry Watson Kent, *What I Am Pleased to Call My Education* (New York: Grolier Club, 1949): 165–66.

13. *Museum News* 40 (Oct. 1961): 26–29. See also 42 (Jan. 1964): 37–38; 44 (Nov. 1965): 6; 46 (Oct. 1967): 42.

14. *Museum News* 40 (Oct. 1961): 27.

15. Ibid.: 26.

## SELECT BIBLIOGRAPHY

*A Survey: 50 Years of the Newark Museum*. Newark, N.J.: Newark Museum Association, 1959.

"Crisis in Newark." *Library Journal* 94 (Mar. 15, 1969): 1081.

Kingdon, Frank. *John Cotton Dana: A Life*. Newark, N.J.: Public Library and Museum, 1940.

Gaby, Daniel. "Newark: The Promise of Survival." *Nation* 219 (Dec. 14, 1974): 619–22.

Hayden, Tom. *Rebellion in Newark: Official Violence and Ghetto Response*. New York: Vintage Books, 1967.

Jackson, Kenneth T. and Barbara B. "The Black Experience in Newark: The Growth of the Ghetto, 1870–1970." In *New Jersey since 1960: New Findings and Interpretations*. Edited by William C. Wright. Trenton: New Jersey Historical Commission, 1972.

Kent, Henry Watson. *What I Am Pleased to Call My Education*. New York: Grolier Club, 1949.

Lynes, Russell. "After Hours: How to Make Politics from Art and Vice Versa." *Harper's Magazine* 239 (Aug. 1969): 21–24.

*Museum News*. Vols. 38–47 (1960–1969).

"Newark City Council Votes to Drop Library." *Library Journal* 94 (Mar. 15, 1969): 1083.

*The Newark Museum: A Chronicle of the Founding Years, 1909–1934*. Newark, N.J.: Newark Museum Association, 1934.

Newark Museum. *A Museum in Action: Presenting the Museum's Activities*. Newark, N.J.: Newark Museum, 1944.

*The Newark Museum, Collections and Exhibitions, 1959–1968: Survey 60*. Newark, N.J.: Newark Museum, 1969.

Perambo, Ron. *No Cause for Indictment: An Autopsy of Newark*. New York: Holt, Rinehart and Winston, 1972.

Price, Clement A. "The Beleagured City as Promised Land: Blacks in Newark, 1917–1947." In *Urban New Jersey since 1970*. Edited by William C. Wright. Trenton: New Jersey Historical Commission, 1975.

"Victory from the Jaws of Defeat: A Tribute to the Newark Public Library." *Wilson Library Bulletin* 45 (Apr. 1969): 740–47.

Whitehead, Ralph. "Behind the Violence in Newark: Anatomy of a Riot." *Commonwealth* 86 (Aug. 11, 1967): 492–94.

# CHAPTER 11

# Charles Sprague Sargent *Plants an Outstanding Botanical Garden*

## I

James Arnold, a prosperous businessman of New Bedford, Massachusetts, had a charming English-style garden on his eleven-acre estate and took great interest in horticulture. When he died in 1863, he left part of his residuary holding to three trustees to be applied "for the promotion of agricultural and horticultural improvements, or other Philosophical or Philanthropic purposes."[1] George B. Emerson, the leading trustee, was a part-time botanist who wrote the book, *Trees and Shrubs Growing Naturally in the Forests of Massachusetts* (1846), and in 1872 he persuaded his fellow trustees to bestow the bequest on Harvard University to establish an Arnold Arboretum. Harvard decided to set aside 137 acres of its land in Jamaica Plain west of Boston and six miles from the university. The Arnold bequest came to about $50,000 but at first yielded only $3,000 yearly. According to the agreement of the trustees and the university, the arboretum was to contain "as far as practicable, all the trees, shrubs, and herbaceous plants, either indigenous or exotic, which can be raised in the open air" at Jamaica Plain.[2] Charles Sprague Sargent was made director of the Harvard Botanic Garden, professor of horticulture, and director of the new arboretum.[3]

Born in Boston, April 5, 1841, Sargent was the son of Ignatius and Henrietta (Gray) Sargent. Ignatius was a wealthy East India merchant, banker, and financier; both he and his wife were descended in prominent families and were members of the city's top social elite. Ignatius in 1845 purchased "Holm Lea" ("Inland

Island Pasture"), a 130-acre estate in Brookline, and developed there an outstanding garden. Young Charles was sent to Epes Sargent Dixwell's School for boys and in 1858 entered Harvard. He took Latin, Greek, French, Spanish, Italian, chemistry, astronomy, physics, metaphysics, and four courses of rhetoric (in which he failed to learn to speak in public). He had no work in botany. He was a wretched student and for a time appeared likely to be expelled for lack of application, but he managed to graduate in 1862, standing eighty-eighth in a class of ninety.

Soon after graduation, he enlisted in the Union Army as a first lieutenant assigned to the Second Louisiana Infantry. As aide-de-camp to General Nathaniel P. Banks in New Orleans, he took part in the Teche and Louisiana Red River campaigns, the siege of Port Hudson, and the capture of Mobile. He rose to be a brevet major, praised for his "faithful and meritorious service" against Mobile, and was honorably discharged in 1865. He then spent three years traveling in Europe. Upon his return, he apparently could not decide upon a career but settled for the time being upon managing the Holm Lea estate. There, however, he began to be interested in botany and horticulture and was meticulous in calling plants by their Latin names.

Why Sargent was appointed to his three positions at Harvard remains somewhat of a mystery. He had been a poor student and had only limited experience, though he did belong to Boston's upper class. He was liked by Francis Parkman, the historian, a neighbor deeply interested in horticulture who had served as professor of that subject for a year at Harvard. He may have nominated Sargent as his successor.[4]

Soon after that, Sargent made a promising marriage to Mary Allen Robeson, a dozen years younger than he, whose father owned prosperous cotton mills. Sargent himself could often be dour, uncommunicative, and unsociable, while Mary was always cheerful and outgoing. She had considerable artistic talent and later did watercolor illustrations for Sargent's Collection of Woods. She communicated well with their two sons and three daughters and shielded them from their father's sometimes petulant corrections.

In 1874 the Sargents made a combined business and honeymoon trip to Europe. He was much impressed by the Royal Botanic Garden at Edinburgh and thought it even surpassed the one at Kew. He got along well with Sir Joseph Hooker, Kew's director, and with his son-in-law and eventual successor, William Thiselton-Dyer, who was about his age. He also visited Alphonse de Candolle, the Swiss botanist, at Geneva and Joseph Decaisne at the Jardin des Plants in

Paris. Sargent always made it a point to meet the leading botanists and horticulturists of the world and to keep in touch with them.

Sargent maintained a close relationship with Professor Asa Gray of Harvard, who practically tutored him in the science of botany. He made many improvements in the Botanic Garden and stocked its nursery with plants that he planned to use in the arboretum. In 1877 the university dropped him as professor of horticulture before he did any teaching there, and soon he gave up direction of the Botanic Garden and concentrated all his efforts on the arboretum. As he wrote on its fiftieth anniversary:

> He found himself with a worn-out farm partly covered with natural plantations of native trees nearly ruined by excessive pasturage, to be developed with less than three thousand dollars a year available for the purpose. He was without equipment or the support and encouragement of the general public which knew nothing about an Arboretum and what it was expected to accomplish.[5]

Sargent then made a move that greatly improved the arboretum's chances for success. Frederick Law Olmsted, the landscape architect, conceived the idea of a continuous park system for Boston that would run from the city center for some seven miles. The arboretum lay in the path of that development, and he asked Sargent to join him in making it part of the park system. It would be open for recreation to city citizens, and in return Boston would pay for laying out roadways and footpaths, maintaining and policing them, and furnishing a water supply. Sargent backed the plan enthusiastically and enlisted Asa Gray to help persuade a reluctant President Charles Eliot of Harvard to adopt it. When the City Council voted against the development, Sargent cannily devised a petition in its favor, for which he secured the signatures of 1,305 of the most influential taxpayers. The council changed its mind, and in 1882 Harvard transferred 120 acres of arboretum land to the city, which purchased another 45 acres for the tract, the whole of which was leased to the university for 1,000 years, renewable for the same period, at one dollar per year.

Sargent at once began to develop his project with great energy. He planned for the arboretum to fulfill four functions—as a museum of living plants, a scientific station, school of forestry and arboriculture (which did not develop), and popular educator. He had surveyed the property and found only 123 species of woody plants. He quietly dropped the provision of the 1872 agreement that called for herbaceous plants. He set out new trees in groups to show their natural sequence, usually with a dozen specimens for each species. By the time the arboretum reached its fifteenth anniversary, he had planted 120,000 trees and shrubs. Sargent was a shrewd judge in choosing assistants, and he scored a real hit when he hired as superintendent Jackson Dawson, who took charge of the nursery and proved a marvelous propagator, serving faithfully until his death in 1916.

In order to make the arboretum a scientific center, Sargent began to accumulate a herbarium and wrote his close friend, Dr. George Engelmann, the German-trained physician and botanist, who was helping Henry Shaw develop the Missouri Botanical Garden in St. Louis, that he proposed to confine the herbarium "(for many years at any rate) to trees & shrubs of 1st North America and the whole temperate zone."[6] He also began to gather a library of important and often rare books. Both herbarium and library were his personal property, which he kept in a room at Holm Lea until 1890, when he gave them—by then 1,000 herbarium specimens and 6,000 volumes—to the arboretum. They were to be housed in a new administrative building that had been donated by Horatio Hollis Hunnewell. The new facility welcomed botanists, landscape designers, park superintendents, nurserymen, and students, providing them with a commodious room where they could spread out specimens and books. Sargent himself, always ready to discuss their problems and advise them, and Charles Edward Faxon, a scholarly naturalist, had their offices in the new building. Faxon was the curator and an accomplished botanical artist who provided drawings for Sargent's various books; he served until his death in 1918.

In the educational field, the arboretum made steady progress. In 1886 Sargent added a young Canadian botanist, John George Jack, as his third principal assistant, who lectured on arboriculture and instituted field classes. His knowledgeable and enthusiastic teaching with walks through the arboretum was an instant success. Sargent also started a weekly magazine, *Garden and Forest*, in 1888 with himself as "conductor" and William Augustus Stiles, a skilled journalist, as editor. The conductor contributed frequent short notices on "New or Little Known Plants," usually with engravings or photographs, "Notes on American Trees," "Notes on Forest Fauna of Japan," book reviews, and unsigned editorials that supported his numerous forestry interests. The magazine was published in New York City without arboretum sponsorship but was a strong supporter of its program; unfortunately, it lost money steadily (much of it Sargent's) and was abandoned after ten years.

Sargent's biggest problem with the arboretum was financial. The endowment at most brought in only about $8,000 yearly, and expenditures often were double that. Sargent contributed much money himself (estimated at about $250,000 throughout his lifetime) and frequently called upon his friends for funds. When he faced a shortage, he would give a dinner party at which he outlined the problem and the amount he was giving; his guests would then agree to contribute. He readily admitted that his assistants were badly underpaid, but although they grumbled, they remained loyal.

The arboretum under Sargent was a one-man institution. In the office he worked long hours and on weekends and holidays. He took care of a mountain of correspondence. While his assistants admired "the Professor" and his single-minded devotion, he was sometimes gruff and despotic, a true czar though often a wise one. He admired and trusted his staff but did not regard them as social equals or invite them to Holm Lea for dinner.

## II

While the arboretum was getting underway, Sargent began to examine the forests of North America, and he became a leader in the movement to preserve them. His first publication, *A Few Suggestions on Tree Planting*, appeared in 1875, and the Massachusetts Society for Promoting Agriculture, of which he was a trustee, reprinted 10,000 copies for public distribution. The society elected him president and soon began to make annual contributions of at least $2,500 to the arboretum.

Asa Gray suggested Sargent to the United States Department of the Interior to report on the forests for the Census of 1880, and he agreed to undertake that large and difficult mission. He enlisted botanists to examine the trees in defined regions and persuaded the government to publish his preliminary *Catalogue of the Forest Trees of North America* to guide them. In the summer of 1880 he journeyed west with his friends Engelmann and Charles C. Perry to "examine the trees in the mountainous regions of Utah, Washington, Oregon, British Columbia, California, and Arizona. Engelmann was then seventy years old, rheumatic, and overweight; Perry reported that he was "quite lively but does not enjoy the push and hurry of Sargent," and Engelmann wrote Gray of "the terrible strain Sargent's restlessness and energy put us under. . . . he rarely took or allowed more than '5 minutes' for anything. . . . Well, with all that, we had a glorious time."[7] Sargent's resulting *Report on the Forests of North America (Exclusive of Mexico)* made him known throughout the country. The 612-page volume was an extensive examination of 412 species of trees, the properties of their wood, and their uses. The problem of forest fires was considered, and he urged that the Federal Government investigate the effect of forests upon rivers. The *Report* was by far the best treatment that had appeared, and retained its usefulness for many years.

Sargent had a reactionary and distrustful attitude toward government and its part in American affairs. As he wrote his friend Thiselton-Dyer in 1898:

> If I lived in England I should be a jingo. It is the business of England to civilize the world and boss the inferior races. We are not equipped for that sort of work . . . and the curse of universal suffrage is always with us—a perfect millstone around America's neck—a splendid thing in theory and for small communities where everybody is more or less educated and honest. It is a grievous failure, however, in our big cities, and it will prevent our ever having a public service which will enable us to compete with the rest of the world in the government of colonies. Americans are capable of doing a lot of good work; it is done, however, by corporations and individuals quite outside the government. There is no better proof of the correctness of this statement than the quality of the scientific work done by Government as compared with that produced by the Universities. . . . We are going to have serious trouble sometime in this country. Lots of people are going to be killed and a lot of wealth wasted. If this results in the end in restricted suffrage the sacrifice won't be too great.[8]

Sargent obviously was a nineteenth-century Victorian, comfortable in his wealth, absorbed in a successful scientific career, and certain that responsible individualism was far superior to any possible governmental supervision in the hands of mere politicians. Descended from English stock in the colonial period, he was suspicious of increasing immigration from all over Europe, contemptuous of "inferior races," and fearful of "universal suffrage."

As soon as Sargent had dispatched his census report to Washington in 1883, he left for Montana as a member of the Northern Transcontinental Survey, a project sponsored by railroad interests. The expedition made its way across the Rockies, through northern Washington, and over the Cascades to Portland. When the railroad backers lost interest, no publication of its findings appeared, but Sargent wrote an article in the *Nation* which made the first suggestion of what is now Glacier National Park. He emphasized the breathtaking beauty of the area and argued that a forest preserve there would protect the three great rivers of the continent—the Missouri, Columbia, and Saskatchewan.[9] Eventually, the park was established in 1910.

In 1883 Morris K. Jesup, president of the American Museum of Natural History, persuaded Sargent to head a commission to investigate what New York State should do about an Adirondack Forest Reserve. The state already owned about 40,000 acres there and was adding private land forfeited for nonpayment of taxes. The commission's report of 1885, much of it Sargent's work, stressed the value of the forest and warned against the great numbers of fires and the lax lumbering practices. It rejected state control but favored a three-man, unpaid, nonpolitical commission to manage the forest and enforce fire protection and good lumbering on both state-owned and private tracts. The residents of the area, lumber interests, and railroads transporting timber successfully opposed the report and obtained a compromise with five well-paid, political commissioners and weak restrictions on fires and lumbering. Sargent was disgusted and even more convinced that government action in such areas was only too often fruitless.

Meanwhile, President Jesup had conceived adding a new Collection of North American Woods at the American Museum, and he asked Sargent to gather it. Jesup at first impressed Sargent as a fine businessman and able administrator, "one of the very few Americans who wants to make the best use of his money & spend it for something better than nice houses and bad pictures."[10] Sargent saw to securing some 106 specimens of trees. He had whole tree trunks six feet tall properly cut and polished to show vertical, horizontal, and diagonal sections; they were illustrated by life-size watercolors of their foliage, flowers, and fruit, ultimately painted by Mary Sargent. All of the rapidly mounting bills were paid by Jesup. During the fifteen years the two men worked together, frequent quarrels took place, Sargent insisting upon a full and meticulous scientific collection and Jesup trying to reduce the heavy costs. The Jesup collection opened in 1885 amid plaudits from the press but never had much popular appeal. One consolation for Sargent was that he acquired a collection of smaller specimens of the woods for his museum at the arboretum.

Sargent then decided to write a sylva of North American forests as an expansion of his census report, for he thought the nation badly needed a scientific description of its trees. He had gathered seeds or plants of many of them on his trips to the Northwest, and he began systematically to visit the West Indies, North Carolina, Florida, Louisiana, Alabama, and Texas, securing specimens and making notes. Sometimes he took Faxon along to provide sketches; on other tours his wife accompanied him. He also explored trees in northeastern Mexico, as well as in England, France, Italy, and Germany. In 1891 the first volume of the *Silva* appeared, dedicated to "Asa Gray, Friend and Master." The finished work ran to fourteen volumes with 585 specimens and 740 plates. In the preface, Sargent wrote:

> To be really understood, trees must be studied in the forest; and therefore . . . I have examined the trees of America growing in their native homes from Canada

> to the banks of the Rio Crande and the mountains of Arizona, and from British Columbia to the islands of southern Florida. I have watched many of them in the gardens of this country and those of Europe, and there are hardly a dozen . . . I have not seen in a living state.[11]

The reviewers were enthusiastic about the book. Nathaniel L. Britton predicted that it would "rank with the works of science and art that are recognized the world over." John Muir, the naturalist, then becoming a close friend of Sargent, wrote a flowery review in the *Atlantic Monthly*, which said: "Though accustomed to read the trees themselves, not written descriptions of them, I have read it through twice as if it were a novel, and wished that it were longer."[12]

In 1894 the Secretary of the Interior asked the National Academy of Sciences to devise a "rational forest policy for the forest lands of the United States."[13] Sargent was appointed chairman of the investigatory commission along with three other academy members. He got Gifford Pinchot, a non-academy man, added to the commission, a move which he later regretted. The group followed the northern Rockies along the Canadian border and then through Washington, Oregon, California, and Arizona to Colorado. Early in 1897 their preliminary report urged President Cleveland to proclaim thirteen new forest reserves of more than 21 million acres. Cleveland was about to retire from the presidency, but he dared to issue the proclamation. The Western states and Congress objected strenuously and brought pressure on incoming President McKinley to rescind the proclamation, but Sargent secured an interview and finally convinced him to let it stand. The commission's final report called for good methods of forest management and protection and for the use of federal troops until a trained forest corps could be created. It also proposed parks for Mount Ranier and the Grand Canyon. Congress refused to pass any of the proposed legislation. To make things worse, Pinchot, though he had signed the report, a few days later got the Secretary of the Interior to allow him to prepare "what was described as a practical plan for the national domain."[14] Sargent was outraged by what he considered Pinchot's betrayal. He gave up further efforts to obtain a rational forest policy and devoted his energies to improving the arboretum and to scientific writings about forests and trees.

## III

In developing the arboretum's living collection, Sargent at first gave attention only to American plants. But soon he decided that, in accord with the agreement of the trustees and Harvard, the arboretum ought to contain all the trees and shrubs, either indigenous or exotic, which could be raised in the New England climate. William S. Clark, former president of the Massachusetts College of Agriculture, sent him seeds from Japan, and Dr. Emil Bretschneider of St. Petersburg, many of north China trees. In 1892 Sargent decided to go himself to Japan. Professor Gray had early noticed "the extraordinary similarity between the Floras of Eastern North America and Japan."[15] Sargent and his young nephew, Philip Codman, who was studying landscape architecture with Olmsted, spent ten weeks on Hokkaido and Nippon, the two principal Japanese islands. They visited forests, gardens, and nurseries; made a valuable acquaintance in professor Kingo Miyabe, a botanist in the college of Sapporo, and scaled Mount Hakkoda with young James Herbert Veitch, nephew of the head of a prominent English nursery firm.

Sargent returned to the arboretum with about 200 varieties of plants and 1,225 herbarium specimens. He wrote an account of the trip in an attractive, informal style for *Garden and Forest* and then issued it in book form.[16] He stressed Japan's need for flood control and building materials and pointed out that timber to China and Australia and staves to California would be valuable exports. The living collection of the arboretum gained greatly from Sargent's trip, raising many new species, to name a few: *Acer nicoense*, Japanese barberry, *Magnolia selicifolia*, and the Kaemfer azaleas. Sargent returned to Japan in 1903 during a six-month round-the-world journey with his son Robeson, who had studied landscape design, and his old friend John Muir. They went to England, through Europe to St. Petersburg, Moscow, the Crimea, across Siberia by rail, Manchuria, Peking, Korea, Japan, Shanghai (from which Muir set off on his own), Singapore, Java, and home.

During this same period of time, Sargent also wished China more thoroughly explored for the arboretum. He kept in touch with the Veitches in England, who selected a young botanist, Ernest Henry (later nicknamed "Chinese") Wilson, for their plant hunter. He had been well trained in nurseries and studied botany in university classes. In 1899 he set out for China by way of Boston, where in five days he met Professor Sargent, who became a hero in his eyes, and visited the arboretum and Holm Lea with its garden. Wilson got on well with the Chinese and, despite the unsettled conditions of the Boxer Rebellion, reached the Ich'ang area in central China. He stayed there until 1902, secured plentiful seeds of the Dove Tree (*Davidia*) which the Veitches had hoped he would find, and returned to London with hundreds of other seeds and nearly 2,600 kinds of herbarium specimens. He made a second tour in 1903 with instructions to bring back the Yellow Poppywort and went much farther west, using Loshan near Tibet as a base. He made many perilous journeys, found plentiful seeds of the Poppywort and of 2,000 other species, and collected 5,000 herbarium specimens.

In 1905-1906 Sargent spent six months, accompanied by Robeson, in western South America—Ecuador, Peru, and Chile. They returned via England, where they persuaded Wilson to go to China for the arboretum at greatly increased pay. He spent 1907 in central and western China, sending the arboretum 2,262 packages of seeds, 1,473 varieties of living plants, 2,500 species of herbarium specimens, and 720 photographic plates. He returned to Boston in 1909 but departed again the next year. He had sent Sargent 1,285 packets of seeds when a landslide on the main road left him with a badly broken leg; he could not get back to Boston until the spring of 1911. Unsettled conditions prevented his return to China, but he took two successful tours of Japan, coming back with fifty species of the spectacular Khrume azalea. He also visited Korea and Formosa, and then in 1920 went to Australia, New Zealand, India, Kenya, Rhodesia, and South Africa. As a result of seven Chinese journeys, Wilson introduced more than 1,000 new species in England and the United States, and "succeeded in collecting and introducing a greater number of plants than any other collector."[17]

Sargent also sent out several other plant explorers to China. One of the most capable was the experienced Austrian botanist and collector, Joseph Francis Charles Rock, an authority on Hawaiian flora who could speak Chinese. He left in 1924 to explore the mountain ranges of northwestern China and southern Tibet. He found few trees there but secured seeds and cuttings of hardier forms of species that would do well in New England. But he did not return to Boston until after Sargent's death.

## IV

In examining the first fifty years of the arboretum in 1922, Sargent thought that it had become the greatest existing collection of hardy trees and shrubs, many of them new plants obtained through explorations. Much still needed to be done, of course, assembling information about trees in many parts of the world and examining tropical forests which were disappearing at an alarming rate. The expanded living plant collection was a major factor in increasing the arboretum's worth as a scientific institution. Sargent considered the herbarium the largest and most important in the world; its specimens numbered about

200,000. The library contained more than 37,000 books and 8,400 pamphlets and was perhaps unsurpassed in its field. These resources attracted more and more scholars and serious students who received a warm welcome and friendly assistance. In looking ahead, Sargent called for a department to study diseases in trees, another to examine dangerous insects and their control, and a third for breeding new species of plants.

In the educational area, the arboretum sought to teach both scholars and the general public. In 1911 Sargent began publishing a *Bulletin of Popular Information* (the name later changed to *Arnoldia*) with short articles on plants in bloom and other current news, and in 1919 he founded a scientific quarterly, *Journal of the Arnold Arboretum*, which also served as an outlet for staff research. Though Sargent was the nominal editor, Alfred Rehder did most of the actual work. A German immigrant, he had begun as a day laborer in 1898, but Sargent had put him in charge of the *Bradley Bibliography*, a guide to the woody plants of the world. An accomplished and tireless scholar, he wrote more than a thousand articles during his service; upon Faxan's death, he also became curator.

Sargent himself continued to produce publications, two of the most important: *Manual of the Trees of North America* and *Trees and Shrubs of New or Little Known Ligneous Plants*. He had an amusing experience with the Mount Vernon Ladies' Association of the Union. At the invitation of its regent, he visited Mount Vernon in 1901 in order to consider making its trees conform to those known to George Washington. He generously waived any fee, but when he demanded a free hand in the project, the headstrong Ladies refused his services. A new regent in 1914 persuaded him to try again and worked with him to defeat quarrelsome Ladies' committees from time to time. He made a plan, based on the Washington Diary, showing where each tree should stand and greatly improved the historical authenticity of the Mount Vernon grounds. In this case as in his previous experiences with the Federal and New York State governments, he could not understand why an expert should be called in and then have his advice ignored.

Sargent had much influence in the botanical scientific field through his voluminous correspondence and his generosity in sending out seeds, plants, and advice. How the process worked is well shown by the 328 letters he wrote between 1914 and his death in 1927 to personnel of the Rochester (New York) Park System. He enlisted their close collaboration, requested information on various plants, kept them informed of Chinese Wilson's explorations, sent numerous seeds and plants, and advised them on their trips around the country. Yet he insisted that the arboretum must also help the ordinary gardener and plant lover to learn more about trees and shrubs and their uses. For popular enlightenment, he depended heavily upon the plantings themselves. Their year-round changes not only brought out-of-town visitors but thousands of Boston citizens who came to regard the arboretum as a great civic attraction.

The greatest need of the arboretum, thought Sargent in 1922, was more endowment. It had increased, through his efforts, from $103,848 to $808,176, with an extra construction fund of $129,257 immediately available for improvements. (The endowment finally did exceed one million in 1926). In summarizing what had happened in the first fifty years, Sargent concluded:

> The Arnold Arboretum is . . . a station for the study of trees as individuals in their scientific relations, economic properties and cultural requirements and possibilities. . . . It has been managed not merely as a New England museum but as a national and international institution working to increase knowledge of trees in all parts of the world and as anxious to help a student in Tasmania or New Caledonia as in Massachusetts. An institution with such ambitions must be equipped to answer any questions about any trees growing in any part of the world which may be addressed to it. During the first fifty years of the Arnold Arboretum only the foundations of such an establishment have been laid.[18]

Sargent's last years were not too happy. In 1918 Robeson, his son and close companion, died suddenly, and two years later, Mary Sargent also passed away, at age sixty-six. The next seven years were lonely ones for him, though except for persistent gout, he enjoyed remarkably good health. The last two of his fifty-five years at the arboretum, he came to the office for shorter periods and had to be driven around the grounds in a small automobile. Finally, on March 22, 1927, he died peacefully. He left the arboretum $30,000, two-thirds for the library and the other third to be invested to grow for 100 years. Then, of the new total, all could be used for running expenses except $10,000 which was to increase for another 100 years.

Sargent's career was indeed a remarkable one. By persistent hard work, careful planning and a pervasive sense of order, good administration and sound judgment of personnel, and cooperation with the botanical gardens and leading scientists in the field, he acquired the botanical and horticultural knowledge that he needed. And his willingness to share know-how as well as seeds and plants with others did much to establish his leadership.

The arboretum has continued since as a leading botanical garden of the nation and the world, and the new emphasis mankind is placing on population and environmental puoblems makes it ever more valuable. Though enlarged in scope since Sargent's day, the Arnold Arboretum still maintains the high standards and aspirations that he gave it.

## NOTES

1. Quoted in Stephane Barry Sutton, *Charles Sprague Sargent and the Arnold Arboretum* (Cambridge, Mass.: Harvard University Press, 1970), 30. We are fortunate to have this well-researched and insightful biography.

2. Charles S. Sargent, "The First Fifty Years of the Arnold Arboretum," *Journal of the Arnold Arboretum* 3 (Jan. 1922): 127–71.

3. Other chief works on Sargent and the Arboretum are: Arnold Arboretum, *Bulletin of Popular Information* (May 2, 1911–Dec. 13, 1940), 8 vols.; Arnold Arboretum, *Journal of the Arnold Arboretum* 1 (July 1919); W. T. Councilman, "Charles Sprague Sargent, 1841–1927," in M. A. De Wolfe Howe, ed., *Later Years of the Saturday Club, 1870–1920* (Freeport, N.Y.: Books for Libraries Press, 1968; first published, 1927), 286–94; A. DesCares, *A Treatise on Pruning Forest and Ornamental Trees*, introduction by Charles S. Sargent, 3d ed. (Boston: A. Williams, 1881); Frances Duncan, "Professor Charles Sprague Sargent and the Arnold Arboretum," *Critic* 47 (Aug. 1905): 115–19; *Garden and Forest: A Journal of Horticulture, Landscape Art and Forestry* (Feb. 9, 1888–Dec. 29, 1897), 10 vols; Richard A. Howard, "The Arnold Arboretum at the Century Mark," *Longwood Program Seminars* 3 (Dec. 1971): 33–35; Alfred Rehder, *The Bradley Bibliography: A Guide to the Literature of Woody Plants of the World* (Cambridge, Mass.: Riverside Press, 1911–1918), 5 vols.; Charles Sprague Sargent, *Excerpts: Letters of, to Rochester Park Personnel* (Rochester, N.Y.: Rochester Chapbooks, 1961); Sargent, *Forest Flora of Japan: Notes on* (Boston: Houghton, Mifflin, 1894); Sargent, *Manual of the Trees of North America (Exclusive of Mexico)* 2d ed. enlarged (Boston: Houghton, Mifflin, 1933; first ed., 1905); Sargent, ed., *Plantae Wilsonianae: ... Woody Plants Collected in Western China for the Arnold Arboretum ... 1907, 1908, and 1910 by E. H. Wilson* (Cambridge, Mass.: Harvard University Press, 1913–1917), 3 vols.; Sargent, *Report on the Forests of North America (Exclusive of Mexico)* (Washington, D.C.: Government Printing Office, 1884); Sargent, ed., *Scientific Papers of Asa Gray* (Boston: Houghton, Mifflin, 1889), 2 vols.; Sargent, *The Silva of North America: ... Trees Which Grow Naturally in North America Exclusive of Mexico* (Boston: Houghton, Mifflin, 1891–1902), 14 vols.; Sargent, ed., *Trees and Shrubs of New or Little Known Ligneous Plants* (Boston: Houghton, Mifflin, 1905, 1913), 2 vols.; Sargent, *The Trees of Mount Vernon*, rev. ed. (Mount Vernon: Ladies' Association, 1926); Sargent, *The Woods of the United States: ... Their Structure, Qualities, and Uses* (New York: D. Appleton, 1885); Stephane Barry Sutton, *The Arnold Arboretum: The First Century* (Jamaica Plain: Arnold Arboretum, 1971); Elswyth Thane, *Mount Vernon: The Legacy* (Philadelphia: J. B. Lippincott, 1967); E. H. Wilson, *America's Greatest Garden: The Arnold Arboretum* (Boston: Stratford, 1925); Wilson, *A Naturalist in Western China*, introduction by Charles Sprague Sargent (New York: Doubleday, Page, 1913), 2 vols.; Donald Wyman, *The Arnold Arboretum Garden Book* (New York: D. Van Nostrand, 1954).

4. Sutton, *Sargent*, 28–29.

5. Sargent, "First Fifty Years," 132.

6. Quoted in Sutton, *Sargent*, 64.

7. Quoted in Sutton, *Sargent*, 87–88.

8. Quoted in Sutton, *Sargent*, 192–93.

9. *Nation* 37 (Sept. 6, 1883): 201.
10. Quoted in Sutton, *Sargent*, 106.
11. Sargent, *Silva*, 1: v.
12. *Garden and Forest* 3 (Dec. 3, 1890); John Muir, *Atlantic Monthly* 92 (July 1903): 9–10.
13. Quoted in Sutton, *Sargent*, 159.
14. Quoted in Sutton, *Sargent*, 167.
15. C. S. Sargent, "Asa Gray," *Garden and Forest* 1 (Feb. 29, 1888): 1.
16. Sargent, *Forest Flora of Japan*.
17. Alfred Rehder, "Ernest Henry Wilson," *Journal of the Arnold Arboretum* 2 (Oct. 1920): 185.
18. Sargent, "First Fifty Years," 168–69.

## SELECT BIBLIOGRAPHY

Arnold Arboretum. *Bulletin of Popular Information*. May 2, 1911–Dec. 13, 1940. 8 vols.
Arnold Arboretum. *Journal of the Arnold Arboretum*. Vol. 1 (July 1919).
Councilman, W. T. "Charles Sprague Sargent, 1841–1927." In *Later Years of the Saturday Club, 1870–1920*. Edited by M. A. De Wolfe Howe. Freeport, N.Y.: Books for Libraries Press, 1968. First published, 1927.
DesCares, A. *A Treatise on Pruning Forest and Ornamental Trees*. Introduction by Charles S. Sargent. 3d ed. Boston: A. Williams, 1881.
Duncan, Frances. "Professor Charles Sprague Sargent and the Arnold Arboretum." *Critic* 47 (Aug. 1905): 115–19.
*Garden and Forest: A Journal of Horticulture, Landscape Art and Forestry*. Feb. 9, 1888–Dec. 29, 1897). 10 vols.
Howard, Richard A. "The Arnold Arboretum at the Century Mark." *Longwood Program Seminars* 3 (Dec. 1971): 33–35.
Rehder, Alfred. *The Bradley Bibliography: A Guide to the Literature of Woody Plants of the World*. Cambridge, Mass.: Riverside Press, 1911–1918. 5 vols.
_____. "Ernest Henry Wilson." *Journal of the Arnold Arboretum* 2 (Oct. 1920): 185.
Sargent, Charles Sprague. *Excerpts: Letters of, to Rochester Park Personnel*. Rochester, N.Y.: Rochester Chapbooks, 1961.
_____. "The First Fifty Years of the Arnold Arboretum." *Journal of the Arnold Arboretum* 3 (Jan. 1922): 127–71.
_____. *Forest Flora of Japan: Notes on*. Boston: Houghton, Mifflin, 1894.
_____. *Manual of the Trees of North America (Exclusive of Mexico)*. 2d ed. enlarged. Boston: Houghton, Mifflin, 1933. First ed., 1905.
_____. *Report on the Forests of North America (Exclusive of Mexico)*. Washington, D.C.: Government Printing Office, 1884.
_____. *The Silva of North America: ... Trees Which Grow Naturally in North America Exclusive of Mexico*. Boston: Houghton, Mifflin, 1891–1902. 14 vols.
_____. *The Trees of Mount Vernon*. Rev. ed. Mount Vernon: Ladies' Association, 1926.
_____. *The Woods of the United States: ... Their Structure, Qualities, and Uses*. New York: D. Appleton, 1885.
_____. ed. *Plantae Wilsonianae: ... Woody Plants Collected in Western China for the Arnold Arboretum ... 1907, 1908, and 1910 by E. H. Wilson*. Cambridge, Mass.: Harvard University Press, 1913–1917. 3 vols.

_____. ed. *Scientific Papers of Asa Gray*. Boston: Houghton, Mifflin, 1889. 2 vols.
_____. ed. *Trees and Shrubs of New or Little Known Ligneous Plants*. Boston: Houghton, Mifflin, 1905, 1913. 2 vols.
Sutton, Stephane Barry. *The Arnold Arboretum: The First Century*. Jamaica Plain: Arnold Arboretum, 1971.
_____. *Charles Sprague Sargent and the Arnold Arboretum*. Cambridge, Mass.: Harvard University Press, 1970.
Thane, Elswyth. *Mount Vernon: The Legacy*. Philadelphia: J. B. Lippincott, 1967.
Wilson, E. H. *America's Greatest Garden: The Arnold Arboretum*. Boston: Stratford, 1925.
_____. *A Naturalist in Western China*. Introduction by Charles Sprague Sargent. New York: Doubleday, Page, 1913. 2 vols.
Wyman, Donald. *The Arnold Arboretum Garden Book*. New York: D. Van Nostrand, 1954

CHAPTER 12

# William Temple Hornaday *Founds a Varied and Popular Zoo*

## I

William Temple Hornaday was born on a farm near Plainfield, Indiana, on December 1, 1854, the son of William and Martha (Varner) Hornaday; the family later moved to Iowa. As a boy, Hornaday spent time between Indiana where he was familiar with turtles, yellow perch, croppies, squirrels, and little green herons and Iowa with its prairie chickens, quail, ground squirrels, and pocket gophers. His brother Calvin taught him to hunt, but he later maintained, perhaps in exaggeration because of his support for the conservation of wildlife, that he had shot only one gray squirrel, one blue jay, one little green heron, two prairie chickens, and one woodpecker in order to examine how they were made. Modern guns, he said, made killing game for sport too easy, and he later did so only to obtain scientific specimens.

By the time he was fourteen, both his parents were dead; he attended public school in Knoxville, Iowa, and then in 1870 went to Oskaloosa College for one year. There he received a sound grounding in English that later helped him fluently write many books and articles. He also was entranced to watch a professor skin and mount a crow. As a boy, he had seen two beautifully mounted ducks in Ambrose Ballweg's game store in Indianapolis, but could not find out how the taxidermy was done. In 1871 Hornaday entered Iowa State College at Ames. He studied botany, zoology, museums and museology, paleontology, anthropology, and geology. President Walsh saw him mount a great white heron successfully, relying upon his memory of the crow and with an Audubon engraving of a heron as a guide. The president hired him for work in the college museum at nine cents per hour. By the end of his second year, he was resolved to pursue museology, especially taxidermy, as a career, rather than to engage in business and making money.[1]

He decided, however, that instead of finishing his last two years of college, he would go to Professor Henry A. Ward's world-famous Natural Science Establishment in Rochester, New York, and become an apprentice taxidermist. Ward hired him at six dollars per week. The young man was thrilled to see the work of experienced taxidermists such as Frederic S. Webster, an expert at mounting birds, and John Martens, who had come from Hamburg bringing along iron squares to which leg irons of mounted carcasses could be attached; and he made several close friends, among them Frederic A. Lucas, who would become director of the American Museum of Natural History. Some of the good-natured apprentices posed partially nude for Hornaday when he was working on an orangutan group, and he occasioned amusement among his friends when he sent home from South America a capybara with two pairs of left legs, fore and aft.

In 1874 Professor Ward sent Hornaday out as a collector for a six-year period at first to Florida, Cuba, Barbados, Trinidad, Venezuela, and British Guiana, and then to India, Ceylon, the Malay Peninsula, and Borneo. The professor accompanied him part way on the India trip, and they collected natural history specimens while visiting museums and art galleries in Liverpool, London, Paris, and a half dozen Italian cities. In the Far East, Hornaday hunted widely and got along well with the natives, whom he paid to collect for him; he preserved all specimens with care and returned with the richest zoological collection yet made by one man—a huge mass of skins, skeletons, and skulls of mammals, birds, reptiles, fishes, crustaceans, starfishes, corals, and a few insects. He described his travels so vividly in a book, *Two Years in the Jungle* (1885), that it ran through a dozen printings.[2]

When Hornaday got back from the East Indies, he was married, on September 11, 1879, to Josephine (jokingly called "Empress Josephine") Chamberlain of Battle Creek, Michigan. He dedicated the jungle book "To My Good Wife Josephine whose presence both when seen and unseen has ever been the sunshine of my life." The union lasted until his death; they had one daughter who provided them with three grandchildren. Hornaday took great pride in being a devoted family man.[3]

In 1880 the young naturalist worked on a pioneering habitat group of orangutans that he had collected in Borneo and which his fellow taxidermists helped model. It was called "A Fight in the Tree-Tops" and attracted much attention when shown at a meeting of the American Association for the Advancement of Science in Saratoga. He and some seven others formed the Society of American Taxidermists, which soon held competitive exhibitions at Rochester, Boston, and New York. At the last one (1883), Hornaday's "Coming to the Point," a grouping with a hunting dog and six partridges, won a special medal, and the elephant "Mungo" that he had modeled with a manikin process he had invented received a silver medal as "best piece in the entire Exhibition."[4]

In 1882 Hornaday became chief taxidermist at the Smithsonian Institution's United States National Museum, where he worked harmoniously and happily with George Brown Goode, the museum's director, and Spencer Fullerton Baird, secretary of the Smithsonian. He made many advances in the science of taxidermy, one of the most important being the use of clay as a filling material on the outside of a manikin, which made it possible to affix the hide with all the proper curvatures and indentations of the living animal. The manikin itself consisted of a wooden center board with wires running to the legs, the whole covered with excelsior tied with cords and surmounted by clay. Those developments made it possible to produce a convincing replica of the animal in a lifelike pose. He believed that taxidermists ought to receive credit on museum labels for their work, and Brown Goode adopted that rule for the National Museum.[5]

Hornaday did much to develop the concept of habitat groups, so popular today in natural history museums. About 1886 he completed a small group of three coyotes in a natural setting, an exhibit widely studied and much admired. He made a three-month hunting trip that fall and winter to the Big Dry badlands of Montana to secure specimens of American bison; his buffalo group exhibit included buffalo grass and other authentic accessories. Morris K. Jesup, president of the American Museum of Natural History, came down to inspect the coyote and buffalo groups with enthusiasm.[6]

Hornaday also had the idea of enlarging the small number of live animals kept in a paddock beside the Smithsonian building into a genuine zoological park. In 1888 Congress appropriated $200,000 for a Rock Creek Park site of 168 acres, and the National Zoological Park was soon formed, to be operated by the Smithsonian with Hornaday as designer and director. He wished to attract the general public rather than only professional zoologists and collectors, and he insisted upon letting the animals roam freely in the park's large ranges. He secured a woven wire fence that would contain the beasts but allow the public to view them. But alas! Hornaday did not get along with Baird's successor as

Smithsonian secretary, Samuel P. Langley, who, according to Brown Goode, "wished him to subordinate himself more than he was willing." And so, Hornaday resigned in 1890 because of "great Langley disillusionment" and "the death of my plans for a really great Zoological Park." He supposedly left zoology and taxidermy forever and moved to Buffalo to become secretary of the Union Land Exchange, a large real estate business.[7]

In saying goodbye, Hornaday made another contribution to zoological science when he wrote *Taxidermy and Zoological Collecting* (1891), "a complete handbook for the amateur taxidermist, collector, geologist, museum-builder, sportsman, and traveller." Its 362 pages described, with admirable clarity and sometimes eloquence, hunting and collection, the selection and study of specimens, treatment of skins in the field, and the whole mounting process in the laboratory. Dedicated to G. Brown Goode, "whose liberal policy has done so much for American taxidermy," the book became the acknowledged classic on the subject and had seventeen printings by 1909.

## II

The New York Zoological Society was formed in 1895 as a result of a movement led by Madison Grant, a young lawyer, who was determined to protect American big-game animals from senseless slaughter and possible extermination. The Boone and Crockett Club, an organization of wealthy, concerned sportsmen with Theodore Roosevelt as president, hoped that a zoological garden might be established in one of the parks acquired by New York City in 1888. The cause received a great boost when Henry Fairfield Osborn of the American Museum of Natural History walked into Grant's office and volunteered his help. The society's executive committee adopted the "new Principle" that the larger wild animals "should be shown not in paddocks but in the free range of large enclosures, in which the forests, rocks, and natural features of the landscape will give the people an impression of the life habits and other native surroundings of these different types." As soon as the State Legislature and the city agreed upon the creation of the society, the appointment of an executive director became all important. Hornaday's work with the National Zoological Park was well known, and after a thorough investigation by Osborn and a search committee, he was appointed and took office in April 1896.[8]

The society now had three energetic, strong-willed, and driving men sharing its direction: Professor Osborn as chairman of the executive committee, Madison

Grant as its secretary, and Hornaday. Their opinions clashed violently now and then. Osborn and Grant stood behind Hornaday in his quarrels with the public and appreciated his aggressive actions in behalf of wildlife conservation, but he was always vocal and would throw an occasional tantrum. Grant found him difficult and soon made any complaints he had to Osborn who then, with a combination of tact and firmness, persuaded Hornaday to do as they thought best. Grant once wrote Osborn: "The best way is to let Mr. Hornaday speak his mind, and then we can meet privately and decide what we are going to do."[9]

The new director's first important action was to visit the different New York parks to choose the one most suitable for a zoological garden. When he spent a day in the southern section of Bronx Park (the northern part had been given to the Botanical Garden), he was astonished and enchanted to find an unbroken wilderness with virgin woods, spacious meadows separated by rocky ridges, and abundant ponds, bogs, and streams on the 264-acre tract. He at once enthusiastically recommended that site over Van Cortlandt Park, which a committee of experts previously had suggested. The executive committee ratified his choice and sent him off to Europe with a purse of $13,000 with which to buy animals. In two months he visited fifteen zoos in England, Belgium, Holland, Germany, and France, noting carfully their management, means of support, buildings, methods of exhibition, pleasure grounds and restaurants, and maps and plans. He was much encouraged when some of the European directors told him: "With such ground, and the money New York will give you, you can do anything you choose."[10]

During the next year the city agreed that the society should raise $250,000 over a three-year period for animals and buildings, the latter to belong to the city. It would provide roads, grading, fences, and water, as well as police protection. Admission was to be free of charge for five days each week. Most important, the society should choose and direct all personnel and have entire management of the garden's affairs. Through the years, the arrangement became similar to that worked out for several New York museums with buildings, maintenance, and protection furnished by the city and the collection, museum, and educational programs provided and managed by the private board of trustees.[11]

Hornaday made a plan for the garden that was examined critically but only slightly modified by several experts and the executive committee. It called for a Baird Court bordered by a Lion House (patterned after London's), Elephant House (after Antwerp's), Antelope House (after Frankfurt's), and Reptile House (after London's but with improvements). Hornaday was proud that Our Bird House, Monkey House, sub-tropical House, Winter House for Birds, Administration Building, Bear Dens, Wolf and Fox Dens, Alligators' Pool, Burrowing Rodents' Quarters, Squirrel installations, Beaver Pond and Aquatic Rodents' Ponds, all are features absolutely new, both in design and general arrangement. There also was a Flying Cage for Birds 150 feet long, 75 wide, and 50 high that contained living trees and a flowing stream.[12]

The next problems were to secure a capable staff and animals. Hornaday enlisted three talented young men to serve as assistant curators and take much of the responsibility for hiring keepers, caring for animals, and handling the everyday administration. J. Alden Loring was in charge of animals; he had worked eight years for the Biological Survey as a field naturalist and two years as an animal keeper in London's zoo. Raymond Lee Ditmars took over the reptiles; he had been an assistant at the American Museum of Natural History and a reporter for the New York *Times*; he gave his own collection of forty specimens of reptiles to the society. Charles William Beebe, a graduate student of Professor Osborn's known for his restless energy and interest in birds, supervised the birds. Hornaday appointed his nephew, H. Raymond Mitchell, who was a clerk, cashier, and agent of the Santa Fe Railway, as the garden's chief clerk (later manager) to handle financial matters, and added other important specialists—veterinarian, photographer, and cook to prepare the animals' food.[13]

Hornaday was a czar who ruled his staff with an iron hand, supervised closely, and was quick to reprimand shortcomings. Still, he stood behind decisions of the principal staff members, tried to pay them adequately (though their salaries were much lower than for comparable work in commerce and industry), and took an interest in their personal affairs. He occasionally had difficulties with Grant and Osborn about personnel. A few months after Loring's appointment Grant became dissatisfied with "the very careless way" in which he handled the animals. In November 1900, while Hornaday was on an animal-buying trip in the West, Grant, with Osborn's concurrence, suspended Loring. When the director heard about it, he wrote Osborn a blistering letter about "the new kind of madness" that caused the two executive committee members to interfere with his administration "without any sort of warning to me." The decision, however, was not reversed, and Beebe took charge of the animals as well as the birds. Modern museum professionals must sympathize with Hornaday and conclude that Grant and Osborn, despite their zeal for the society, went too far in their almost daily attention to administrative matters properly left to a director.[14]

In May 1899 Hornaday began to stock the garden with animals, obtained either by gift or purchase. The first two accessions were white-tailed prairie dogs

Birds and smaller animals arrived in great numbers, and rarer acquisitions included a giant anteater from Venezuela, three gray wolves, four California sea lions, nine American elk, six pronghorn antelopes, three young orangutans (which Mrs. Hornaday took home to care for), a Bengal tiger, two polar bears, and two huge reticulated pythons (twenty-six and twenty-two feet long). Hornaday was especially interested in American bison and began to assemble a sizeable herd, which ranged in a twenty-acre enclosure.

Hornaday did not succeed in raising a herd of pronghorns, moose, caribou, or mule deer and concluded that it was exceedingly difficult to acclimatize those animals on the Atlantic Coast. Though a fine beaver pond was scooped out in a natural bog between two ridges, that exhibit was not popular because beavers are nocturnal animals seldom visible during daytime visiting hours. Animal escapes always attracted much public attention. A young female wolf terrified the neighborhood for five days; a policeman fired at her but missed, and she ran into a cellar where she was recaptured. Sea lions escaped from their pool, and one of them spent three weeks in the Bronx River before being retaken. Hornaday himself helped subdue a Borneo sun bear but was bitten in the hand; unfortunately, the bear died from exhaustion.[15]

The opening day ceremonies for the Zoological Park on November 8, 1899, attracted a crowd of about two thousand, led by city officials, representatives from other museums and institutions of higher learning, and wealthy donors intent upon seeing what their money had bought. Professor Osborn, as chief speaker, pointed out that the park was projected on a larger scale than ever attempted by the small, confined gardens of Europe.[16] Hornaday himself did not speak, but he must have been elated to see his dearest charge progressing so well. His fertile ideas and abundant energy were paying off. His demanding but imaginative administration; his personal handling of a mountain of correspondence; and his hard-hitting interviews, letters to press and public, and magazine articles were keeping the park in the news, usually in a favorable light. He was determined to accumulate and disseminate animal lore for millions. The park, though open to experts and collectors, would stress popular zoology in writing, photography, editing, printing, lecturing, and broadcasting. In an article he wrote after his retirement, he said that a director could make or break such an institution. His greatest worry was the death of his animals, his chief delight receiving wonderful new arrivals; the highest praise he could receive was: "Your animals are looking fine."[17]

## III

Hornaday was always a positive person, often dogmatic, aggressive, and belligerent. He believed in putting everything in writing—orders to all members of his varied staff and answers to correspondents, newspaper notices, and comments that in any way concerned the park or himself. He insisted that his curators leave all public correspondence to him and often wrote or dictated his way through an enormous pile of letters and memorandums. He also sent off a stream of letters to the editor and magazine articles, to say nothing of writing some twenty long and detailed books. His fierce energy kept him working, usually twelve or more hours a day at the office or at home on weekends and holidays. In his quarrels with Osborn and Grant, Hornaday might lose on some issues, but he frequently won because he was on the spot, decisive, and prompt to take action. So far as the curators and other staff members went, he supervised closely; in 1923 they begged to have half days off on Saturday, but he reluctantly but firmly refused because of the cost. He also was adamant about newspaper interviews or articles that the curators might originate. Their names were not to appear blatantly, but all credit must be given to the society and perhaps to its director.

Hornaday's tiffs with the newspapers and their reporters were frequent. He wished them to remember to use "New York Zoological Society" or "Park," never that despicable term, "Bronx Zoo." He also decried amusing but silly stories about his animals that reporters might dream up, and he reminded them often that truth frequently is stranger than fiction. The public also had to conduct itself in seemly fashion at the park. First of all, no photographs were allowed; that prohibition led to many quarrels, but he insisted that the society had photographs for sale and was entitled to that income. Then he had trouble with the park's neighbors; packs of dogs managed to enter the garden and attack deer, and certain vagrants drifted in to shoot songbirds. Finally, a Rubbish War erupted as visitors carelessly dropped paper containers and other trash along park pathways. Hornaday designed a three-foot-high trash basket in the shape of a tree stump and distributed 200 of them about the park. He had to put up with a good deal of silliness from the public. Some said that the giraffes were suffering from tonsilitis, and the Tonsilene Company sent a bottle of its product to help them. A great Smells Battle took place when a well-meaning correspondent maintained that he could cure the peculiar musky odor secreted by civet cats in the Small Animal House. But in any case the public was deeply interested in the park and its animals.[18]

The beasts themselves frequently furnished controversy. In 1904 "Gunda," the elephant from India, began to become unruly, especially during recurring periods of sexual excitement or musth. He knocked down one keeper and nearly killed another. He was whipped on the trunk and then had his feet chained to the floor of the cage. The public protested to the newspapers that the keepers were treating him cruelly. Hornaday explained why such measures were necessary, but the protests continued. When Gunda's behavior became worse, he had to be shot. "Khartoum," a huge elephant from the Blue Nile, took delight in breaking every zoo fence and door until Hornaday had 4,567 needle-pointed spikes installed in strategic spots. Was Hornaday's treatment of elephants and other animals too violent? Perhaps so, by modern standards, but in those days it was agreed that animals must always obey their keepers.[19]

In 1906 an unusual incident took place. An African Pygmy from the Congo, named Ota Benga, was exhibited (Hornaday preferred the word "employed") playing with his own chimpanzee and other apes in a cage. The practice continued for less than a week, because black ministers insisted that it was a flagrant case of race bigotry. Ota Benga moved to the Colored Orphan Asylum, then to several other places, and finally committed suicide. When David Garnett's novel entitled *A Man in the Zoo* (1924) caused a New Yorker to volunteer to put himself on exhibition, Hornaday refused, saying that the book aroused "Bitter Reflections" of his "first offense in the display of Man as a Primate."[20]

In 1918–1920 the Zoological Society was investigated by the Tammany administration under Mayor John F. Hyland and his commissioner of accounts, David Hirshfield. They objected to the society's keeping the income from restaurant, animal rides, photographs, and the like, while other city parks let such concessions to the highest bidder who turned over profits to the city. They argued that the city ought to assume the operation of the park and run it under the rules of the Municipal Civil Service Commission. The society cited its legal grant of 1897 and pointed out that it had donated more than $700,000 to the park, had seen that city monies were spent with honesty and care, and so far had instructed and entertained nearly 25 million visitors. The Hirshfield Report asserted that "Hornaday rules the Zoo and the City's park lands like an autocrat—a monarch in his own principality—and looks down with disgust upon common people." One witness said of the employees: "Everybody trembles when they see him." But the New York newspapers that had fought with Hornaday so often stood up for him and the society. They asked scornfully: "Shall we Hylandize the Zoo?" and characterized the report as an obvious attempted power grab.

The whole investigation was often painful, but the Zoological Park and its director emerged stronger than ever in the loyalty and affection of most New Yorkers.[21]

Throughout the years the park and society maintained that they were operating the greatest zoo in the world. Hornaday moved steadily to secure the buildings to complete his original plan, and he added many new features. In 1900 the park pioneered in hiring a veterinarian to look after its animals and soon added Dr. W. Reid Blair, trained in that science at McGill, who later became assistant director and succeeded Hornaday when he retired. The society took over the Aquarium in Castle Garden at the Battery and appointed its director upon Hornaday's recommendation. He also gave artists, sculptors, zoologists, and students special privileges in the park, and Ernest Thompson Seton, Carl Rungius from Germany, Charles P. Knight, and others painted murals and made sculptures for the various buildings. For a time the park had an art gallery financed by park members. Grant and Hornaday also enthusiastically created an old-fashioned "National Collection of Heads and Horns," raised $10,000 for it, and contributed their own considerable holdings of such trophies. But neither the art gallery nor the heads and horns attracted the public, and they were eventually dropped.[22]

In the research field, Hornaday founded *Zoologica: Scientific Papers of the New York Zoological Society* in 1907. William Beebe was its chief contributor; a skilled and prolific researcher and writer, he produced impressive scientific articles and volumes. In 1919 he partially cut his ties with the park, became honorary curator of birds, and began to spend most of his time at his Tropical Research Station in British Guiana. Lee Saunders Crandall, Beebe's assistant, was his successor; he had begun as an unpaid student keeper in 1908 and went on to serve the society for sixty-one fruitful years.[23]

The Zoological Society made considerable educational progress. Ditmars, the former reporter on the New York *Times*, provided his friends of the press with many striking, yet authentic, stories about the zoo and its animals. He also proved expert at producing motion pictures; his forty-three reels of the "Living Natural History" series were shown in the park and at theatres and schools throughout the country. Hornaday in 1925 allowed himself and the staff to make weekly broadcasts for the Radio Corporation of America, and some of the curators continued to appear occasionally. But a curator of educational activities was not added to the staff until 1939 under Dr. Blair's administration.[24]

The entry of the United States into the First World War sent Hornaday into a frenzy of patriotic activity. He tried to cut down the food rations of the animals but when they lost weight, he had to give up that move, though he added economical cornbread to their diet. Half of the Lion House was turned over to the Red Cross. He formed Company A of the Zoological Park Guards, uniformed and equipped with rifles; they drilled frequently and conducted armed patrols from sunset to sunrise. Hornaday participated in seven defense organizations and wrote pamphlets such as "A Searchlight on Germany" (50,000 copies and reprinted in 13 newspapers) and "Awake! America." He urged zoos not to patronize German dealers and wished to cut off the society's subscriptions to German books and periodicals (President Grant refused to do so). When the war ended, the park sent 329 mammals, birds, reptiles, and amphibians to restock the Antwerp Zoo.[25]

In his 1920 Annual Report, Hornaday put down his basic philosophy for zoological gardens, as follows:

> The first, the last and the greatest business of every zoological park is to collect and exhibit fine and rare animals. Next comes the duty of enabling the greatest possible number of people to see them with comfort and satisfaction. In comparison with these objects, all others are of secondary or tertiary or quaternary importance. The breeding of wild animals is extremely interesting, and the systematic study of them is fascinating, but both these ends must be subordinated to the main objects.[26]

Without any doubt, Hornaday attained his chief objectives. On the outbreak of war in 1914, the park contained 4,729 specimens of 1,290 species, and by the time of his retirement in 1926, annual attendance had reached 2.5 million. But as Kenneth J. Polakowski has pointed out recently:

> Many zoos at this time [about 1985] began to move away from the traditional goals of providing recreation and entertainment while amassing large varieties and numbers of species. The quality of a zoo is no longer measured by the number of species it contains, but rather by the quality of its exhibits, its educational programs, its propagation results, and its research and conservation activities.[27]

Thus Hornaday did not value the various zoo functions as zoo leaders do today. Of course, the depletion of wild animals in what were once primitive areas of the earth has greatly increased since his day, and the modern zoo has become a center for the conservation and propagation of endangered species.

Nor did Hornaday adopt the latest methods of exhibition of wild animals. Carl Hagenbeck's private zoo at Stelligen in Hamburg in 1907 largely did away with bars and cages; it used moats to keep predators and prey apart as well as animals and the public. Hornaday praised Hagenbeck for having "the temerity to build . . . a private zoological garden so spectacular and attractive" and considered him the greatest zoological park creator in the world. Later, in 1919, Hornaday's intense anti-German feelings may have influenced the advice he gave the director of the St. Louis Zoo against building moated and barless bear pits. Hornaday said that when he was erecting his own bear dens in 1899, Hagenbeck had strongly urged his methods, but Hornaday had rejected them because of the great disadvantage of "having our bears separated from our visitors by a distance of sixty or seventy feet"; he preferred using the woven wire fence. (St. Louis went ahead to build moated dens with realistic concrete rockwork.) He also successfully opposed Dr. Blair's desire to experiment with moats. Since then, however, Blair's successors have used them extensively, as in the "African Plains" exhibits with its "Lion Island," or in "Tropical Asia."[28]

It is not too harsh a judgment to say that in Hornaday's later years, the Zoological Park was beginning to fall behind the more progressive zoos of the world. Fortunately, its new president Fairfield Osborn and several later innovative directors brought it back to its former eminence. It is now generally agreed that the Bronx Zoo, the San Diego Zoo and Wild Animal Park, and the National Zoo at Washington are the three great American leaders.[29]

## IV

Hornaday early decided that a most important part of his duties at the Zoological Society was the conservation of American wildlife. In 1905 he became chief executive of the American Bison Society and helped set up buffalo herds in Oklahoma, Montana, and South Dakota. He opposed sportsmen, boys, market hunters, plumage gatherers, and egg collectors who were slaughtering birds and animals. He did much to secure state and national laws and international treaties to protect animals threatened with extinction and tried unsuccessfully to obtain a federal law to establish game preserves in national forests. He wrote two books on *Our Vanishing Wild Life* (1913) and *Thirty Years War for Wild Life* (1931) in his best battling, no-holds-barred style. After his retirement, he devoted most of his time to various conservation projects.[30]

The magazine *Outdoor Life* in 1930 summed it up well:

> In the long and often weary annals of conservation progress, no man has been less bowed beneath reverses or less satisfied with success than Dr. Hornaday. Determined and intransigent, it was never his policy to go around or under an

> opponent; smashing straight through his opposition, he has left a long trail of personal enemies in his wake—but has never looked back. Sold out by game-hogs in high places, rebuffed by organizations purporting to have conservation purpose, deserted even by high-principled and well-intentioned leaders who felt him too radical and truculent for his time, much of Dr. Hornaday's far-seeing effort has been single-handed. In his day of triumph, let his indomitable persistence be remembered.[31]

Thus in the sixty-four years of his active career from apprenticeship until his death in retirement, Hornaday had made countless contributions to zoology in America and the world—improving the theory and practice of taxidermy, developing a great zoological garden, and conserving wildlife threatened with extinction. Many honors came to him—gold medals, honorary degrees, and honorific membership in zoo and conservation organizations around the world. A 10,000-foot peak in Yellowstone Park was named "Mount Hornaday." And Iowa State College, proud that as a student there he had found his calling, placed a large boulder in front of the College Library with a bronze plaque that justly commemorated "his contributions to zoology and conservation which have been of immeasurable benefit to America."[32]

## NOTES

1. For Hornaday's early life, see William T. Hornaday, "My Fifty-Four Years of Animal Life: Personal Reflections of a Big Game Hunter and Naturalist," *Mentor* 17 (May 1929): 3–5; Hornaday, *Camp-Fires on Desert and Lava* (Tucson: University of Arizona Press, 1983; original edition, 1908), xxiii-xxiv; Hornaday, *Taxidermy and Zoological Collecting* (New York: Charles Scribner's Sons, 1891), 62–64; "William Temple Hornaday," *Who Was Who in America* (Chicago: A. N. Marquis Company, 1942), 1 (1897–1942): 588; "Dr. Hornaday" (obituary), *Commonwealth* 25 (Mar. 19, 1937): 583; Fairfield Osborn, "William Temple Hornaday" (obituary), *Science* 85 (Mar. 7, 1937): 445–46; Edward A. Preble, "William Temple Hornaday: An Appreciation" (obituary), *Nature Magazine* 29 (May 1937): 303–04; William Bridges, *Gathering of Animals: An Unconventional History of the New York Zoological Society* (New York: Harper & Row, 1974), 20–24.
2. William T. Hornaday, "Masterpieces of American Bird Taxidermy," *Scribner's Magazine* 78 (Sept. 1925): 262–63; Hornaday, *Two Years in the Jungle: The Experiences of a Hunter and Naturalist in India, Ceylon, the Malay Peninsula, and Borneo* (New York: Charles Scribner's Sons, 1885); Hornaday, "My Fifty- Four Years," 5–6; Hornaday, *Desert and Lava*, xxiii-xxiv; Hornaday, *Taxidermy and Zoological Collecting*, 10, 52, 135, 175, 195–96, 221–24, 272; Osborn, "Hornaday," 445; Preble, "Hornaday," 303; Bridges, *Gathering of Animals*, 21.
3. Hornaday, "My Fifty-Four Years," 7; Hornaday, *Two Years in the Jungle*, iii; *Who Was Who*, 1: 588; Preble, "Hornaday," 304.
4. William T. Hornaday, "Masterpieces of American Taxidermy," *Scribner's Magazine* 72 (July 1927): 6; Hornaday, *Taxidermy and Zoological Collecting*, 221–22, 230–33.

5. Hornaday, "Masterpieces of American Bird Taxidermy," 272; Hornaday, *Taxidermy and Zoological Collecting*, 112–13, 127, 130–31, 140–42, 163, 174, 211, 213–14; Bridges, *Gathering of Animals*, 22.

6. Hornaday, "Masterpieces of American Bird Taxidermy," 265–66; Hornaday, "Masterpieces of American Taxidermy," 8–9; Hornaday, *Taxidermy and Zoological Collecting*, 233–35, 245–46.

7. Bridges, *Gathering of Animals*, 17, 20, 24, 55–56; Hornaday, "My Fifty-Four Years," 7; William T. Hornaday, *Thirty Years War for Wild Life: Gains and Losses in a Thankless Task* (New York: Arno and the New York *Times*, 1970; original edition, 1931), 167–68; Osborn, "Hornaday," 445–46.

8. Quotation in Bridges, *Gathering of Animals*, 16. See also, 1–30.

9. Ibid., 43–44, 64–68, 79–82, 300; "Dr. Hornaday's Retirement as Director of the New York Zoological Park," *Scientific Monthly* 23 (July 1926): 88–93.

10. Bridges, *Gathering of Animals*, 40 (quotation); see also, 29–40, 130–31; William T. Hornaday, "The New York Zoological Park," *Century Magazine* 39 (Nov. 1900): 85–102.

11. Bridges, *Gathering of Animals*, 36–37; William T. Hornaday, "The New York Plan for Zoological Parks," *Scribner's Magazine* 46 (Nov. 1909): 590–605.

12. Bridges, *Gathering of Animals*, 40–42, 46–50, 86, 118.

13. Ibid., 57–64, 76–77; Raymond L. Ditmars, *The Making of a Scientist* (New York: Macmillan, 1937), 11–48; Robert Henry Welker, *Natural Man: The Life of William Beebe* (Bloomington: Indiana University Press, 1975).

14. Bridges, *Gathering of Animals*, 64–67.

15. Ibid., 68–76, 82–84; William T. Hornaday, "Behind the Scenes in a Great Zoo," *Mentor* 15 (Aug. 1927): 3–4.

16. Bridges, *Gathering of Animals*, 89–98.

17. Hornaday, "Behind the Scenes," 8.

18. Bridges, *Gathering of Animals*, 172–91, 362–63, 406; Hornaday, "Behind the Scenes," 9–10.

19. Bridges, *Gathering of Animals*, 231–32, 247–56; Hornaday, "Behind the Scenes," 5.

20. Bridges, *Gathering of Animals*, 223–30, 388.

21. Ibid., 338–45.

22. Ibid., 141–64, 306–13, 329–33, 337–38; Hornaday, "My Fifty-Four Years," 9; William T. Hornaday, "Wild Animal Models at the Zoo: How New York Painters and Sculptors Work from Nature in Their Representations of Wild Life," *Scientific Monthly* 122 (Feb. 7, 1920): 134.

23. Bridges, *Gathering of Animals*, 290–305, 388–97; Lee Saunders Crandall, *The Management of Wild Animals in Captivity* (Chicago: University of Chicago Press, 1964); Crandall in collaboration with Bridges, *A Zoo Man's Notebook* (Chicago: University of Chicago Press, 1966), 1–5.

24. Bridges, *Gathering of Animals*, 402–05, 417, 425; Ditmars, *Confessions of a Scientist*, 221–41.

25. Bridges, *Gathering of Animals*, 364, 369–79.

26. Ibid., 414.

27. Ibid., 362; Kenneth J. Polakowski, *Zoo Design: The Reality of Wild Illusions* (Ann Arbor: University of Michigan School of Natural Resources, 1987), 5, 21–22.

28. Bridges, *Gathering of Animals*, 377, 387–88, 411–13; Polakowski, *Zoo Design*, 8, 82–83.

29. A good description of the later Bronx Zoo is Bernard Livingston, *Zoo Animals: People, Places* (New York: Arbor House, 1974), 263–79.

30. Bridges, *Gathering of Animals*, 204–06, 257–73, 276–78; William T. Hornaday, *Campfires in the Canadian Rockies* (New York: Charles Scribner's Sons, 1906), 7–8, 213–64; Hornaday

"My Fifty-Four Years," 9; William Temple Hornaday, *Our Vanishing Wild Life: Its Extermination and Protection* (New York: New York Zoological Society, 1913), x, 208–397; Hornaday, *Thirty Years War*, 150–56, 168–70, 179–81, 199–206, 223–30.

31. Hornaday, *Thirty Years War*, iv.

32. Bridges, *Gathering of Animals*, 409–10, 440; "Dr. Hornaday," *Commonwealth* 25 (Mar. 19, 1937): 583; Hornaday, "Behind the Scenes," 5; "Hornaday—Conservationist," *Nature Magazine* 21 (May 1933): 256; "Dr. Hornaday's Retirement," 88–93; Osborn, "Hornaday," 445–46; Preble, "Hornaday," 303–04.

## SELECT BIBLIOGRAPHY

Bridges, William. *Gathering of Animals: An Unconventional History of the New York Zoological Society*. New York: Harper & Row, 1974.

Crandall, Lee Saunders. *The Management of Wild Animals in Captivity*. Chicago: University of Chicago Press, 1964.

Crandall, Lee Saunders, with William Bridges. *A Zoo Man's Notebook*. Chicago: University of Chicago Press, 1966.

Ditmars, Raymond L. *The Making of a Scientist*. New York: Macmillan, 1937.

"Dr. Hornaday's Retirement as Director of the New York Zoological Park." *Scientific Monthly* 23 (July 1926): 88–93.

"Hornaday—Conservationist." *Nature Magazine* 21 (May 1933): 256.

Hornaday, William T. "Behind the Scenes in a Great Zoo." *Mentor* 15 (Aug. 1927): 3–4.

_____. *Camp-fires in the Canadian Rockies*. New York: Charles Scribner's Sons, 1906.

_____. *Camp-Fires on Desert and Lava*. Tucson: University of Arizona Press, 1983 (original edition, 1908).

_____. "Masterpieces of American Bird Taxidermy." *Scribner's Magazine* 78 (Sept. 1925): 262–63.

_____. "Masterpieces of American Taxidermy." *Scribner's Magazine* 72 (July 1927): 6.

_____. "My Fifty-Four Years of Animal Life: Personal Reflections of a Big Game Hunter and Naturalist." *Mentor* 17 (May 1929): 3–5.

_____. "The New York Plan for Zoological Parks." *Scribner's Magazine* 46 (Nov. 1909): 590–605.

_____. "The New York Zoological Park." *Century Magazine* 39 (Nov. 1900): 85–02.

_____. *Our Vanishing Wild Life: Its Extermination and Protection*. New York: New York Zoological Society, 1913.

_____. *Taxidermy and Zoological Collecting*. New York: Charles Scribner's Sons, 1891.

_____. *Thirty Years War for Wild Life: Gains and Losses in a Thankless Task*. New York: Arno and the New York *Times*, 1970 (original edition, 1931).

_____. *Two Years in the Jungle: The Experiences of a Hunter and Naturalist in India, Ceylon, the Malay Peninsula, and Borneo*. New York: Charles Scribner's Sons, 1885.

_____. "Wild Animal Models at the Zoo: How New York Painters and Sculptors Work from Nature in Their Representations of Wild Life." *Scientific Monthly* 122 (Feb. 7, 1920): 134.

Livingston, Bernard. *Zoo Animals: People, Places*. New York: Arbor House, 1974.

Polakowski, Kenneth J. *Zoo Design: The Reality of Wild Illusions*. Ann Arbor: University of Michigan School of Natural Resources, 1987.

Welker, Robert Henry. *Natural Man: The Life of William Beebe*. Bloomington: Indiana University Press, 1975.

"William Temple Hornaday." *Who Was Who in America*. Chicago: A. N. Marquis Company, 1942. Vol. 1 (1897–1942): 588.

CHAPTER 13

# Paul Joseph Sachs *Teaches a Pioneering Course in Museum Studies*

## I

PAUL J. SACHS WAS one of the greatest teachers of museum studies who has yet appeared in America. For nearly a quarter century, starting about 1921, his museum course at Harvard University and its Fogg Art Museum trained graduate students who became curators and directors in the leading art museums of the country. "Uncle Paul," as he was affectionately but surreptitiously called by the students, was an unusual personality, only five feet, two inches tall, always immaculately dressed with a pearl stick pin in his tie, a passionate and prescient collector of master prints and drawings, famed gourmet, and possessed of a volcanic temper. But his deep love for art, enthusiastic spirit, and generosity brought him friends throughout the cultural world and among his students as he placed them in promising positions and continued carefully to follow their careers. An observer at the exhibition that honored his seventieth birthday described him as follows: "His closely cropped white hair makes a handsome contrast with emphatically black Groucho Marx-like eyebrows and a neatly trimmed bushy gray mustache; behind rimless eyeglasses dart snappingly alert eyes—eyes that have especially looked lovingly at art."[1]

Professor Sachs had a few pioneering predecessors in the field of museum studies. Mrs. Sarah Yorke Stevenson, assistant curator of the Pennsylvania Museum (now the Philadelphia Museum of Art), in 1908 began to help young men and women with at least a high school diploma prepare for work in art museums.

She gave lectures on museum techniques, demanded critical reports of visits to all the Philadelphia museums, and had the students perform practical tasks in her own institution. The course soon expanded to two years, with one year devoted to art history, and continued until Mrs. Stevenson's death in 1921.

Professor Homer K. Dill, director of the Museum of Natural History at the State University of Iowa in Iowa City, in 1908 experimented with a class in museum studies; within three years it had developed into a four-year program with the degree given in natural science but a minor concentration in museum work that included taxidermy, exhibit techniques, freehand drawing, and modeling. That course had no difficulty in placing its graduates and still continues today.

Miss Myrtilla Avery at the Farnsworth Museum in Wellesley College began to train young women to be art museum assistants in 1910 in her "Museum and Art Library Methods" course. The students were to acquire educational, library, clerical, and exhibition skills. Upon graduation, however, they experienced difficulty in obtaining museum employment. The course was dropped and reinstated several times, and last offered in 1941.

Another museum studies course of much importance, roughly contemporary with that of Sachs, was begun at Newark, New Jersey, in 1925 by John Cotton Dana, the director of both the public library and museum there. The program, supervised directly by his assistant, Katherine Coffey, involved apprenticeship; it accepted students with a college degree and paid them a monthly stipend. For one academic year they listened to lectures on phases of museum work and actually assisted in the various departments of the museum. The two weeks between semesters were devoted to visiting other museums. At first, all the apprentices were women, but men later participated. By 1942, 108 young women and men had been graduated, and most of them were working in museums in the United States and Canada.

In general, however, most museum trustees and directors agreed with Frederic A. Lucas, chief of the Brooklyn Museum, who insisted in 1910 that curators were "born and not made," could not be produced by training courses alone, and were "the result of the combination of natural ability and circumstances." For the most part, museum directors and curators continued to be turned out in subject-matter courses (preferably in graduate school), and they learned the nuts-and-bolts side of museum work on their first job.[2]

Professor Sachs demanded that his students add to their year-long graduate museum course subject-matter competence in art history with a thorough knowledge of museum history, functions, and ethics. He offered "Museum Work and Museum

Problems" weekly during the academic year, often at his home, Shady Hill. The course treated the history and philosophy of art museums, their organization and management, their buildings, and the functions of collection, installation, conservation and storage, recordkeeping, educational policies, and museum ethics. Sessions were supposed to last three hours, but Sachs's enthusiasm, ingenious approaches, and encouragement of lively student discussion often prolonged the meetings for another hour or so. Directors and curators from the Fogg and other leading museums in this country and abroad occasionally came to lecture and lead the discussion, and during university winter and spring vacations, Sachs took the students to visit museums (preferably behind the scenes), private collectors, dealers, and auction halls. The students were responsible yearly for two major exhibitions at the Fogg, for which they did the research, installation, labels, and catalogues. Each student was required to spend $50 on an object for his collection; Sachs told Agnes Mongan, his research assistant, "that when it hit your own pocketbook, you'd consider things you wouldn't think of with someone else's money."[3] They were also to visit a gallery and write an essay explaining which of its two or three paintings they would wish to obtain for their own museum. All in all, the course was stimulating, demanding, and mind stretching, indeed memorable.[4]

## II

Paul Joseph Sachs was born in New York City on November 27, 1878, the eldest of three sons of Samuel and Louisa (Goldman) Sachs. His father was a partner in the international banking firm of Goldman Sachs Company, and his mother, the niece of another partner, Henry Goldman. Paul, at age eight, began to attend the Sachs School conducted by his Uncle Julius; he later described the school as "a second home, a Paradise."[5] In 1894 his father took him to Europe, where he visited the great museums. The next year, he took the entrance examination for Harvard, passing in German, French, and history but failing Latin, Greek, algebra, geometry, and physics. In 1896 he succeeded in conquering the tests and entered Harvard, where he studied French, other modern languages, philosophy, and especially the fine arts which captured his ardent attention. His professors included Charles Herbert Moore, an accomplished artist, and Martin Mower, who "more than any one man, taught me to see."[6] He shyly attended a reception given by the venerable Charles Eliot Norton, the first teacher of art in an American university, at his home, Shady Hill, which Sachs was later to occupy.

When Sachs was graduated in 1900, Professor Moore offered him an assistantship, but it paid only $750 and his father refused to supplement that meager sum. As a consequence, the young man joined the Goldman Sachs firm and was sent to Boston. His first notable success there was selling some railroad bonds, the commission for which he spent chiefly on a portrait painted by his mentor, Professor Moore. The next year, he was transferred to New York and in 1904 made a partner. He also was married then to Meta Pollack, who joined him in exploring museums and visiting print dealers. She was an outgoing, friendly person who made their guests feel at home—a splendid contrast to his sometimes shy and reticent manner.

Sachs had collected stamps as a boy, and his bedroom walls were covered with reproduced wood engravings clipped from magazines and auction catalogues. During college he had begun to buy prints and drawings; he used the $700 accumulated from his grandfather's $25 annual birthday gifts to buy etchings by Dürer, Cranach, Rembrandt, and Claúde . Alfred Barr later recalled that Sachs once told the class of his triumph in outbidding the British Museum, Berlin, and Dresden at the Earl of Pembroke's sale for Antonio del Pollaiuolo's drawing, *Fighting Nudes*. On another occasion, he was chagrined to find that he had bought a forgery of Dürer's *The Riders of the Four Horses of the Apocalypse* but kept it for use later to help train his students to detect frauds.[7]

Edward Waldo Forbes had become director of the Fogg Museum at Harvard in 1909.[8] He was a wealthy collector who presented a somewhat rumpled appearance and dreamy expression but was determined to make the Fogg the best university art museum in the country. He proved to be tenacious and ingenious as well as an excellent money raiser. The Fogg that he took over was a discouraging place—"a building," he said, "with a lecture hall in which you could not hear, a gallery in which you could not see, working rooms in which you could not work, and a roof that leaked like a sieve."[9] Forbes persuaded Sachs to join the museum's visiting committee in 1911, and he soon became its chairman. The two men, so different in personality, got along well together, and Forbes was soon urging Sachs to become his assistant director. When the Harvard Board made that appointment in December 1914, Sachs resigned his partnership at Goldman Sachs, spent several months in Italy and the United States studying other museums, and then moved Meta and their three small daughters to Shady Hill in Cambridge. Sachs later praised Forbes and asserted that "it is to him that I owe the best years of my life which have been spent in the service of the University."[10]

## III

Paul Sachs's second career developed in three main directions: teaching, museum administration, and collecting. Soon after his arrival at Harvard, he was asked to give a paper before the Archaeological Institute of America; he was somewhat apprehensive about undertaking it, but, upon Meta's urging, agreed to do so. As a result, some of his listeners invited him to join the Wellesley College faculty as an instructor in art, and he lectured there in 1916–1917. After service as captain and then major in the Red Cross during the First World War (he was too short to be accepted in the regular armed services), he was made an assistant professor of fine arts at Harvard. At his courses in French art and in drawings and prints, he strode back and forth in front of the class, consulted copious notes, and used slides and a pointer. If an assistant showed the wrong slide, a violent eruption might occur, and at the end of the session, a broken pointer might be found on the floor. But his teaching proved exciting to the students because of his contagious enthusiasm and his ability to make them see and appreciate the quality of art objects.

Sachs moved steadily up the academic ladder as associate professor, professor, and department chairman. Special honors came to him for his teaching; in 1929 he gave the Lowell Lectures at Harvard; in 1932–1933 he was exchange professor at the Sorbonne in Paris, with side appearances in Berlin and Bonn; and in 1942 Harvard gave him an honorary doctorate as a "lover of the fine arts, who deserted a business career to become an accomplished teacher."[11] After he retired from the Fogg in 1945, he continued teaching at Harvard for three more years.

In museum administration, Sachs was most competent. His business experience had trained him in advance planning, and he was always well organized, prompt, energetic, and decisive. The Fogg Museum ran smoothly and efficiently under the joint command of Forbes and Sachs. They devoted themselves and their fortunes to the museum but did not duplicate each other in teaching students. Forbes trained them in art conservation, and Sachs prepared them for curatorship. Both men did well in raising funds, and, beginning in 1923, they headed a campaign that secured ten million dollars for Harvard, two million of which went for the new Fogg building opened in 1927 and its endowment. President Lowell called Forbes and Sachs "those exuberant mendicants, the Siamese twins."[12] They both were generous in giving the museum many outstanding works of art, and they left a distinguished building, a superb collection, a library rich in books, slides, and photographs, and a reputation for scholarly activity enhanced by their own efforts and those of their staff and students.

Sachs's success as a museum administrator brought him many extracurricular duties. He was one of the seven founders of the Museum of Modern Art in New York in 1939. Its director, Alfred H. Barr Jr., and curator of graphic arts, William S. Lieberman, had been his students, and its print and drawing galleries were named for Sachs. He served on the Administrative Board of Dumbarton Oaks for nearly twenty-five years and on the Editorial Board of the *Art Bulletin* for more than twenty. And scores of university presidents and deans as well as museum trustees and directors from here and abroad came to secure his advice. He was a trustee of the Museum of Fine Arts, Boston; Cincinnati Museum; and of Smith, Wellesley, and Radcliffe colleges. He also worked with various health groups and with the National Urban League. The Metropolitan Museum of Art tried to procure him as head of its new print department with the likelihood of his succeeding to the directorship, but he suggested his close friend, William M. Ivins, Jr., who accepted the appointment. Sachs continued to be seriously considered for that and other museums' directorships, but he chose to remain at Harvard.

As a collector, Sachs had a passionate love for quality in art objects. He thought that his keen eye and understanding of quality had been developed under the tutelage of Carl Dreyfus of the Louvre and the French painter, Leon Bonnat, whom he visited often. A young student, he said, could profit greatly from "contact with an older, more experienced and enthusiastic collector."[13] When he came to work at Harvard and the Fogg, Sachs already had an excellent collection of prints and drawings. He believed that he did not have enough money to collect master paintings and sculptures but that master prints and drawings were abundantly available and reasonable in price. He began to circulate his collection among his students. He discovered, however, that he had many duplicates of prints in the Fogg and Boston's Museum of Fine Arts. He therefore decided to concentrate upon collecting drawings and began to sell his prints and use the proceeds for more drawings. At the time, there were few American collectors in that field, and Sachs became a great connoisseur and leader; in fact, no one did more to make master drawings appreciated and cherished. Through the years, Sachs was most generous in giving prints and drawings to the Fogg and early decided that it was to receive his whole collection. Yet he insisted that no credit be given him for loans and gifts on either labels or in catalogues. (He took a similar attitude in giving anonymously many fellowships to students for study or travel.) He also collected books, many of them outstanding rarities, and gave them to the Fogg or Harvard; when he moved from Shady Hill, 4,000 volumes went to the university. So modest had he been that when the catalogue of the Memorial Exhibition honoring him was published, even his closest friends were astonished to learn the range of his collection and the magnitude of his gifts to the Fogg. Altogether, the checklist of his contributions contained more than 2,690 art objects, and that did not include textiles and furniture.[14]

Sachs retired from the associate directorship of the Fogg (he and Forbes left at the same time) in 1945. A great celebration and exhibition was held three years later on his seventieth birthday. Soon after that, Meta and he moved from Shady Hill to a comfortable apartment overlooking the Charles River. But he continued collecting to the last. For a time, another print connoisseur, W. G. Russell Allen, and Sachs often sought art works together. Allen was six feet, four inches tall, and, as Agnes Mongan says, they made a "picturesque pair" as they visited museums, called on dealers, and attended auctions.[15] Sachs's students continued to visit him at the apartment, bringing news of the latest doings in the art and museum worlds. Meta Sachs died at age eighty-one in 1961, and Sachs himself, in his library surrounded by books, prints, drawings, and other art objects, peacefully expired on the morning of February 17, 1965, at the age of eighty-two.

## IV

Sachs experimented in 1921 with a museum course, which he permanently established two years later and continued teaching through the 1944–1945 academic year. He may have decided to offer it because of a conversation he had during a train ride with Henry Watson Kent, secretary of the Metropolitan Museum. The course covered all aspects of museum work as well as personalities in the art field, but also placed strong emphasis on art history and art objects. He told Agnes Mongan, a favorite collaborator of his: "First use your eye and your sensitivity, then the book learning."[16] The class was small, usually two dozen or fewer, and often met at Shady Hill, the students occupying comfortable chairs in front of Professor Sach's desk. After each class, an assistant distributed detailed mimeographed notes covering the lecture, discussion, and any announcements.

At the opening session of the course, Sachs sketched the basic requirements. Each student should develop a specialty but be acquainted with the whole field of art history, including its bibliography. He should know everything going on at the Fogg Museum and make personal contacts with many dealers. He should cultivate visual memory, master the long reading lists, make the issues of *Art News* a virtual textbook, and form the habit of taking notes. And Sachs later stressed the need for good organization in student papers and sorrowfully noted lapses in their use of English. He was generous in allowing students to use his library at Shady Hill.

Sachs gave his students a heavy load of assignments. They must make written reports on their reading of books and periodicals, on histories of great museums, visits to museums, and conversations with dealers. They needed to prepare book reviews suitable for the *Saturday Review* or an article for *The Arts* on an art object of special interest to them. The Fogg offered a multitude of projects—drawing an architectural plan; cataloguing a photograph; deciding whether art books should be checked out from Harvard or the Fogg; moving, rearranging, and labeling exhibit cases; commenting on flooring, chairs, and lighting; and scores of other tasks, both theoretical and practical. At the end of the course, when the students made suggestions for its improvement, they wished fewer written reports. Sachs pointed out, in reply, that he did not require examinations in the course and said that he deliberately overloaded them because museum workers needed to become accustomed to being overloaded.

Sachs shared his own museum problems with the students. He would bring in his correspondence for two or three days and ask how it should be answered. He would get the students to write a presentation to a granting agency for a new building for the Museum of Modern Art, and after it had been fully discussed in class, present it to the Museum's Executive Committee, on which he was serving. He would request volunteers to investigate an actual museum problem, write out a solution, talk it over with the class, and then go to discuss the result with the institution's board. Sachs also showed the class hundreds of slides of art objects, demanding their identification and provenance. He gave personal thumbnail sketches of numerous collectors, dealers, and other personalities in the art field. At the end of the course, he asked the students to list the most significant events of the past year in the art world in America and abroad. All of these various approaches captured intense student attention and made them feel part of the museum community that they were planning to enter.[17]

The ideal graduate of the course, Sachs thought, should be a scholar connoisseur, able both to recognize and appreciate the quality of art objects and to conduct accurate research on their physical characteristics and historical provenance. He considered that his own strengths lay in teaching and administration but that he was inadequate in the field of historical research. He admired greatly Agnes Mongan, who often acted as co-author with him, and praised "her unflagging zeal and her special capacity for research."[18] As John Walker, one of his students, put it: "He was someone who could really make you want to be a collector. None of the rest could. They could teach you the history of art, but Paul was the one that made us all want to be collectors."[19] He thought that visual memory was all-important for art museum professionals, and he would ask the students to memorize all the objects on exhibition at the Fogg. And Sachs might pick at random any of scores of art objects in his living room at Shady Hill and demand that the students identify them and their place in history.

Many leaders of the art world visited Sachs, such as Dr. Adolf Goldschmidt of the University of Berlin, Professor A. M. Hind of the British Museum, and W. G. Constable of London's National Gallery. They would participate in the classroom teaching. Later on, he invited some of his successful students to return in that role. Sachs was also a famed gourmet, who once said more or less jokingly: "Anyone who professes an interest in the fine arts and is indifferent to the joys of the palate is suspect with me."[20] Meta and Paul's dinner parties at Shady Hill were renowned, and students were invited now and then to share in the delicious food and stimulating conversation. After Stravinsky had dined there on one occasion, he composed a piece in honor of the evening. Other cultural celebrities who came included Courtauld, Kenneth Clark, Erwin Panofsky, and Sigfried Giedion.

Sachs gave up his winter and spring vacations in order to take the students on tours of museums, private collections, dealers, and auction houses. They would visit outstanding collectors such as the Robert Lehmans, Grenville Winthrop, Lord Duveen, the Stephen Clarks, the Philip Lehmans, the Sam Levinsons, the John D. Rockefellers Jr., Joseph Widener, the Carroll Tysons, and Henry McIlhenny.

The students took their exhibitions at the Fogg most seriously and organized themselves so as to get the most from them. Thus in 1944 the team that produced *Blake to Beardsley: A Century of English Illustration* had William S. Lieberman as director, Richard McLanathan, secretary, and Felice Stampfle, catalogue supervisor. Sachs demanded that such projects be clearly defined and closely supervised; he distrusted the internships provided by many institutions that allowed a student to float about a large museum "as a kind of spare part."[21]

Sachs believed that any museum director must have training in curatorship, that "he should enter upon his directorial duties only through the curatorial portal." He had no confidence in the bright young man who became director of a small museum and then gradually assumed much larger responsibilities without a thorough knowledge of art history, a trained eye, and a real understanding of art objects. "If such a man ends with a staff of competent curators, he does not know what their work is or why they do it," said Sachs. On the other hand, he thought his students should "look upon the educational department of a museum as intimately related to, and a part of their official work as future curators." They must not retreat into esoteric scholarship or superciliously look down their noses at museum educators, public relations personnel, or even directors. They always should hold high the torch of quality and remember that "museums exist, not so much to amuse as to educate the public, to give it some sense of excellence."[22]

Sachs summed up his philosophy with consideration for the broader purposes of museums as follows:

> While yielding to no one on the importance of forming usable collections of quality and bringing to bear upon their interpretation the highest curatorial and scholarly standards, one should never forget that in America at least, the museum is a social instrument highly useful in any scheme of general education. . . . The primary need of our museums is guidance through the scholar's approach. . . . I find it unreasonable to fear that with scholars in control of museums, the vital need for sound popular education in the humanities and in social studies would be put in jeopardy.[23]

In another place, he advised against any dilution of museum quality when he wrote:

> Let us be ever watchful to resist pressure to vulgarize and cheapen our work through the mistaken idea that in such fashion a broad public may be reached effectively. That is an especially tempting error because of the intense competition for public attention in America. In the end a lowering of tone and standards must lead to mediocrity.[24]

Sachs was not always close to his students during their stay, and John Walker complained that he "could never remember who I was, a disheartening experience for a student who had come to Harvard especially to sit at his feet."[25] Yet when Lincoln Kirstein, Edward M. M. Warburg, and Walker formed the Society of Contemporary Art at Harvard, Sachs joined Forbes in helping them raise funds and had the Fogg staff pack and ship their exhibits. He also served on their board with Miss Lizzie Bliss, Frank Crowninshield, Mrs. John D. Rockefeller Jr., and Conger Goodyear, all of whom were important in founding the Museum of Modern Art. Sachs's action was generous and even courageous, for Boston patrons and the Museum of Fine Arts showed real animosity toward modern art and for Picasso, Matisse, Mogliani, Braque, et al. Sachs was interested chiefly in European art of an earlier period but was broad-minded enough to back his students in offering more contemporary artists.

Sachs set a demanding standard for the students so far as their museum careers were concerned. They must work in behalf of their institutions all the time and with all their heart Agnes Mongan, with an A.B. from Bryn Mawr and M.A. from Smith, had returned from a year abroad when Sachs hired her as research assistant at the Fogg in 1928. He told her then: "I shall *never* ask you what hours you are keeping or how you are spending your time. I shall assume that as long as you work for us, wherever you are and whatever you are doing, you are working for the good of the Fogg Museum."[26] She afterwards realized that he was following the same rule for himself at both Harvard and the Fogg.

Sachs was especially helpful to his students when they began to go abroad or to apply for jobs. On one occasion, he wrote 103 letters and 107 cards of introduction for a student traveling to Europe. He served as a one-man placement agency and frequently mentioned job openings to his classes; for example, Edith Standen in 1928 noted five vacancies that he had listed—museums at St. Louis, Cincinnati, and Seattle and teaching positions at Amherst College and Pittsburgh University. Sachs wrote by hand long, carefully crafted letters on the students' behalf and sometimes even accompanied an applicant to meet a Board of Trustees. He also advised and supported former students when they ran into difficulties on the job. He suggested Alfred Barr for the directorship of the Museum of Modern Art, stood by him when he encountered trouble with his board, and helped him retain an influential place on the staff. Perry Rathbone corresponded frequently with Sachs as he made his way upward as director of the Detroit Institute of Art, St. Louis Art Museum, and then Museum of Fine Arts in Boston.

Sachs's students came to hold top curatorial and directorial spots in the art museum world. Among them were James J. Rorimer and Edith A. Standen at the Metropolitan Museum; John Walker at the National Gallery; Barr and Lieberman at the Museum of Modern Art; Perry Rathbone; John Coolidge at the Fogg; Jean S. Boggs at the National Gallery of Canada; Richard Howard at the Birmingham Museum of Art; Thomas Howe at the California Palace of the Legion of Honor; Otto Wittmann at the Toledo Museum of Art; Gordon Washburn at the Albright-Knox Art Gallery; Henry Trubner at the Seattle Art Museum; A. Everett Austin at the Wadsworth Atheneium; Charles C. Cunningham and John M. Maxon at the Art Institute of Chicago; Felice Stamfle at the Pierpont Morgan Library; Leslie Cheek Jr. at the Virginia Museum of Fine Arts; Richard McLanathan at the American Association of Museums; and Samuel Sachs II (Paul's grandnephew) at the Minneapolis Institute of Art. As Leslie Cheek pointed out, the former students constituted a network of art museum professionals who kept in touch with one another.[27]

Paul Sachs could indeed be proud of his museum course. He had trained several scores of young men and women who became the leaders in the American and Canadian art museum field for a generation. He had insisted that they know art history and understand art objects, but also had actually experienced the nitty-gritty, practical side of museum work. By his own example, he made them see the satisfaction and even the joy of working in the new profession, and he set sensible but lofty standards for teachers who were to follow him in the American museum studies field.

## NOTES

1. "Paul Joseph Sachs" (New York *Times* obituary, Feb. 19, 1965), 35.
2. Karen Cushman, "Museum Studies: The Beginnings, 1900–1926," *Museum Studies Journal* 1 (Spring 1984): 8–16; Melinda Young Fry, "Women Pioneers in the Public Museum Movement," in Smithsonian Institution, *Women's Changing Roles in Museums: Feb./April Proceedings* (Washington: Smithsonian, 1986), 11–17; Jane R. Glaser, "Museum Studies in the United States: Coming a Long Way in a Long Time," *Museum* 156 (1987): 268–74. For John Cotton Dana, see Edward P. Alexander, *Museum Masters: Their Museums and Their Influence* (Nashville: American Association for State and Local History, 1983), 377–411.
3. Ada V. Ciniglio, "Pioneers in American Museums: Paul J. Sachs," *Museum News* 55 (Sept./Oct. 1976): 70.
4. The chief works describing Sachs and his career are: Edward P. Alexander, "A Handhold on the Curatorial Ladder," *Museum News* 52 (May 1974): 23–25; Ciniglio, "Paul J. Sachs," 48–51, 68–71; Cushman, "Museum Studies," 12–13; Agnes Mongan, *Memorial Exhibition: Works of Art from the Collection of Paul J. Sachs, 1878–1965* (Cambridge, Mass.: Harvard University, Fogg Art Museum, 1965), 7–13; Mongan, "Paul Joseph Sachs (1878–1965)," *Art Journal* 25 (Fall 1965): 50–52; New York *Times*, Feb. 13, 1965; Paul J. Sachs, *Modern Prints & Drawings: A Guide to a Better Understanding of Modern Draughtsmanship* (New York: Alfred A. Knopf, 1954); Sachs, Museum Course, Typescript Copy of Notes (1930), 243 leaves; Sachs, "Preparation for Art Museum Work," *Museum News* 24 (Sept. 1, 1946): 6–8.
5. Ciniglio, "Paul J. Sachs," 49.
6. Ibid., 50.
7. Ibid.
8. Harvard University, William Hayes Fogg Art Museum, *Edward Waldo Forbes: Yankee Visionary* (Cambridge, Mass.: Harvard University, 1971).
9. Ibid., vii.

10. Agnes Mongan and Paul J. Sachs, *Drawings in the Fogg Museum of Art: A Critical Catalogue*, 3 vols. (Cambridge, Mass.: Harvard University Press, 1940), 1: xii.
11. Ciniglio, "Paul J. Sachs," 69.
12. New York *Times*, Feb. 19, 1965.
13. Mongan and Sachs, *Drawings in the Fogg Museum*, 1: viii-xii.
14. Mongan, *Memorial Exhibition*, 199–214.
15. Ibid., 7–13.
16. Ciniglio, "Paul J. Sachs," 69.
17. This analysis of the class is based upon Sachs, Museum Course Typescript, 1930.
18. Mongan and Sachs, *Drawings in the Fogg Museum*, 1: xii.
19. Ciniglio, "Paul J. Sachs," 69.
20. New York *Times*, Feb. 19, 1965.
21. Sachs, "Preparation for Art Museum Work," 6–8.
22. Ibid.
23. Ciniglio, "Paul J. Sachs," 71.
24. New York *Times*, Feb. 19, 1965.
25. John Walker, *Self-Portrait with Donors: Confessions of an Art Collector* (Boston: Little, Brown, 1974), 24–25; Ciniglio, "Paul J. Sachs," 70–71.
26. Mongan, *Memorial Exhibition*, 13.
27. Park Rouse, *Living by Design: Leslie Cheek and the Arts, a Photobiography* (Williamsburg, Va.: Society of the Alumni of William and Mary College, 1985), 46.

## SELECT BIBLIOGRAPHY

Edward P. Alexander. "A Handhold on the Curatorial Ladder," *Museum News* 52 (May 1974): 23–25.

______. *Museum Masters: Their Museums and Their Influence*. Nashville: American Association for State and Local History, 1983.

Ciniglio, Ada V. "Pioneers in American Museums: Paul J. Sachs." *Museum News* 55 (Sept./Oct. 1976): 70.

Cushman, Karen. "Museum Studies: The Beginnings, 1900–1926." *Museum Studies Journal* 1 (Spring 1984): 8–16.

Fry, Melinda Young. "Women Pioneers in the Public Museum Movement." In Smithsonian Institution. *Women's Changing Roles in Museums: Feb./April Proceedings*. Washington: Smithsonian, 1986.

Glaser, Jane R. "Museum Studies in the United States: Coming a Long Way in a Long Time." *Museum* 156 (1987): 268–74.

Harvard University, William Hayes Fogg Art Museum. *Edward Waldo Forbes: Yankee Visionary*. Cambridge, Mass.: Harvard University, 1971.

Mongan, Agnes. *Memorial Exhibition: Works of Art from the Collection of Paul J. Sachs, 1878–1965*. Cambridge, Mass.: Harvard University, Fogg Art Museum, 1965.

______. "Paul Joseph Sachs (1878–1965)." *Art Journal* 25 (Fall 1965): 50–52.

Mongan, Agnes, and Paul J. Sachs. *Drawings in the Fogg Museum of Art: A Critical Catalogue*. 3 vols. Cambridge, Mass.: Harvard University Press, 1940.

Rouse, Park. *Living by Design: Leslie Cheek and the Arts, a Photobiography*. Williamsburg, Va.: Society of the Alumni of William and Mary College, 1985.

Sachs, Paul J. *Modern Prints & Drawings: A Guide to a Better Understanding of Modern Draughtsmanship*. New York: Alfred A. Knopf, 1954.

_____. Museum Course, Typescript Copy of Notes (1930).

_____. "Preparation for Art Museum Work." *Museum News* 24 (Sept. 1, 1946): 6–8.

Walker, John. *Self-Portrait with Donors: Confessions of an Art Collector*. Boston: Little, Brown, 1974.

A BRIEF EPILOGUE:

# The American Museum Progresses

IN LOOKING TO THE FUTURE, the American museum should stress several principles. First of all, each individual museum ought to define clearly its mission and see that its board, director, and staff fully understand it. Then the function of each of these components should be carefully defined and differentiated: the board to provide financing, appoint the director, and approve all general policies; the director to choose his staff and control the day-to-day administration; and the staff to see to the functions of collection, preservation, research, exhibition, and education. The staff also must strive for high professionalism both in its training and in keeping in touch with the latest activities of regional, national, and international museum organizations. The museum should play a far-reaching role in its community and make public service a key goal of its educational programs.

If considerable success can be attained in following these principles, the future of American museums will be assured.

# Index